From Many, One

LATIN AMERICAN AND CARIBBEAN SERIES

Christon I. Archer, General Editor

ISSN 1498–2366

This series sheds light on historical and cultural topics in Latin America and the Caribbean by publishing works that challenge the canon in history, literature, and postcolonial studies. It seeks to print cutting-edge studies and research that redefine our understanding of historical and current issues in Latin America and the Caribbean.

No. 1 · **Waking the Dictator: Veracruz, the Struggle for Federalism and the Mexican Revolution** Karl B. Koth

No. 2 · **The Spirit of Hidalgo: The Mexican Revolution in Coahuila** Suzanne B. Pasztor · Copublished with Michigan State University Press

No. 3 · **Clerical Ideology in a Revolutionary Age: The Guadalajara Church and the Idea of the Mexican Nation, 1788–1853** Brian F. Connaughton, translated by Mark Allan Healey · Copublished with University Press of Colorado

No. 4 · **Monuments of Progress: Modernization and Public Health in Mexico City, 1876–1910** Claudia Agostoni · Copublished with University Press of Colorado

No. 5 · **Madness in Buenos Aires: Patients, Psychiatrists and the Argentine State, 1880–1983** Jonathan Ablard · Copublished with Ohio University Press

No. 6 · **Patrons, Partisans, and Palace Intrigues: The Court Society of Colonial Mexico, 1702–1710** Christoph Rosenmüller

No. 7 · **From Many, One: Indians, Peasants, Borders, and Education in Callista Mexico, 1924–1935** Andrae Marak

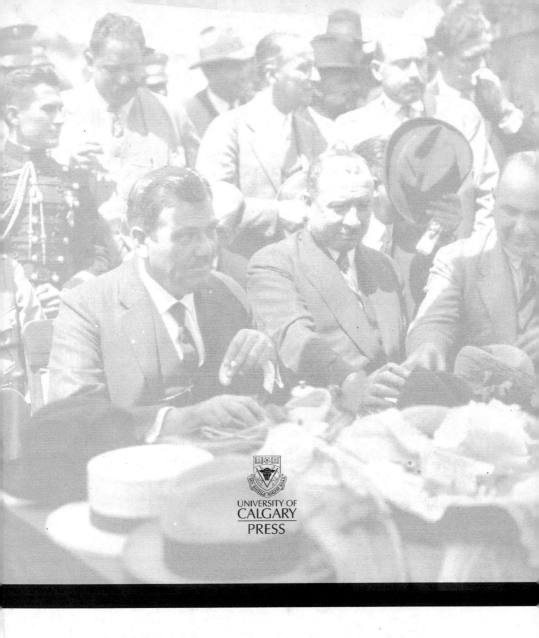

From Many, One

Indians, Peasants, Borders, and Education in Callista Mexico, 1924–1935

ANDRAE M. MARAK

University of Calgary Press
2500 University Drive NW
Calgary, Alberta
Canada T2N 1N4
www.uofcpress.com

LIBRARY AND ARCHIVES CANADA CATALOGUING IN PUBLICATION

Marak, Andrae M., 1968-
    From many, one : Indians, peasants, borders, and education in Callista Mexico, 1924–1935 / Andrae M. Marak.

(Latin American and Caribbean series, 1498-2366 ; 7)
Includes bibliographical references and index.
ISBN 978-1-55238-250-9

    1. Education and state–Mexico–History–20th century. 2. Indians of Mexico–Cultural assimilation–History–20th century. 3. Indians of Mexico–Education–History–20th century. 4. Peasantry–Education–Mexico–History–20th century. 5. Nationalism and education–Mexico–History–20th century. 6. Mexico–Politics and government–1910-1946. 7. Education–Mexico–History–20th century. I. Title. II. Series: Latin American and Caribbean series 7

LA421.8.M37 2009   379.7209'042   C2008-908083-1

The University of Calgary Press acknowledges the support of the Alberta Foundation for the Arts for our publications. We acknowledge the financial support of the Government of Canada through the Book Publishing Industry Development Program (BPIDP) for our publishing activities. We acknowledge the financial support of the Canada Council for the Arts for our publishing program.

Printed and bound in Canada by Marquis Printing
This book is printed on Silva Enviro paper

Cover design by Melina Cusano
Page design and typesetting by Melina Cusano

FOR FLANNERY

TABLE OF CONTENTS

PREFACE

Similar to many other first monographs, *From Many, One: Indians, Peasants, Borders and Education in Callista Mexico, 1924–1935*, is the culmination of my dissertation undertaken at the University of New Mexico in the late 1990s. It really began, however, in 1992 when political scientist Michael Fleet assigned our undergraduate class Alan Riding's *Distant Neighbors* in an introductory Latin American politics course. Riding's account of what the Peruvian novelist Mario Vargas Llosa called in 1990 the "perfect dictatorship," Mexico's one-party state, led me to explore the idea that people might (or might not) be willing to give up some (or many) of their political freedoms in exchange for economic stability and growth (or in our present post–9/11 world, for security). On what terms and in exchange for what would people be willing to give up their right to vote in meaningful elections? In what ways was U.S. society more open than Mexican society and vice versa? Was democracy naturally better than a corporatist vision of society if corporatism led to improved economic living conditions? Were Mexicans co-opted or coerced into accepting the "perfect dictatorship"? In what ways did the *Partido Revolucionario Institucional* (PRI) and its predecessors use (and abuse) the Mexican Revolution (1910–17) and its ideals to gain (maintain) their popularity? Thus began my fascination with Mexican politics and history.

At Syracuse University I took a traveling graduate seminar in Mexico with David Robinson and a half dozen other students. We spent six weeks visiting Yucatán, Quintana Roo, Campeche, Mexico City, Morelos, Michoacán, Jalisco, Guanajuato, and Colima. I went with the express purpose of exploring the sea change in the previous two elections. Most international observers agreed that the PRI had stolen the 1988 elections, which put Carlos Salinas de Gortari (1988–94) in power, but had not needed to do so in 1994 when Ernesto Zedillo (1994–2000) handily won the presidency. Yet, as we crossed Mexico in 1995, the community schools and meeting places constructed through Salinas's public works program (PRONASOL) to promote his neo-liberal adjustment program and to ensure the election of Zedillo were locked and abandoned. The vast majority of people that I met disliked the PRI and its sleight of hand but they were resigned to its maintenance of power. Many of them had, in any case, voted for Zedillo, knowing full well that the outward façade the PRI placed on its neo-liberal adjustment program was just that. Perhaps, as Scott Morgenstern has argued, Mexicans were more comfortable with the devil they knew than the angel they did not. In any case, in spite of their dislike of current Mexican politics, most Mexicans still believed in the Mexican Revolution and its goals. Their popular aspirations, they believed, had been undermined by corrupt politicians. Repeatedly, the locals all across Mexico whom I talked to referred to the Mexican Revolution when describing their political rights, privileges, and duties and how the Mexican government *should* function. It did not take long for me to understand that in order for me to understand current Mexican politics, I would have to come to understand the Mexican Revolution and the construction of the post-revolutionary state.

My interest in modern Mexican politics had quickly led me to historical research on the construction of the post-revolutionary Mexican state and this monograph. I quickly realized three things. First, although there was an abundance of scholarship on Lázaro Cárdenas (1934–40), Plutarco Elías Calles (1924–28) built the institutional structures upon which Cárdenas based the construction of the corporatist state during his presidency and the Maximato. Second, there was a dearth of English-language scholarship on the era dominated by Calles, especially on his social policies. What did exist – scholars have produced much quality work since then, especially Jürgen Buchenau's recently published biography of Calles – treated him either as a middle-class sellout who abandoned the revolution's transformative goals or as an anti-religious radical who imposed his Jacobin program on Mexico's Catholic campesinos. The truth, of course, was more nuanced. Calles was not in favor of many of the revolution's goals, especially major changes in property and class structures. Nevertheless, he was willing to use education as an alternative to more radical social changes. He was also an anti-religious radical, who was not afraid to use anticlerical and anti-Chinese campaigns and the promotion of socialist education to cover for his retreat from land reform. He was unable to impose his Jacobin ideals on Mexican society; Lázaro Cárdenas would be more successful, though he would also fail. Calles and his followers implemented a developmentalist education model, an advancement over the religious-dominated elite-based system that preceded it, but not one with transformative goals such as those later implemented in post-revolutionary Cuba and Nicaragua (and perhaps under Cárdenas in Mexico). Third, scholars had yet to study in depth the impact of the U.S.-Mexican border on Calles' nation-building project. I argue that Calles engaged in nation building in two ways along Mexico's northern frontier. He attempted to incorporate and unify by bringing in previously unassimilated indigenous groups into the nation. These indigenous groups were quite different from those in central Mexico because they were deemed less redeemable due to their "barbaric" past, one not based on the sedentary practice of agriculture. Calles also used the border to define Mexico against what it was not, the United States. This latter kind of Mexican nationalism and nation building has been little discussed in the literature on education.

My realization that Calles, though a radical of sorts, was unable to impose his project on campesinos and borderlands residents was balanced, however, with the realization that policy implementers were often incredibly insensitive or just plain ignorant of campesino mores and realities. Depictions of campesinos and indigenous people by government educators, inspectors, engineers at the *Archivo Historico de la Secretaría de Educación Pública, Archivo General de la Nación, Archivo Historico del Agua, Fideicomiso Archivos Plutarco Elías Calles y Fernando Torreblanco, Archivo Historico General del Estado de Sonora*, the *Archivo del Congreso del Estado de Sonora*, the *Patronato de la Historia del Sonora* and the *Silvestre Terrazas Colleción* at the *Museo Nacional de Antropología e Historia*, and the *Archivo de la Palabra* at the *Instituto Mora* [not to mention similar negative depictions of the Tohono O'odham in the *Bureau of Indian Affairs* papers in the *National Archives and Records Administration – Pacific Region (Laguna Niguel)*] were consistently derogatory and dehumanizing. No wonder they often had little success.

Scholars have convincingly argued that, in addition to the failure of government officials to understand the everyday lives of the people they were trying to change, campesino resistance also played a major role in shaping government policies. A perhaps strange mixture of scholarship that underlines the power of everyday people to reshape government agendas heavily influenced my work. This is the result of my pursuit of a dual degree doctorate in Latin American Studies at the University of New Mexico, where I worked with historians, political scientists, and educational anthropologists. Historians will recognize the impact of Alan Knight, Florencia Mallon's explanation of Gramscian hegemony, collected works on "everyday forms of state formation" put together by Gilbert Joseph and Daniel Nugent, James Scott's "weapons of the weak," Alexander Dawson's examination of the "mediating role" played by indigenous leaders vis-à-vis the state and their own people, and Mary Kay Vaughan's insights on the campesinos' adoption of a common language of consent and dissent in their discussions (and struggles) with state officials. Political scientists will recognize the influence of literature on state-society relations, Kevin Middlebrook's work on state formation, and Joel Migdal's work on strong societies and weak states that comprises much of the developing world. Educational theorists will notice the influence of David Labaree's insights into the multiple purposes of education and the ways in which everyday people work the system to their own advantage.

The long-term results of Mexico's corporatist state and the education policies that it created in conjunction with its campesinos and indigenous people are, perhaps, not much better today than they were in 1935. On a research trip during the summer of 2005 in Sonora, I noted that Tohono O'odham tribal members regularly visited the *Unidad de Información de Pueblos Indigenas* in Hermosillo, knowing full well that they would find a sympathetic ear as well as a willingness on behalf of the staff to purchase the arts and crafts on which many Tohono O'odham eke out a living. When I went to Bahia Kino to visit with the Seri, I discovered that the government had removed them from their ancestral lands to make way for tourist development.

Acknowledgments

This book would not have been possible without the help of numerous people in the United States, Mexico, and Canada. I am grateful to my dissertation advisor Linda Hall and my mentor Bob Himmerich y Valencia, who had faith in me and my desire to earn an interdisciplinary degree even when others did not. Others at the University of New Mexico who were central in my development as a scholar are Ken Coleman, Sam Truett, Ken Roberts, Mark Peceny, Jaime Grinberg, Bob Kern, Carlos Salomon, Elaine Carey, Javier Marion, Gary VanValen, and Pat Killinger. At Syracuse University Jeff Stonecash introduced me to research methodology while David Robinson gave me the opportunity to experience Mexico through a traveling graduate seminar in which we visited and studied nine of Mexico's 31 states plus the Distrito Federal. Michael Fleet first introduced me to Latin American politics and history at Marquette University where his assigning of Alan Riding's *Distant Neighbors* began my fascination with Mexico. At the Colegio de México Engracia Loyo agreed to serve as my advisor, offered me countless hours of advice, and introduced (and continues to introduce) me to a plethora of Mexican scholars working in the field. Other scholars in Mexico who agreed to meet with me to discuss my project include Luis Aboites, Guillermo Palacios, Alberto Arnaut, Enrique Semo, Ignacio Almada Bay, Eugenia Meyer, Susana Quintanilla, Jean Meyer, Pablo Yankelevich, Benjamín Alonso Rascón, and Carlos Macías Richard.

In Mexico I owe gratitude to the archivists, librarians, and employees at the Archivo General de la Nación, Biblioteca Nación, El Colegio de México, Archivo Histórico del Agua, Fideicomiso Archivos Plutarco Elías Calles y Fernando Torreblanca, Unidad de Información de Pueblos Indigenas, Archivo Historico del Estado de Sonora, Hemeroteca Nacional, Fototeca Nacional, Museo Nacional de Culturas Populares, Archivo Historico de la Secretaria de Educación Pública, Museo Nacional de Antropología e Historia, and Instituto Dr. José María Luis Mora. I owe special thanks to Norma Mereles Torreblanca de Ogarrio, Roberto Pérez Aguilar, Macrina Restor, and Gwen Pattison for their always being willing to assist me in finding additional material and the folks at the New Mexico Economic Development Office in Mexico City for facilitating my transition to Mexico. In the United States, the staff at the National Archives and Records Administration Pacific Region (Laguna Niguel) and the libraries at Cornell University, the University of New Mexico and California University of Pennsylvania were incredibly accommodating. In addition, Stephen Lewis, Alan Knight, Mark Wasserman, David Rich Lewis, Mary Kay Vaughan, Adrian Bantjes, Alexander Dawson, Sarah Buck, Nicole Sanders, Susie Porter, Jocelyn Olcott, Victor Macías-Gonzalez, and Jeff Bannister have also provided feedback on my work. My colleagues at California University of Pennsylvania have supplied me with great advice and have served as wonderful role models. I especially want to thank Laura Tuennerman-Kaplan, Jim Wood, Kelton Edmonds, and Melanie Blumberg. No one played a larger role in assisting me in converting my dissertation into a book manuscript than Ev Schlatter. Ev not only wielded a ruthless editing pen, but also served as a constant source of support and encouragement. The two anonymous reviewers of my work clearly helped me hone my thesis and offered excellent criticism. Christon Archer and Karen Buttner at the University of Calgary Press also proved to be wonderful guides throughout the process.

I received several seed grants from the Latin American and Iberian Institute and the Graduate School at the University of New Mexico. A Fulbright-Robles García grant from the United States Information Agency and the Mexican government funded the majority of the research for this project. Since my arrival at California University of Pennsylvania, I have been supported amply by the Department of History and Political Science, the Office of Provost and Academic Affairs, the College of Liberal Arts, and the Faculty Professional Development Committee.

Of course, none of this would have been possible without the support of my friends and family, who made accommodations in their lives so that I could pursue mine. I would have been unlikely to finish this book had it not been for the many Mexicans who helped me bridge the end of graduate school in 2000 and my start in academia in 2004. I would like to dedicate this book to Gustavo, Luis, Nico, and Martín, whose limited education and lack of economic opportunities (but not their incredible work ethic) forced them to migrate to the United States to make a living, and to the members of my baseball team in Xochimilco who still struggle to make ends meet.

Introduction: The Role of the State and Educational Reform in Mexican Nation Building

This study examines Plutarco Elías Calles' nation-building project of construct-ing an economically prosperous and culturally unified Mexico through a series of national educational policies during his presidency and the Maximato, from 1924 to 1935. It also explores the various power centers inside and outside the Mexican federal government to analyze the responses of teachers, educational inspectors, local governmental officials, priests and church members, large landowners, indigenous people, and everyday Mexican citizens – all of whom played multiple and sometimes competing roles – to those unifying policies. The analysis of the federal government's attempt to promote nationalism highlights both the ways in which the federal government sought to incorporate and unify Mexico through centralization and assimilation and the ways in which it tried to define itself in opposition to what was not Mexican, an especially prominent feature along the U.S.-Mexican border. Analysis of the response to government educational policies focuses specifically on three areas of contention within the national building arena and the field of education. First, it traces the battle over the federal government's political centralization program by capturing the takeover of state primary schools by federal inspectors in Chihuahua in 1933. Second, it scrutinizes the federal government's attempts to promote nationalism through special frontier schools along the U.S.-Mexican border where Mexi-can officials feared the onslaught of U.S. cultural and economic imperialism. Finally, it addresses the federal government's indigenous assimilation program, which aimed at integrating numerous culturally distinct groups into a mono-cultural Mexican nation, and the distinct responses of select indigenous groups – the Tarahumara, Seri, and Tohono O'odham – in northern Mexico.

Between 1924 and 1935, Plutarco Elías Calles and his political cohorts completely rearranged the structure of the Public Education Ministry (the

Secretaría de Educación Pública or SEP), centralizing political power over policy and budgets.[1] Calles (1924–28) and his predecessor, Alvaro Obregón (1920–24), were the first Mexican presidents to be able to extend the primary educational system into the Mexican countryside in a meaningful way, in many places replacing the educational role that the Catholic Church had played since colonial times.[2] Despite the important political and economic changes undertaken by the Mexican government through its educational policies and institutions between 1924 and 1935, until recently, relatively few Mexican historians or political scientists have examined the process of these structural changes or their outcomes. Instead, historians have focused their attention on the presidency of Alvaro Obregón and the initial push into the countryside by his Minister of Education, José Vasconcelos.[3] They have also given in-depth coverage to Lazaro Cárdenas' administration (1934–40), looking at the culmination and radicalization of the federal government's centralization program.[4] Most importantly, almost no one has examined the educational nation-building project during this time along Mexico's northern frontier. This book attempts to address this weakness in the literature by presenting five case studies focusing on educational centralization (Chapter 2), frontier schools in Chihuahua, Sonora, and Coahuila (Chapter 6), and the attempted assimilation of the Tarahumara (Chapter 3), Seri (Chapter 4), and Tohono O'odham (Chapter 5).

This study focuses on the eleven years of Calles' political power from 1924, when he became President of Mexico, through the Maximato to 1935, when Lázaro Cárdenas had finally amassed enough political support to be able to force Calles into exile. The Maximato stretched from 1928 through 1935 and comprised parts of four different presidential administrations; namely, those of interim President Emilio Portes Gil (1928–30), President Pascual Ortiz Rubio (1930–32), interim President Abelardo L. Rodríguez (1932–34), and the beginning of President Cárdenas' administration (1934–35). During the Maximato, Calles ran the federal government and directed its major policy decisions from the shadows of the presidential chair.[5] This book specifically concentrates on primary education in the countryside, in predominately indigenous areas, and along the border of the three northern states of Sonora, Chihuahua, and Coahuila. During this decade, Calles used the educational system as a means of centralizing political and ideological control over the individual states and their communities.[6]

With the exception of the more populated border cities within the geographical area of study – Nogales, Ciudad Juárez, and Piedras Negras – I focus chiefly on the countryside for two reasons. First, prior to Alvaro Obregón's administration (1920–24) no national government had managed to expand the primary education system beyond large urban centers despite over 35 years of discussion about the necessity of doing so. Obregón's rural educational programs, though headed by the vaunted José Vasconcelos and endowed with a budget second only to the Ministry of War and Navy, made a modest impact at best.[7] Second, rural Mexico played a predominant political role in the shaping of Mexico as a nation. The vast majority of Mexicans lived in the countryside, over 75 per cent in 1921, and the political and military mobilization of campesinos during and after the revolution profoundly shaped the revolution's outcome.[8] Later, the responses of the federal government to the political, social, and economic desires of Mexico's campesinos through the creation of extensive social programs and institutions allowed the central government to secure the support of the majority of the peasantry.[9] The federal government also engaged in strategic acts of repression to limit or eliminate dissent from certain sectors of rural Mexican society.[10] The SEP and the *Partido Revolucionario Institucional* (PRI) and its predecessors are only two of the many institutions created by Mexican elites to consolidate the support of Mexicans for the post-revolutionary government.[11] This book tells part of that story.

This book focuses on three of Mexico's northern states for several reasons. First, they were the source of three of the revolution's main political and military forces: namely, the Obregonistas from Sonora, the Carrancistas from Coahuila, and the Villistas from Chihuahua. This shaped Mexico's future in two profound ways. First, the fact that peasants in northern Mexico mobilized during the revolution forced future political leaders to respond to the issues that motivated them to rebel. Second, Obregonistas, Carrancistas, and Villistas played central political roles in the creation and running of the post-revolutionary government. Unique frontier cultural influences shaped the perspectives of both peasants and their political leaders. The leaders of each of the three revolutionary groups paid particularly close attention to the role that education could play in alleviating the social and economic problems that were at the root of the revolution to begin with. In doing so, they applied the lessons that the borderlands region had taught them. For example, Obregón and Calles, who were both from Sonora, applied what historian Jürgen Buchenau has called a *Yori* understanding to post-revolutionary problems. Sonoran indigenous groups, mainly the Mayo and Yaquis, used Yori to denote Spanish-speaking people in Sonora. During the nineteenth century, Yoris were isolated and outnumbered along the frontier.

They earned their citizenship and land by defending whatever amount of land they could manage and offering assistance to local *presidios*, or Spanish military posts. Yoris viewed themselves as *gente de razón*, people with reason, and viewed their task as bringing civilization to indigenous people, whom they viewed as backward and uncivilized. This understanding of frontier citizenship was not unique to Sonora. Ana María Alonso, using gender as an analytical tool, has noted a nearly identical understanding of frontier citizenship in Chihuahua.[12] This understanding of borderlands citizenship had several major impacts. First, peasants from Sonora and Chihuahua often fought in the revolution in order to regain access to the land that they or their ancestors had fought to attain, but which they had lost during the Porfiriato.[13] Second, political leaders from both states would later bring many of the "civilizing" and education programs that they had earlier implemented in their home states to the national political arena.[14] Finally, frontier political leaders often had a different understanding of the causes of the revolution than their counterparts in the center and south. To give just one example, those from the frontier were more concerned about access to water than they were about access to land.[15] Coahuila, meanwhile, was a state that early on was the center of many educational reforms based on the work of U.S. pedagogist John Dewey. Protestant missionaries exposed the state and its people to Dewey's influence through their extensive work. Interestingly, for example, Moisés Sáenz, the sub-secretary of education during the Calles administration and one of the chief advocates of Dewey's *Escuela de Acción*, was a Protestant preacher who served under both Carranza and Obregón.[16] Finally, Pancho Villa saw educational reform as a non-controversial antidote for the ills of the peasants of his home state and as a means of modernizing all sectors of the Mexican economy.[17]

Second, the Mexican north presents a unique series of historical and economic similarities across states while also furnishing some equally unique differences between states. For example, all of northern Mexico underwent a similar economic development during the Porfiriato that focused on foreign investments in mining and railroads as well as the rising importance of large haciendas.[18] Higher levels of foreign investment led to higher per capita revenues, which, in turn, resulted in greater state expenditures on education. Only the Federal District and the Yucatán equaled northern Mexico's educational budgets. These increased expenditures left a legacy of literacy in the north unmatched by central and southern Mexico; 45 per cent of adults were literate in Mexico's northern states, while 27 and 14 per cent could read and write in central and southern Mexico, respectively.[19] In fact, Stephen Lewis has argued that both Sonora and Coahuila, because of their healthy export sectors, were able to create state school systems that outperformed Education Ministry schools into the 1930s.[20] Yet each of the three northern states underwent the process of economic development that resulted in increased educational expenditures in distinct ways, resulting in the initial mobilization of different sectors of societies with diverse revolutionary goals. In Coahuila and Chihuahua, economic elites had ready access to both internal and external markets. In Coahuila, where economic development was centered in the Laguna region, however, discontent first arose among economic elites that had been shut out of the dialogue over political and economic issues, mainly dealing with water rights.[21] In Chihuahua, on the other hand, the Terrazas-Creel family had a stranglehold on economic and political resources, resulting in widespread dissatisfaction among campesinos. These campesinos would eventually supply disaffected regional elites with the "armies of rural dwellers" necessary to fight against the dominant regime.[22] Meanwhile, Sonora's remoteness resulted in its having had little access to Mexico's internal markets, forcing Sonoran entrepreneurs into a position of greater interdependency with their equally isolated neighbors in Arizona.[23] This history of greater economic and social interdependence may have led to the moderate stance vis-à-vis the United States on issues of trade and capital investment by Mexico's eventual leaders with Sonoran roots.

Third, the choice of these three northern states also provided other areas of interest. For example, in 1933 Chihuahua's state primary school system was the first to be completely federalized.[24] This event permitted further examination of one of the main theoretical thrusts of this book, the struggle between the federal, state, and municipal governments over control of education. When Obregón first attempted to advance the federalization of primary education, he was forced to include constitutional provisions for the non-interference with state sovereignty.[25] Over time, Calles was able to use the federal budget and his control over the disbursement of educational money to further centralize and federalize the national primary education system.[26]

Fourth, the presence of a wide range of indigenous groups who call Sonora and Chihuahua home afforded the opportunity to examine the Mexican government's educational assimilation program through the varying cases of the different tribes, their leaders, and those who acted as cultural brokers. Several rather distinct indigenous groups had settled permanently in northern Mexico. Each of those that I study here had very different educational experiences. The Tarahumara had some control over the local curriculum as Ignacio León, a Tarahumara himself, worked for the Education Ministry as both a teacher and inspector. On the other hand, SEP officials relied on outsiders to administer their program to the Seri and Tohono O'odham. In the Seri case, Robert Thompson, a local rancher and a friend, acted as an interlocutor between state officials, the federal government, tribal members, and other local ranchers. Among the Tohono O'odham two community leaders from Arizona allied with a modernizing, Protestant segment of the group, acted as spokesmen for tribal members living south of the U.S.-Mexican border and attempted to play the U.S. and Mexican governments off against each other. In spite of the different cases, these states had some things in common. They had one of the lowest overall concentrations of purely indigenous people in all of Mexico, especially compared with central and southern Mexico. Because sedentary indigenous groups, who were viewed as the largest stumbling block to economic and social progress, did not make up a majority of northern Mexico's inhabitants, it provided an environment in which the predominance of mestizos should have granted the federal government its best chance of success with its rural modernization program.[27] Furthermore, it furnished an ideal arena in which to compare and contrast the educational, political, and economic outcomes of indigenous versus non-indigenous communities under the influence of the federal government's programs.

Finally, the proximity of the U.S. border to these states also gave me the opportunity to address the Mexican government's attempts to counteract U.S. cultural and economic imperialism.[28] During Calles' presidency, the SEP organized *escuelas fronterizas* in all the major border towns along the U.S.-Mexican border. These schools provided an alternative for Mexican parents who were sending their children to schools on the U.S. side of the border, an alternative that would teach their children Spanish and Mexican songs, hymns, and history as opposed to English and the U.S.'s Pledge of Allegiance. Mexican officials often defined what was Mexican in contrast to what was not Mexican. Interestingly, parents in these communities often disagreed. For example, while they viewed themselves as being authentically Mexican, they pushed the SEP to hire native-speaking English teachers to teach their children. By threatening to keep their children in U.S. schools if the Education Ministry failed to comply, they partially undermined the original intentions of the federal government even as they were redefining what it meant to be Mexican.

I now turn briefly to the history of education leading up to the Calles presidency and the Maximato. The near decade of intermittent war and political, social, and economic upheaval that comprised the Mexican Revolution served to disable and undermine nearly every institution established by the previous federal government during the Porfiriato.[29] In addition, the revolution served to mobilize the masses across most of rural Mexico, creating new popular forces that post-revolutionary political elites and policy makers had to contend with in reconstructing a nation out of the detritus of war.[30] Given that Porfirio Díaz's government had not fully penetrated the daily lives of rural Mexicans, in hindsight it is rather surprising the success, though varied and uneven, that the post-revolutionary leaders of Mexico had in putting the political pieces back together after the revolution, though as we will see, this success in many ways did not extend into the field of education.[31]

The Porfiriato (1876–1910) ushered in a period of relative educational advancement based primarily on the implementation of the liberal policies of the Reforma in urban areas. Díaz's positivist governmental approach of "Order and Progress" helped to create a seemingly strong, centralized state that was fiscally sound, allowing him to put his educational plans in place where both his liberal and conservative predecessors had been unable to do so. The Reform Laws of 1867 declared that primary education was not only to be free, but also obligatory. Nevertheless, lawmakers first implemented them during the Porfiriato and then only in the Federal District. In 1888, Díaz signed into law a bill that encompassed the principle of the 1867 law of free and obligatory primary schooling in the Federal District with the additional restrictions that no member of any religious cult or anyone who had taken a religious vow could teach in these lay schools.[32] In order to further advance scientifically based education, Díaz created the National Preparatory School and the Normal School for Professors, which promoted the spread of positivism, the development of patriotism and moral progress, and the eradication of ignorance.[33]

The Primer Congreso Nacional de Instrucción Pública, which met June 1, 1889, provides an excellent case for reviewing the strengths and weaknesses of Porfirian educational policy as a national project. Not only did members of the congress address the important issue of primary education, they also spoke to the need for increased access to education in rural areas and the need for better teacher training and pay.[34] They noted that widespread access to free and obligatory primary schooling in rural areas faced numerous challenges, not the least of which were: 1) the diversity of languages spoken by indigenous groups; 2) the general ignorance of campesinos; 3) the large distances and lack of adequate roads between rural schools; and 4) the need for campesinos and their children to work long hours in order to maintain even a "miserable subsistence."[35] These issues would remain paramount through the Maximato and beyond. The members of the congress proposed establishing mixed rural schools of boys and girls to make education more accessible and affordable. In addition, they placed a greater emphasis on Instrucción Primaria Superior where the "sons of workers and artisans" could "justly satisfy" their "legitimate aspirations."[36] While the members of this meeting understood what the shortcomings of the Mexican educational system were, they were unable to address them in any systematic way other than the passing of a new series of laws. Education officials almost completely ignored the implementation of rural education; they left the actual implementation policies up to the individual states, which in turn often left them up to the various municipalities; the majority of budgeted rural schools continued to exist only on paper.[37] By the end of the Porfiriato, only 16 per cent of Mexicans were literate, and they were highly concentrated in urban centers.[38]

The supposedly liberating positivist "New School" pedagogy created by Mexican intellectuals Enrique Rébsamen, Carlos Carrillo, and Gabino Barrera, but drawing heavily on European models, spread throughout the nation during the Porfiriato. According to Justo Sierra, a leading writer and politician and the Secretary of Public Education (1905–1911), the "New School" was an advance over previous liberal educational models because its scientifically based epistemological approach augmented learning in children. With the "New School" approach the child proceeded,

> from the concrete to the abstract through observation and experimentation with natural and man-made phenomena. Designed to equip the student with a scientific understanding of the universe and consequent skills for manipulation of the environment, the program was also supposed to develop habits of self-restraint, altruism, discipline, punctuality, and industriousness to create a balance of initiative, order, and harmony in work tasks within a modernizing society.[39]

In theory, this approach was liberating because it stimulated the different talents of individual students instead of creating a particular type of man. The teacher would no longer be the forger of men but rather the "evoker" of naturally latent talents, much as Socrates had been in ancient Greece.[40]

In practice, of course, the "New School" pedagogy was less liberating than it appeared on paper. The tacit objective of promoting this educational approach was to "permit all men to act in accordance with their natural qualities." Empirically measurable abilities, however, were the only basis for natural qualities. Thus, as the Minister of Public Instruction, Ezequiel Montes, complained, they left no room for moral questions such as "the existence of God, the soul, [or] the destiny of man."[41] And, although the "New School" pedagogy was officially not a tool for the molding of men, in practice it focused on inculcating self-restraint, a trait that was supposedly missing in religious and indigenous people. Educators hoped that increased self-restraint would create a people who believed in the necessity of work, savings, and accumulation so essential to Díaz's emerging capitalist economy.

While Díaz was congratulating himself on the number of primary schools he had opened in the Federal District, 337 by 1904, his educational agenda was limited and often ineffective, especially given that the federal government only had control over schools in the Federal District and the federal territories.[42] Governmental elites knew the importance of education as a means of expanding federal governmental control and ideology. Nonetheless, they were unable to expand education beyond urban centers. Despite his failings, Díaz did leave one important institutional legacy, the *Secretaría de Instrucción Pública y Bellas Artes*. Created in 1905, it would, after being abolished during the course of the Mexican Revolution, be resurrected to good effect by Vasconcelos and later used by Calles to extend the national educational policy across the Mexican countryside, albeit unevenly, for the first time.

The period from 1911 to 1920 brought a series of revolutionary and counterrevolutionary governments to power. All of these governments espoused expanded access to free secular primary education. Some also advocated social and structural changes that, if implemented, would have provided an environment within which increased access to education could have made a positive impact in the lives of the majority of rural Mexicans. In reaction to the centralizing tendencies of the Porfiriato, the period also saw a return to the liberal idea of decentralization. States would have control over, and be responsible for funding and supervising, their own educational programs. In the case of rural education, this was hardly anything new. Nevertheless, the lack of financial resources due to continued military confrontations, plus an inability by revolutionary leaders to reach a consensus about the necessary extent of social and structural changes, made progress difficult. In fact, the decentralizing nature of educational reforms during this period resulted in the creation and strengthening of institutional power centers (i.e., local, state, and church educational bureaucracies) that post-revolutionary federal governments would later have to contend with in trying to regain political control over the country.

A new wave of liberals had arisen during the Porfiriato. They no longer believed that society was naturally hierarchical due to scientific and evolutionary laws. Instead, they held that "individual entrepreneurship, competition, and political democracy" served as the basis for society and that education was the key to the success of their revolutionary programs.[43] Ricardo Flores Magón, in his *Programa y Manifiesto del Partido Liberal Mexicano*, argued that Mexicans must build a new, modern Mexico with productive workers created by a good system of primary education.[44] In addition to Flores Magón and his followers, other groups of liberals also released manifestos. The *Manifiesto del Club Liberal Ponciano Arriaga* had as one of its foremost goals the improvement of education, while the *Manifiesto del Partido Democrático* insisted that education was the only means of creating a better government. All of these liberal groups wanted to loosen the central government's stranglehold on the country. Moreover, although it existed more on paper than in fact, they proposed the end to the centralization of the federal education system and its replacement with a decentralized system.[45] Calles, as the centerpiece of his educational policies, would later adopt many of these liberal educational ideologies, though he would eschew decentralization.

When Francisco Madero came to power in 1911, he noted that the Mexican people could not be civilized at the points of bayonets; textbooks would have to serve in their place.[46] In 1912 he announced his educational program for the country, calling for school lunches for poor children, additional funding for superior schools and universities, and the creation of additional "rudimentary" schools in the countryside. Madero created the *Sección de Instrucción Rudimentaría* and asked its members to formulate a plan that would most efficiently bring the most basic level of education into rural areas. Although most of this came to naught as budget reductions undermined nearly his entire educational program, Madero did manage to undertake the building of an average of ten rural schools in each state.[47] Despite his optimistic educational outlook, Madero's education budget represented only 7.8 per cent of his regime's total overall budget, a miniscule improvement over the 7.2 per cent allocated to education during the final year of the Porfiriato.[48]

When Victoriano Huerta came to power in 1913 through a military uprising, he named José María Lozano as his Minister of Public Instruction and vowed to continue Madero's plan of creating more primary schools in the countryside. Both his and Madero's administration were reacting to a genuine clamor by peasants for increased funding for rural schooling. In Zacatecas and Tlaxcala, for example, entire communities organized in hopes that the federal government would open *Escuelas Rudimentarias*.[49] In a liberal democratic move designed to give the power back to the people in 1914, Huerta's government put in place the *Reglamento para la Inspección Moral del Personal de los Establecimientos de Educación Pública*. This program called for the parents of students to make regular classroom visits to ensure that teachers were not abusing the moral authority of their position. While these public relations moves may have looked good on paper, they merely underlined the difficult political and economic position that Huerta had placed his government in and the inability of his government to implement or oversee much of anything, within or outside of education, anywhere in the country.[50]

The Carranza administration made several educational policy changes aimed at improving his regime's military readiness and economic development. For example, in 1917 he created the *Dirección General de Enseñanza Militar*, which was to be in charge of providing military training for all males and nursing training for all females in primary, superior, and preparatory school. He also reduced the number of years necessary to receive a degree at the National Preparatory School from five to four in an attempt to increase the number of graduates in the workforce. In addition, Carranza scrapped the *Escuela Nacional de Artes y Oficios* – designed in 1867 specifically for the advanced education of men – and created in its place the *Escuela Práctica de Ingenieros Mecánicos y Electricistas and the Escuela Nacional de Ciencias Químicas*. His emphasis on industrial and technical training mirrored the educational changes that he had undertaken as governor of Coahuila from 1911 to 1913.[51] Finally, in 1919 he enacted a normal school reform law that brought the pedagogical approach up to date. Specifically, he was interested in changing teacher training to reflect the newly emerging "action" pedagogy. Followers of "action" pedagogy argued that students must use their intuition to learn the subjects to which they were most naturally inclined. They also noted that children learned best through doing, rather than through memorization and recitation. Thus, the true teacher should not be a giver of lectures, but rather the "promoter of experiences."[52] Carranza also took steps so that education more strongly stressed Mexican nationalism and tradition by creating an editorial department that produced a series of inexpensive books, newspapers, and pamphlets that promoted popular culture for teachers to use in the classroom.[53]

The fall of Carranza in 1920 and the onset of the interim presidency of Adolfo de la Huerta set the stage for the educational push of Obregón and Vasconcelos. In September 1920, de la Huerta named José Vasconcelos, the rector of the National University, to begin a campaign against illiteracy in the rural areas. Vasconcelos advanced a literacy campaign that enlisted 2,000 honorary teachers in the task of teaching 10,000 campesinos how to read and write over the next four months.[54] Vasconcelos asked these volunteers, mostly teachers from Mexico City, to find rural counterparts who could read, write, and do basic math to continue the work in their own communities begun by the volunteers.[55] A child who provided documentation that she had taught five other children to read received a certificate declaring her a "good Mexican," while an adult volunteer needed to teach successfully 20 students to receive the same honor.[56] This program served the dual purposes of advancing rural education without seriously threatening already existing institutional power centers that were not under the control of the federal government.

All the educational programs put forward between 1911 and 1920 had two things in common: contemporary liberal thought permeated them and they advanced the goal of local control over local education. The hopes of revolutionary leaders that a liberal, decentralized education system would pave the way toward Mexico's future economic development and the preservation of social order had a short life. Obregón and Calles turned education into a tool aimed at centralizing the federal government's control over the country, increasing economic output, civilizing campesinos and indigenous people, and creating patriotic citizens. Obregón named Vasconcelos the minister of the newly created Education Ministry in 1921. Lawmakers gave the SEP jurisdiction over schooling throughout all of Mexico, bringing to a close the revolutionary program of educational decentralization.[57]

Obregón's presidential term (1920–1924) saw the rise in importance of education to levels never previously seen in Mexico. The two ministries with the highest budgets during this period were that of War and Navy and the Education Ministry.[58] In fact, Obregón budgeted 13 per cent of the national expenditures for education during his term. The need to gain U.S. recognition, which meant spending more on external debt reduction than Obregón would have liked, and the need to put down a military rebellion in 1923, however, diverted much of the money originally earmarked for educational purposes.[59] Despite these budgetary constraints, Obregón and Vasconcelos did manage to take the first steps in advancing a federal education program in rural areas that had as its primary aim the creation of a Mexico without racial distinctions and the advancement of classical education.[60] Vasconcelos adopted a humanist approach to education that focused on the reprinting of positivist textbooks from the Porfiriato and the translation and reproduction of ancient Western classics.[61] By the end of Vasconcelos' term at the helm of the SEP, 37,984 illiterate peasants had been introduced to the world of reading and writing.[62]

In 1921, Vasconcelos also created another important department, the Department of Indigenous Culture. This department, whose main goal was "the incorporation [of indigenous people] into the dominant European culture," was responsible for running most of the federal schools located in the countryside. The policy of the Hispanization and "modernization" of indigenous people in rural Mexico underlined Vasconcelos' belief that the creation of separate indigenous schools as already being practiced in U.S. Native American boarding schools would only serve to maintain pre-capitalist structures in the countryside and hold back Mexico's eventual evolution into a modern country on a par with western Europe.[63] An important factor in achieving modernity was the forging of a true Mexican nationality and patriotism that crossed class and racial lines. In order to consummate this plan, the government created special normal schools to train teachers who planned to work in rural areas. These specially trained teachers were to undertake the task of teaching not only rural children, but their parents as well. In addition, education was to penetrate and radically transform the social milieu of rural communities by moving outside of classroom walls, teaching them more advanced home management techniques, better methods of agriculture, and more sanitary forms of personal hygiene. By 1924, the Department of Indigenous Culture had created 1,926 rural schools and had trained 2,388 teachers to work in them.[64]

In 1923, the Obregón administration officially endorsed "action" education as the official pedagogy. Mary Kay Vaughan argues that the promotion of John Dewey's action pedagogy in Mexico is proof of the dependency mindset of most Mexican intellectuals and politicians during the post-revolutionary period. Instead of looking at the historical and structural reasons for the economic backwardness of their country, Mexican leaders, she argues, reached into the United States for an educational theory that pointed to the "behavioral deficiencies of the Mexican."[65] The adoption of action education, however, is better explained by the northern frontier mentality of Obregón, Calles, and other important members of the government. Thus, the inculcation of positive work habits, diligence, and industry in a people whom they viewed as being more interested in idleness and drinking was the classical Yori understanding that gente de razón had of their yet-to-be-civilized rural and indigenous counterparts. The fact that they drew on theories first promulgated in the United States only underscores that, like many of their borderlands brethren, they had stronger cultural connections to the United States than their fellow compatriots outside of the region.

In the end, the long arm of the federal government's educational bureaucracy would touch the lives of a vast majority of Mexican campesinos, for better or worse, over the next decade or more. Although the nation-building program, begun under Obregón but solidified under Calles, met with varying degrees of success and failure in different regions, states, and communities, it nonetheless had a strong influence on the future course of Mexican political history and the way in which the federal government would interact with civil society. Perhaps the program's failures were most important. Calles' attempts to unify Mexico at times met with abject failure. These failures were the result of a combination of things: a weak state, conflicts with local power holders and economic interests, and resistance to the Education Ministry by many of the people it targeted (and sometimes by those who were supposed to implement its policies). In spite of the fact that the SEP, which Stephen Lewis has called the "the federal government's chief state- and nation-building institution," failed to promote meaningful rural economic development or implement lasting agrarian and labor reforms prior to the mid-1930s, its institutionalization allowed the federal government to extend its reach into the countryside and made Cárdenas' populist program possible.[66] As Alexander Dawson has demonstrated, these failures also, in time, led the federal government to promote a more inclusionary vision of nationalism, one which, for example, indigenous leaders had a hand in forging.[67] Now we turn to an overview of Calles' attempt to extend the reach of the federal government, through the Education Ministry, into the countryside.

1

The Callista Program

To Plutarco Elías Calles, the motives behind the Mexican Revolution and Mexico's future economic progress were synonymous. He fought in the revolution to overthrow a political regime that stifled the economic prospects of Mexico's burgeoning middle class and commercial farmers and that prevented Mexico's campesinos from becoming commercial farmers or members of the middle class.[1] Unlike Zapatismo and Villismo, the agrarian problem was never a central focus in Calles' home state of Sonora.[2] In order to achieve the economic advances demanded by his Yori understanding of the revolution, Calles would need peace and political stability.[3] In some ways, these goals mirrored those previously embraced by the dictator Porfirio Díaz, but Calles' methods were different. Whereas Díaz used the idea of *"pan o palo,"* the enticement of political rewards backed up by the threat of severe political punishment for non-compliance, Calles believed in the efficacy and transformative nature of education to achieve his goals. Calles realized that the weak private sector he inherited with his presidency in 1924 could provide little assistance in the reconstruction of the national economy.[4] Thus, he mobilized the state and used it both to fill the vacuum of those parts of Mexico's private sector that were historically underdeveloped or destroyed by the revolution and as a means of supplementing the future growth of the private sector by providing it with the necessary infrastructure.[5] His education program was meant to make his economic and infrastructure projects more effective by providing Mexico with trained workers to carry them out.[6] He focused his reforms on agricultural credit, new irrigation systems, dams, and roads.[7]

Calles advanced a modernization project that centered on the role of education as an inculcator of economic advancement, pride, and patriotism. To Calles, this project – much like the positivist project advanced by Díaz's *científicos* – was apolitical and would lessen the need to change the predominant social structure of rural Mexico through wholesale land distribution and transfers of wealth.[8] This project would also develop Mexico's inherent productive strengths and take advantage of her natural sources of wealth, mainly mining, agriculture, and oil.[9] These were the seeds of the future corporate Mexican state, a state that would mitigate class conflict through a centralized state apparatus that provided citizens with social programs and promises of a better life.[10] To make it happen, Calles would need to advance policies that resulted in the accumulation of private capital.[11] More than anything, however, Calles was interested in turning the denizens of Mexico's countryside into U.S.-style independent farmers, mirroring successful commercial farmers from his home state of Sonora. He believed that the main reason for Mexico's economic backwardness was the ignorance of campesinos and their inability to make use of advanced agricultural techniques.[12] Furthermore, he thought that a modernized peasantry could provide the engine of growth for Mexico's modernizing economy, arguing that the "economic well-being of the peasants ... [would] form a more prosperous and happier" Mexico, overcoming the economic chaos caused by the revolution and propelling her into the economic and social realm of the world's leaders.[13]

Calles hoped to achieve several goals through the expansion of rural education. First, he wanted to provide the basic service of teaching people how to read and write. Though campesino loss of land to greedy elites during the Porfiriato was the main cause of the revolution in many parts of Mexico, rural Mexicans had been clamoring for increased educational opportunities for over 40 years. Calles hoped that the vast expansion in the number of federal schools would fill this gap. Furthermore, he believed that if campesinos knew how to read and write they would better be able to defend themselves in legal matters against large landowners. Second, Calles wanted to improve Mexico's rural economic production. He viewed increased agricultural output as both the primary motor for the national economy and a means of overcoming class conflict by providing a brighter economic future for those harmed most by the policies of the Porfiriato. Third, Calles wanted to undermine the power of the Catholic Church as well as other hostile local power holders. Like many other liberals, Calles believed that the teachings of the Catholic Church were one of the major causes of Mexico's economic backwardness. Moreover, he viewed the Church's vast wealth as unproductive and wanted to harness it to improve Mexico's economy. In addition, Calles proposed strong state intervention into the Mexican economy, which would only be effective if local political authorities hostile to his regime did not undermine it. Fourth, Calles dreamed of creating a single national culture. Mexico had long been a country of strong regionalism. In this respect, Calles hoped that inculcating a single national culture in

Mexican primary schools would transform the local loyalties of Mexicans into an ardent patriotism and love for Mexico as a nation. In response, he focused his attention on those who had the least reason to be patriotic – Mexico's numerous indigenous groups. Calles understood that indigenous people were the victims of centuries of neglect and abuse at the hands of Spanish and then Mexican settlers and thus called for their incorporation into Mexico's Hispanic heritage (without doing anything actually to stem the tide of further abuse at the hands of Mexican capitalists, of which he was one). Part of his dream of a single national culture, however, included the civilizing process of the vast majority of Mexico's rural dwellers, whom Calles viewed as being only a little more advanced than their indigenous counterparts.

Calles' educational thought clearly favored the teaching of practical matters. His predisposition toward "rational" and practical schooling began with his teacher training at the Colegio de Sonora in 1889.[14] Sonoran Governor Ramón Corral, one of Diaz's strongmen, created the Colegio to put Sonora on the road to "civilization," advance the "cult of progress," and counteract the influence of a newly founded Catholic school in Hermosillo.[15] The positivism taught in the Colegio promoted the idea that Europe and the United States were superior to Mexico because their greater "order" had led to economic and social "progress," that elites had been chosen to rule through Darwinian natural selection, and that only scientific (rather than humanistic or religious) knowledge would result in "order and progress."[16] In fact, he believed that humanistic and religious knowledge impeded progress.[17]

As an assistant teacher at the Colegio de Sonora in 1896, he began applying his positivist training in the classroom. Historian Jürgen Buchenau argues that it was in the classroom that Calles first realized that education was an extraordinary milieu within which to mold the hearts and minds of Mexico's future citizens. It was also during this time that he came to focus on the family as the central unit for inculcating positivist beliefs and morals.[18] In 1901, Calles co-edited *Revista Escolar* with his long-time associate, Fernando F. Dworack, who would later serve as the Director of Federal Education in Sonora. In the magazine, Calles argued that "the family unit should be the basic foundation of society" and that "to the degree that family life is better organized, society will be better off."[19]

During his tenure as the Governor of Sonora (1915–19), Calles published a program called *Tierra y libros para todos* (*Land and Books for Everyone*) as a basis for his government. The program stressed the state's dual role of promoting

PLUTARCO ELÍAS CALLES FLANKED BY LÁZARO CÁRDENAS AND OTHER POLITICAL
AND MILITARY LEADERS AT A PUBLIC WORKS SIGNING CEREMONY. PHOTO COURTESY
OF FIDIECOMISO ARCHIVOS PLUTARCO ELÍAS CALLES Y FERNANDO TORREBLANCA.

public education and agricultural improvement for the betterment of the public good.[20] Even at this early stage, Calles was arguing that agriculture was "the principal element of national wealth" around which Mexico's social renovation, modernization, and progress should be based.[21] In addition to these mainstays, Calles promised to support the improvement of infrastructure, public health, and commerce in hopes of creating a vibrant economy in Sonora. In 1917, he established the Cruz Gálvez Vocational and Arts School for orphans, where teachers trained boys to farm, type, and do carpentry and girls to perform domestic tasks.[22] He had enough faith in the school that he placed his own daughters in it.

Calles' Sonoran program provided a blueprint for the multiple goals that Calles wanted to achieve through his educational policy as President of Mexico. To take the place of the Catholic Church as the molder of hearts and minds the state would need to expand citizens' access to lay primary schools. Calles' *Tierra y libros para todos* promised that the state would pay for a lay primary school in any location with more than 500 inhabitants or 20 children unless it was located on the land of a company, hacienda, or mine; in these cases, the owners of the business would have to pay for the school.[23] Primary schools would also be required to provide night classes for adults. To make sure that the education available in these schools was satisfactory, the state government would create a normal school for the training of teachers. In addition, each municipality would be required to maintain a public library. Finally, to prepare students for the state's workforce, Calles mandated that the managers of railroads, mines, and factories would provide vocational training for youth.

Calles combined educational policy with social and moral renovation. He outlawed the importation, manufacture, or sale of intoxicating beverages, the penalty being five years in jail.[24] He followed this decree with another that forbade the playing of games of chance, allowing state citizens to play only the higher-class games of dominos, chess, raffles, billiards, bowling, and checkers, but only if there was no wagering involved.[25] Calles backed his promises of moral reform and increased educational opportunities for Sonorans by allotting a whopping 22 per cent of the state's budget to education.[26] Following his positivist belief in the superiority of the United States, the normal school that he founded was based on a school in Gary, Indiana, that he had visited.[27]

Also while governor, Calles attacked religion in Sonora. First, Calles allowed Luis Monzón, a firm anticleric, to run the state's normal school. Monzón insisted that teachers who attended the normal school fill out questionnaires to insure that they held the proper liberal and anti-religious beliefs.[28] In 1918, Calles signed an expulsion order for all the Catholic and Protestant priests who worked in the state's 83 temples and churches. Calles stated publicly that it was necessary to rid Sonora of their presence because they had failed to take an active role in pursuing the economic, political, military, or educational goals of the state. Instead, he argued, they served to "foment American intervention."[29] The truth, however, was that the majority of these priests were against the policies being put in place by Calles. Many of them had actively undermined the liberal and anti-religious tenets of his educational, economic, and political policies. In 1919, he retracted the expulsion, but continued to limit the number of priests and ministers allowed in the state.[30]

As a presidential candidate in 1923 and 1924, Calles argued that "Mexico could not be a great country" as long as 80 per cent of all Mexicans were illiterate.[31] Accordingly, he advanced a more thorough version of his previous educational and social program for Sonora. On September 6, 1923, when he declared himself a candidate for the Mexican presidency, he announced in *Excélsior* that the spread of elementary schools would be a "primary and determining" factor in the advancement of "our humble classes" by teaching utilitarian and practical skills. Calles wanted these schools to wage war upon the moral vices, religious fanaticism, and petty crimes that stood in the way of Mexico's progress.[32] Later, in *El Democrata*, he promoted the incorporation of Mexico's indigenous population, arguing that only if they were united with the rest of the country could they come to understand their duties.[33] While most Mexicans saw the numerous indigenous groups as obstacles to progress, he asserted that their economic backwardness was the product of 400 years of persecution. Calles, adopting the main argument of Justo Sierra's *Political Evolution of the Mexican People*, argued that, given a proper education, indigenous people could be "elevated" to the level of men of dignity; their incorporation into the civilized world would help to "form a happy and respected nation for all the people" of Mexico.[34]

As president-elect, Calles continued to outline the educational program that he planned to implement. In an interview with U.S. journalists in New York City, he noted that he was an ally of schooling in Mexico, arguing that the federal government would establish schools where they did not yet exist and improve them where they already did.[35] Upon accepting the presidency, Calles guaranteed that education policy under his administration would not only "fight against illiteracy, but also achieve the development of a harmonious spirit among our campesino and indigenous population in order to ...

Escuela Ofici

STUDENTS, SOME IN BLACKFACE, IN FRONT OF THEIR SCHOOL IN SINOQUIPE, SONORA. PHOTO COURTESY OF FIDIECOMISO ARCHIVOS PLUTARCO ELÍAS CALLES Y FERNANDO TORREBLANCA.

FROM MANY, ONE

1 de Sinoquipe Son

incorporate them completely into our civilization" and that extending rural schooling to the extent that Mexico would fulfill its full economic potential would be a "constant preoccupation" for him and his policy makers.[36] During his inauguration address for the school year at the National Autonomous University of Mexico (UNAM) he repeated his pledge to support the "economic liberation and educational development" of the "rural masses, workers, and indigenous people" upon whom the future prosperity of Mexico depended.[37]

After Calles assumed the presidency on December 1, 1924 he said that "the revolutionary movement [had] entered its constructive phase," hinting that the need for revolutionary change in Mexico was over.[38] He was faced with a daunting task. Mexico's total population was over 13 million, of whom an estimated 62.3 per cent were functionally illiterate. Meanwhile, only 5.4 per cent of school age children, between the ages of 6 and 14, were attending federal schools that, in theory, would be offering classes that advanced Calles' educational policies. Many of the federal schools that did exist lacked completed buildings and had to hold classes in the shade of trees or in temporary structures.[39] Meanwhile, the rest of the country's school age children were either attending state primary schools (24.1%) or attended illegal religious schools or lived in areas that did not have schools (70.6%).[40] Furthermore, until October 1924 state-controlled political delegations in each of the states ran federal education, making it nearly impossible for members of the federal government to implement their educational programs.[41] The above statistics overestimate the number of school age children who failed to attend school because private religious schools were illegal and the federal government did not consider them. Regardless, Calles recognized the great strides that federal teachers had made in their local communities. He said:

> Rural teachers of the Republic ... that know how to resolve [problems] in their pueblos, many times without anyone's help and with only duty as a guide ... men that, with only two pesos daily, are capable, outside of school hours, of forming rural cooperatives and various economic and social actions.[42]

To widen the effectiveness of his education program and to provide greater access to schooling for the campesinos, Calles asked the Education Ministry to increase the number of rural schools by 1,000 in each year of his presidency.[43] In fact, his goal of increasing the number of federal schools during his presidential administration often overshadowed the attempts by his educational advisors to improve the quality of education in those schools.[44] Because the SEP lacked proper resources, Calles asked the parents of students to take an active part in numerous leagues and societies, donating their time and resources toward the construction and maintenance of schools.[45] He also shifted the SEP's resources away from school construction, focusing budget expenditures on paying for the new teachers who would give instruction in the schools built by campesinos.[46]

In 1926, Calles founded the Ejidal and Agricultural Bank, based on institutions he had seen during his trips to Germany. He hoped that this bank would decentralize agricultural production by supporting the creation of regionally and locally run agricultural organizations and collectives. By 1927, 17,000 adherents had formed 378 agricultural societies.[47] In addition, the government created two Experimental Agricultural Substations in hopes of improving rural production.[48] Overall, Calles spent $9 million for irrigation projects, $6 million on 20,000 kilometers of roads which stretched from Mexico City to Laredo, Acapulco, and Puebla, and $6 million for maritime ports to bring about the economic advancement of Mexico based upon her agricultural production.[49]

Calles also spent another $6 million on the centerpiece of his educational and agricultural program, the Central Agricultural Schools.[50] The goal of these schools was to train campesinos to become modern farmers who would be able to produce increasing amounts of crops, while simultaneously increasing the purchasing power of Mexico's rural workers who would be the target of new industrial and consumer goods produced in urban areas.[51] Calles envisioned a network of agricultural schools encompassing the entire nation. Each school would adapt its programs of instruction to the varying economic and geographic features of its local area. Each of these schools would also be equipped with an Ejidal Agricultural Bank to enable the students and local campesinos alike to borrow the necessary capital to industrialize their agricultural production.[52] Furthermore, the Education Ministry would supply each of the schools with 500 hectares of arable land and modern farming equipment with which to raise crops and livestock. Finally, each school would have dormitories and classroom space for 200 students between the ages of 10 and 16. Officials hoped that students would return to their communities of origin after graduation to pass on their knowledge and experience.

As we will cover in more detail in the next chapter, federal officials radically changed the structure of the Education Ministry in October 1924 in an effort to centralize the federal government's control over primary schooling. During Obregón's presidency, delegations established and controlled by the individual state governments ran education. SEP officials, however, believed that the individual states were more concerned with consolidating their political power than with spreading education into the countryside. Most of the primary schools opened with federal funds, they argued, were mere concessions to the politically powerful or were gifts to political friends. As a result, state and local officials opened many schools in unnecessary locations, leaving other areas without any educational facilities whatsoever. In addition, most of the teachers who received jobs in these schools received them as political favors and were unqualified.[53] Education Ministry officials decided to transform these delegations into director's offices under the control of the federal government with the responsibility of administering and inspecting primary schools.[54] To rectify the lack of rural educational coverage, José Manuel Puig, the Secretary of Education, dispatched education missionaries to convince campesinos to accept the placement of federal schools in their communities.[55] Puig emphasized that he would not impose federal schools on rural communities, arguing, "We want the school to work for the community and the community to work for the school." The success of federal schools, he hoped, would be the result of increased cooperation between the rich and the poor. They would also provide a locus in which federal teachers could bring modern civilization to the countryside.[56] During the first nine months that the SEP was under Puig's control, the 48 federal missionaries were able to nearly double the number of rural schools under federal control from 1,039 to 2,001.[57]

Campesinos would learn more than reading, writing, and arithmetic in rural schools. In addition, the government entrusted teachers with providing practical and technical training, adapted to the local economy and natural resources of the region, to rural inhabitants to increase economic capacity.[58] Moisés Sáenz, the sub-secretary of education, cited as an example the success of the rural school in the indigenous community of San Francisco Culhuacán near Xochimilco on the edge of Mexico City. Sáenz noted that the teacher there taught the children to read and write in the morning and spent her afternoons teaching the women in the community how to sew and cook. In addition, the teacher had convinced the community members to purchase an icemaker with which they made ice to sell in neighboring communities.[59] In hopes of achieving similar results across Mexico, the SEP set up eight traveling *Misiones Culturales* that offered short classes for teachers to increase their knowledge about both academic and practical subjects.[60] This was doubly important since, given the rapid expansion of the federal school system, few rural teachers actually met the federal government's minimum requirements, which officially included finishing the sixth grade and graduating from a federal normal school.[61] Once federal teachers had received sufficient training, however, Education Ministry officials believed that they would be able to transform rural communities completely in two or three years.[62]

At the root of this rural transformation would be the already mentioned action education pedagogy adopted in 1923. The action school would be an idyllic copy of the community as well as a social center for community members in which teachers would expose children to the various activities that they would take up in earnest when they reached adulthood.[63] According to Puig, the school would provide a milieu in which,

> ... the child might live the rich and complete life of a child; that the child's school activities might form a connection with the home and the community; that the child might have a spirit of wakefulness, activity, and investigation; that the child might observe and compare, and in a real and concrete form consistent with the motives of scholarly work, schools will be centers of interest made available for the acquisition of knowledge; that the child might work spontaneously and freely; that the child might enrich his culture, develop his powers and have a prevocational preparation for the activity to which he is inclined; that it might be the child's own actions that provides the most efficient tool for his education and that he might acquire habits of cooperation, of mutual aid, and constancy in work which will fortify his moral character.[64]

While the action school claimed to improve both the student's learning process and his or her local economy, it accepted, and in some ways reinforced, the economic status quo by teaching the sons of campesinos to be campesinos, the sons of workers to be workers, and the sons of the wealthy to be white-collar workers. In addition, Education Ministry officials often found it difficult to convince older teachers, who had been trained to teach with different techniques and pedagogies, and teachers in the countryside who lacked training and the proper equipment and materials, to implement the action education.[65]

Between 1926 and 1928, the SEP founded Central Agricultural Schools in Durango, Guanajuato, Michoacán, Jalisco, and Puebla. The economic difficulties that began in 1926, however, forced Calles to back off from his dream of expanding their coverage to all the different states. Besides the high cost of these schools, the lack of political and economic support by the different states and the unrealistic entrance requirements – students from rural areas were supposed to have graduated from primary school – resulted in their failure to fulfill their original goals.[66]

In 1926, the SEP began making radio broadcasts asking rural communities to construct voluntarily a federal school building. The broadcasts told campesinos that doing so was part of being a good citizen and that it would give them the chance to practice working together to achieve something that would help everyone in the community.[67] In private, Education Ministry officials acknowledged that they would have preferred to build the schools themselves, but that they lacked the necessary resources.[68] Nonetheless, once the SEP received a promise of school construction from a community or the donation of an already existing building, inspectors formed a Comité Pro-Educación (Pro-Education Committee) with the local parents. Officials charged this committee with arranging for additional donations for the school, including playground and theater equipment, school furniture and supplies, farming and orchard land, and livestock to practice new techniques and raising future revenue for the school.[69] The Pro-Education Committee was just the beginning. In order to gain the support of the local populace and often against the wishes of local caciques, the SEP also demanded that teachers create societies, clubs, banks, newspapers, co-operatives, commissions, and unions as well as hold numerous "social gatherings" among children and adults that stressed proper hygiene, sanitation, dress, and deportment.[70] These would give them a taste of democracy as well as teach them effective administrative skills.[71]

In addition to improving Mexico's overall agricultural output, Calles hoped to attack Mexico's weakest link in the production chain, Mexico's numerous indigenous groups. Calles, like most Mexicans, viewed the non-Hispanized members of Mexico's indigenous groups as economically backward because they failed to use "modern" farming techniques and, more importantly, because mestizos and whites had invaded indigenous areas and confiscated the most productive agricultural land, forcing them into isolated areas where there were less fertile lands and less access to irrigation.[72] He believed that the indigenous races were mentally fit, well organized, and capable of elevating themselves to the intellectual level of their mestizo and white neighbors. Calles hoped that access to education would end the exploitation of indigenous people and give them "the exact comprehension of their duties;" in other words, patriotism.[73] His experience of the late-nineteenth/early-twentieth-century Yaqui racial struggle in Sonora molded his ambivalence toward indigenous people. The Yaquis controlled most of the fertile land in Sonora, and Yoris saw them as an impediment to progress and engaged in an extermination campaign against them to gain access to their land. At the same time, Yoris valued Yaqui labor and often protected individual "civilized" Yaquis from the extermination campaign.[74] If only indigenous people could be "civilized," Mexico could harness their labor and skills.

The SEP's major policy initiative aiming at "civilizing" members of the various indigenous groups was the creation of the *Casa del Estudiante Indígena*. The Education Ministry founded the Casa in Mexico City in 1925. It ran until replaced by indigenous boarding schools in the separate states in 1932. Calles considered the Casa as a "collective psychological experiment" that would prove that indigenous people had the capacity to "acquire the culture and civilization of criollos and mestizos."[75] In many ways, the Casa's goals mirrored the goals of the off-reservation boarding schools that preceded it in the United States. According to educational specialist Joel Spring, boarding schools in the United States had three main goals: 1) teaching Native Americans to use English instead of their tribal language; 2) the eradication of Native American cultures; and 3) the inculcation of patriotism in place of tribal allegiance. Spring emphasizes that the location of boarding schools away from the reservation was consistent with an educational philosophy that focused on destroying Native American children's tribal cultural connections.[76] There were some important differences of emphasis between the U.S. and Mexican programs. Obviously, the Education Ministry wanted indigenous people to learn Spanish, not English. More importantly, the SEP was less interested in completely eradicating indigenous culture. In fact, as Dawson and López have shown, the Mexican government was willing to tap into some aspects of indigenous culture that they deemed superior to mainstream Mexican culture.[77] Nonetheless, it would be dangerous to overemphasize the degree to which the Education Ministry wanted to rescue indigenous culture, as most indigenistas still viewed indigenous people as barbaric and uncivilized.

The SEP asked federal and state officials in each of the states to send "pure blooded Indians" between the ages of 14 and 18 who had already finished second grade to the Casa in order to "civilize them."[78] Their plan was to remove these boys from their homelands and immerse them in the culture of modern Mexico by placing them in "daily contact with criollos and mestizos" in primary, technical, and industrial schools located in the capital.[79] Shortly after the founding of the school, Puig cited the Casa's acceptance of a group of *Huicholes* who arrived in a state of absolute cultural backwardness and impoverishment. Less than two months later, he claimed, these indigenous children could not be distinguished from other Mexican children.[80] Clearly, Puig's claim was part of a propaganda campaign aimed at convincing other educators (and through them the communities – especially, perhaps, indigenous ones – within which they worked) that the SEP's civilizing campaign would be successful and beneficial. Eventually, the SEP hoped to send these "civilized" indigenous students back home to continue the acculturation program amongst their own people. Given the difficulties that most teachers faced, it is hard to believe that Puig persuaded many teachers that the Casa was a magic pill that would eventually solve Mexico's most intractable problem. As we will see, the Casa met with only very limited success.

Three months after the SEP had opened the Casa, Puig outlined the program for indigenous integration that the Education Ministry would attempt to implement during his tenure as Secretary of the SEP. He believed that Mexico's indigenous problem was essentially a social rather than a racial question. He asked readers to recognize that the truth about Mexico's indigenous population lay somewhere between the positive physical and spiritual characteristics attributed to them by the supporters of *indigenismo* such as Manuel Gamio and the negative characteristics of docility attributed to them by skeptics.[81]

The real question, Puig said, was what the Education Ministry should do to help indigenous people recover from centuries of exploitation. Since indigenous people's potential was no different from anyone else's, civilizing them was the key to redeeming, adapting, and converting them into equals and citizens of Mexico.[82] To civilize them, they would need to be rescued (through schooling, of course) from isolation and reintegrated into mainstream Mexican society.[83]

For those indigenous people unable to attend the Casa – the vast majority, since the Casa could take on only 200 children at any one time – Puig suggested that teachers use a different pedagogical approach. The main vehicle of acculturation would be Spanish. Rural teachers with indigenous students would have to sacrifice the practical program of the action school to focus completely on Spanish instruction until their students had a comfortable command of the language. At the same time, Puig expected federal education inspectors to create a cottage industry in each indigenous school to augment the economic capacity of indigenous communities.[84] To overcome the ambivalence of many indigenous communities toward *indigenismo* and acculturation, Puig hoped to harness the abilities of Casa graduates when they returned to their original communities.[85] Finally, Puig argued that empowering indigenous communities was not a zero sum game and asked teachers, inspectors, mestizos, and whites to work together to advance the SEP's indigenous education program.[86]

For some indigenous students, the economic opportunities of Mexico City, and perhaps, their cultural alienation from their own people after being educated, far outweighed any incentive to return home.[87] For other students, however, their extreme isolation from their indigenous societies and cultures was too difficult to overcome. Almost 30 per cent of them quit or fled the Casa.[88] Nonetheless, after the Education Ministry changed the Casa into a normal school for the training of indigenous rural teachers some students did eventually return home to instruct their brethren about the things they had learned. By 1931, however, the SEP realized that training indigenous rural teachers in the capital to confront problems in the countryside was not only inappropriate but also impossible.[89] Despite these problems, Moises Sáenz argued that although the Casa was too expensive to continue, it was a "beautiful and generous experiment ... an experience that has given the most brilliant results" and provided an objective lesson of what indigenous people could accomplish.[90]

Reminiscent of his anti-religion crusade during his governorship of Sonora, President Calles moved to implement the constitutional restrictions against church involvement in education in 1926. His decision brought his administration into direct conflict with Catholic forces throughout much of central and western Mexico in the *Cristero* rebellion from 1926 through 1929 and again in 1932 and 1933.[91] The Cristero rebellion proved to be one of the greatest obstacles to educational and economic progress and political centralization during Callista Mexico, requiring major troop deployments and reallocation of funds that the government could have used for much more productive purposes.

In 1928, the last year of Calles' presidency brought with it serious political and educational problems as well as much reflection on the part of educational authorities. In his annual speech before Congress, Calles incorrectly claimed that neither the Cristero rebellion nor the collapse of the world economy had harmed his education program.[92] The Education Ministry's most recent data (based on 1926) were dire. They showed that 65 per cent of adults (those over nine years of age) were still functionally illiterate and that 62 per cent of all children were not attending school on a regular basis.[93] Thus, the outlook for the future looked quite dim despite all that the federal government had tried to do in the countryside. Puig and Sáenz had focused a lot of their attention on the creation of an efficient system of normal schools for the training of teachers and inspectors. For example, in 1928 alone the SEP had trained 1,224 new rural teachers and 24 new inspectors (to raise the total to 117).[94] Yet, after four years, most of the normal schools still lacked furniture, bathrooms, good buildings, decent libraries, and the necessary materials to give teachers hands-on training.[95] Moreover, the Department of Primary and Normal Schooling noted that the normal schools themselves (as well as the teachers graduating from them) were seldom implementing the action school pedagogy that the entire federal school system was based on. They asked that school inspectors hold those teachers who refused to use these methods accountable.[96] How they should do so given the scarcity of well-trained teachers and their high levels of mobility, however, they left unanswered.[97]

In response to these difficulties, Puig advanced a wholesale program for the betterment of rural communities. He noted that in order for the SEP to be successful, federal teachers would need the full support and co-operation of other federal, state, and local government agencies, though these agencies were often working at cross-purposes.[98] In addition to the reading, writing, arithmetic, and industrial and agricultural skills that the federal rural schools had taught in the past, they would now also focus on teaching campesinos how to improve their domestic lives and personal cleanliness. This new program would specifically focus on changing adults' "customs and … ideals."[99] Teachers would form cleanliness clubs to visit neighborhood homes to make sure that everyone in the community was complying with SEP hygiene standards.[100] This was a drastic shift in rural education. Puig claimed that underlying moral factors were undermining rural education, not the education program itself. He argued that if this new program of changing the domestic living patterns and habits of personal cleanliness of campesinos were successful, the Education Ministry would be able to integrate 50,000 adults into the modernized fabric of Mexican life and in the process rapidly modify the Mexican countryside.[101] To speed along the process of rural change, Puig asked teachers to spend their weekends convincing the members of rural communities to put in telegraph lines, highlighting his belief with regard to indigenous people and campesinos that isolation was a root cause of their perceived backwardness.[102] Yet, Sáenz correctly noted that the intrusiveness of these programs, which included regular home visits to inspect for cleanliness, had already played a central role in the SEP's past failures. Sáenz noted that Education Ministry officials had underestimated the high degree of conflict caused by the great ideological disparities between the federal government's teachers and local inhabitants. While Sáenz went on record as supporting the SEP's new program, he publicly stated that the first goal of every federal teacher should be to maintain good relations with local authorities.[103]

Meanwhile, Rafael Ramírez, having returned from an inspection tour of U.S. rural schools, accepted the post of head of the *Departamento de Escuelas Rurales, Primarias Foráneas e Incorporación Cultural Indígena*, which he would hold until 1934.[104] He argued that Mexico's rural schools were inferior to those in the United States on nearly every count. His trip had impressed upon him that U.S. rural schools had better buildings; were cleaner; were better organized; were being repaired and adapted as necessary; had adequate playgrounds, theaters, and gardens; had better and more equipment, supplies, and books; had better trained personnel; had higher attendance; and were better supported by their local communities. Like Calles, Ramírez aimed to change Mexico's rural schools, using the United States as model of success.[105] In conjunction with Puig, he vowed to eliminate all those "customs, beliefs, and ideas that undermined the improvement of [peasant's] 'productive capacity.'"[106]

The actual implementation of the SEP's programs in the countryside was something else altogether. In southeastern Chihuahua, officials noted that local inhabitants already viewed federal schools in the same manner as churches had been in the past, namely, as institutions that helped and defended them against the vagaries of life. At the same time, however, night classes suffered not only because few schools owned lamps, but also because of teacher and campesino resistance to SEP policies. Furthermore, numerous communities were unwilling to donate the mandatory farming land for the school. Instead of recognizing the intrusiveness of the SEP's program, Education Ministry officials chalked up the problem to the fact that the teachers in the area were women, to whom locals were disinclined to listen.[107]

As noted earlier, Calles' educational policies that met with the most resistance were his anti-Catholic ones. Among the casualties was president-elect Obregón, whom religious fanatic José de León Toral assassinated in 1928. Obregón's assassination ushered in the Maximato, which Calles used to centralize power. In the area of education, for example, Chihuahuan school inspector

Gregorio Lozano and a cadre of three teachers sided with anti-Calles rebels in the wake of the assassination. Calles subsequently fired them.[108]

The replacement of Manuel Puig Casauranc with Ezequiel Padilla as the Secretary of Public Education at the beginning of 1929 marked the further radicalization of primary education in Mexico. Upon taking the job, Padilla announced that during his tenure he would try to accomplish two main goals. First, he would try to extend the use of the action education pedagogy to every school in the country. Second, he would use every available resource to accomplish the federal government's education plans. Like his predecessors, he decried the lack of co-operation that both state and local governments had shown toward the federal government's programs. In this vein, he applauded the advancement of circuit schools that local inhabitants of rural communities would pay for but that would be run by and extend the influence of the federal government.[109] Between February and April 1929, the SEP established 292 circuit schools with 1,477 satellite schools attached to them.[110]

In May 1929, Padilla began to implement a socialist version of the action pedagogy that would later become the official pedagogy of the SEP under Narciso Bassols in 1931. As Lewis has noted, it was never quite clear exactly what socialist pedagogy entailed. In its simplest form, socialist pedagogy merely transformed the individual hands-on learning by doing experiences into group projects. However, it also aimed to mobilize entire rural communities in favor of the federal government's hygiene, anti-alcohol, "Mexicanization," and anti-Catholic programs in addition to encouraging "cultural projects intended to promote rational, scientific thought."[111] Padilla also pushed to use joint public-private ventures as an alternative means of mobilizing people to construct outdoor theaters, playgrounds, and parks and to invest in first aid kits and campaigns against the use of alcohol and infant mortality. Padilla argued that the old individualist pedagogies had resulted in the creation of a social caste system. The new socialist approach, on the other hand, would bring together everyone's interests and would result in the overall betterment of Mexican society.[112]

Padilla also focused on expanding the federal government's primary education system into highly indigenous areas. In all, the SEP had established nearly 800 rural schools with about 75,000 students in indigenous areas, although that did not mean that the students attending these schools were necessarily indigenous. As we will see in more detail in Chapter 3, Education Ministry officials created two Tarahumara boarding schools in the western sierra of Chihuahua. Finally, they proudly announced that they had sent two indigenous students from the Casa to an advanced school to learn modern agricultural techniques, which they were to bring back to their native regions.[113]

In 1930, Aaron Sáenz, the brother of Moisés, became the Secretary of Public Education, replacing Padilla. Aaron began his tenure by noting that education was the basis of Mexico's national consolidation. Promoting "Mexicanization," he argued that primary education should remain the focus of the SEP's program because it served immediately to incorporate the popular masses into the national culture and because it provided a means by which campesinos and workers could satisfy both their material and spiritual needs. Moreover, he philosophized that the Mexican Revolution had created a government that served the people rather than exploiting them. The revolution's chief success in this regard, he said, was the creation of the federal rural school system.[114] He vowed to add a new chapter to the federal government's educational successes by focusing on the expansion of Mexico's normal schools.[115] The main problem with the normal school system was that it did not produce enough teachers to fill the needs of Mexico's primary schools. Equally important, their somewhat centralized locations made it difficult to convince (as well as expensive to send) graduates of the schools to fill the vacancies in faraway states such as Sonora, Sinaloa, Campeche, and Yucatan.[116] The Education Ministry agreed to fund a federal normal school in each state to rectify the situation.[117]

In addition to the improvement of normal schools, Sáenz advanced a detailed plan meant to put into place Padilla's socialist action school. The range of goals that primary schools were supposed to achieve continued to expand. First, policy makers argued that campesinos lacked the necessary "physical vigor" to undertake the necessary transformative labor to modernize the countryside. Profesor Alfredo E. Uruchurtu, the author of many textbooks and lesson plans for primary schools, deemed that turning weak, sickly campesinos into "good animals" was more important than teaching them how to read and write. If rural teachers and parents failed to focus on health and physical education, Mexicans would be unable to undertake their duties as Mexican citizens.[118] Second, rural schools were to familiarize children with "the most important beings, things, and phenomena" of their native environment so that they would be able to take better advantage of it when they were adults than their parents were presently doing.[119] Furthermore, the school was to familiarize children with the tools and instruments that they would most likely use when they grew up. Third, the rural primary school was to provide children with an example of human advancement within the context of a socially homogeneous community.[120] Fourth, the federal education system was to build children's self-esteem and moral character, in the process giving them the skills necessary to "formulate plans and projects ... [as well as] the necessary perseverance to accomplish them."[121] Finally, schooling was to teach children to "use their free time in an adequate manner" so that they would not become victims of the numerous vices that plagued the Mexican countryside.[122]

As we will see in Chapter 6, the Education Ministry also set up four frontier schools on the U.S.-Mexican border to "counteract the foreign influence along the frontier" and to offer young people the chance to finish their primary and secondary schooling without crossing the border to attend better-financed schools in the United States. To accomplish this, frontier schools were given better facilities, offered a wider range of classes, and were staffed with fully trained and better paid teachers. SEP officials also considered turning the frontier schools into combined primary and secondary schools to prevent the graduates of primary school from going to the United States to attend high school.[123]

The following year brought Narciso Bassols to the helm of the SEP with the most radical education agenda of the Callista era. Bassols successfully pushed for the implementation of an anti-religious program and the coeducation of all children. In addition, he advocated, unsuccessfully, for a sex education program throughout the federal school program. The Education Ministry's battle against the Catholic Church had been dormant since 1929 with the end of the Cristero rebellion. Bassols began by pushing for a change in Article 3 of the Constitution (supported by Calles and duly passed by Congress) that outlawed the "sustaining, establishment, or direction [of] primary schools" by any religious corporation or ministry. The previous version of Article 3 had outlawed religious teaching in both public and private schools, but had not restricted the running of schools by religious organizations. The Catholic Church and other religious groups were using this loophole to offer religious training in the schools that they ran.[124] This was certainly true of the Mormon inhabitants of Chihuahua, who managed to continue teaching the Bible in their schools until 1935, when they decided, under pressure from the Cárdenas administration, to place themselves under SEP's authority.[125] The sex education program never emerged from the planning stages due to strong Catholic resistance. Members of the influential *Unión Femenina Católica Mexicana* (Mexican Catholic Women's Union or UFCM) engaged in successful "petitions, school boycotts, and rallies" in Mexico City while the Mexican episcopate asked parents to remove their children from public schools and place them in illegal religious schools until the Education Ministry backed down.[126] The coeducation program, on the other hand, while fully implemented, still taught girls "cooking and women's work" while instructing boys in "farming and the workshop."[127]

SEP officials continued emphasizing the socialist goals of the rural school, arguing that its two main goals were to give campesinos a "communal conscience" and to "dignify and ... ennoble the community." As part of this program, officials asked community members to engage in a further expanded modernization campaign by establishing voluntarily local post offices and postal services, laying telephone and telegraph lines, building roads and local markets, cultivating public gardens, and introducing potable water.[128] One way to measure the Education Ministry's priorities is to look at the time teachers were to allot to the instruction of different subjects. In first and second grade children were supposed to spend 3 hours and 45 minutes (third and fourth graders spent only 2 hours and 15 minutes) every week learning Spanish. At the same time, children in every grade were to spend 9 hours per week learning aviculture and horticulture and maintaining the school's garden.[129] Another means of measuring their priorities is to look at SEP budgets. Between 1927 and 1932, the Education Ministry had redirected its budget to address the needs of Mexico's campesinos. In 1927 primary schools in Mexico City had absorbed nearly half of all federal education spending while rural schools received only 12 per cent of total expenditures. By 1932, the SEP had reduced Mexico City's share of budget expenditures to 29 per cent while simultaneously expanding its rural expenditures to 32 per cent. Furthermore, the Education Ministry had expanded the rural school system to include 7,165 schools while the primary school system in Mexico City continued its work with 438 primary schools.[130] They had accomplished all of this expansion in the face of severe budget cuts brought on by the Depression.

Bassols used the SEP's greater presence in rural Mexico to reinforce the hygiene campaign, prodding supposedly unclean and unsanitary campesinos to clean up their villages, burn their garbage, and receive vaccination shots.[131] To make sure that teachers and inspectors were doing an adequate job, the SEP created the new position of Inspector General (IG) and centralized educational oversight. The IGs, four in all, audited the work of local inspectors and reported their findings directly to Education Ministry officials in Mexico City rather than to the individual heads of federal education in each of the states.[132]

Under Bassols, the Education Ministry also increased its efforts to integrate Mexico's numerous indigenous groups into mainstream culture. Many indigenous children only attended school at irregular intervals because they needed to work long hours just to avoid starvation or because they had to migrate looking for work. The SEP tried to overcome this problem by setting up two further indigenous boarding schools in Chiapas and Guerrero in addition to those already established in the Sierra Tarahumara in Chihuahua. They planned to add another in Oaxaca. They hoped that these schools would more quickly "civilize" the indigenous children by putting them in continual contact with their teachers, who were to eat, sleep, and work with them. In addition to teaching Spanish, the boarding schools served as agricultural and industrial workshops. Education Ministry officials wrongly hoped that agricultural and industrial products made in boarding schools would provide enough income to pay for the children's food and clothing.[133]

In 1933, with presidential elections looming and with them the fear of violence in the countryside, the SEP focused on reminding teachers of their proper role. Education Ministry officials argued that while teachers had the constitutional right to their full civil rights (by which they meant that teachers could vote), they were not to take an active part in any political party or faction or explicitly adopt any creed. Instead, they were to act as leaders and guides for the communities within which they were working and advance the common good of rural Mexicans by advancing the tenets of the federal government's new Six-Year Plan.[134] The plan called for the "improved integration of the nation and of all the people that were part of it." The plan would continue the modernization of Mexico's rural and indigenous denizens through "intensive education and through the better use and distribution of natural resources."[135] Finally, the plan adopted "Mexican socialism" as the official pedagogy of all federal schools.[136] Of course, a teacher's adoption of the federal government's educational program, which called for organizing rural communities in favor of economic development, was inherently political.

Bassols also returned to Calles' early attempts to improve rural agricultural output through the reconstitution of agricultural training schools. The new *Escuelas Centrales Agrícolas* (Central Agricultural Schools) would combine the old *Escuelas Normales Rurales* (Rural Normal Schools) and the *Misiones Culturales* (Cultural Missions). The old Cultural Missions had been traveling teachers' workshops, but numerous SEP officials had complained that the courses that they offered were too short and often did not address the needs of local communities.

Centros de Cooperación Pedagógica (Cooperative Pedagogy Centers) replaced the workshop function of Cultural Missions. Teachers from different schools were to get together each Saturday under the supervision of local inspectors to discuss the difficulties and problems that they had encountered during the week.[137] The new Central Agricultural Schools underlined the fact that the SEP's goal of rural education was to create "an economic base" for improved production. Accordingly, the schools would "orientate, perfect, and intensify [Mexico's economic development] through the action of teachers with a special attitude, ideology, and preparation."[138] Bassols argued that only those teachers who received training in and practiced new agricultural techniques would be able to teach others to do the same.[139] Interestingly, the Education Ministry staffed each of these schools with both a male and female rural organizer, meant to train teachers and to enlist and coordinate peasant support for agrarian reform and federal schools.[140]

In 1933, SEP officials also attempted to harness what they believed was the underutilized economic production of rural women. Since 1923, when officials implemented action education, the Education Ministry had advocated teaching women how to cook and sew (skills that they probably already knew quite well) to improve the overall domestic life of rural dwellers. Now they exhorted rural women to quit wasting their time trying to look beautiful for their men. Instead, if women used their moral authority over men and devoted themselves to doing good works in favor of the local community, then their men could also be convinced to participate in local civic life as well.[141] In addition to tapping into women's moral authority over men, there was also an underlying suggestion that rural men would do whatever it took to have intercourse with their women whether they looked good or not. Thus, rural women could co-opt their mates' sex drives to the advantage of their families and local communities. This presumed that women, unlike men, were naturally less interested in sex for sex's sake. In rural areas, where women had little access to beauty products or money to purchase them, and in a society where women had long been expected to submit to their men's sexual advances, it was dubious (and probably even dangerous) to suggest that through withholding sex from their men, women could improve the civic life of their local communities. Equally important, but consistent with accepted gender ideologies, was the underlying assumption that women were more interested in improving the local community than men were.

Finally, with a slight improvement in the Mexican economy Bassols tried to shore up the retention of federal teachers, the SEP's indigenous education program, and frontier schooling. To this end, 3,502 rural teachers who had in the past been paid between 27 and 41 pesos a month were now being guaranteed a minimum salary of 55 pesos.[142] Bassols argued that the Education Ministry could not rely on teachers who received less than two pesos a day because they often sought other work at the same time that they were supposed to be teaching. In addition, the SEP expanded the number of indigenous boarding schools outside of Mexico City to eleven.[143] These new boarding schools undertook the so-called "economic and social rehabilitation" of indigenous children.[144] Rafael Ramírez argued that boarding schools located in indigenous areas would function better than the Casa del Estudiante Indígena because they would not separate indigenous children from their natural environment and also would not create in them a hatred toward their own people after they had been fully civilized.[145] The SEP was also addressing the indigenous problem by sending out *Promotores Deportivos* (Sports Promoters) to work among Mexico's various tribes. Education Ministry officials hoped to improve the physical well-being of indigenous people, which they viewed as one of the major factors in their future economic advancement. Finally, the Education Ministry opened 30 additional rural schools and two new urban schools along the U.S.-Mexican border. Though they did not officially name them frontier schools, they were nonetheless supposed to continue the work of strengthening the "patriotic sentiment[s]" of Mexicans living near the United States.[146]

In July 1934, Calles adopted his most radical educational position ever in his Grito de Guadalajara. He argued that:

> The Revolution has not ended.... It is necessary for us to enter a new period of the Revolution, which I would call the psychological or spiritual conquest of the revolution; we must enter into that period and seize the consciences of the children and of the youth, because the children are and must belong to the Revolution. It is absolutely necessary to evict the enemy from that trench, and we must assault it with decision, because there is the clergy. I am referring to education. I am referring to the school. It would be a very grave mistake, it would be criminal, for the men of the Revolution to fail to dislodge the youth from the claws of the clergy, from the

claws of the conservatives; and, disgracefully, numerous schools, in many States of the Republic and in this very capital, are directed by clerical and reactionary elements.[147]

In December 1934, the same month that Lázaro Cárdenas took office, government officials changed Article 3 of the Constitution to acknowledge officially the adoption of Calles' new position, establishing that "education which the State imparts will be socialist and in addition to excluding any religious doctrine, will combat fanaticism and prejudices, for which the school will organize teaching and activities in such a way as to create in youth a rational and exact concept of the Universe and social life."[148]

All of the institutional changes put in place between 1924 and 1934 set the stage for Cárdenas' renewed effort at mobilizing rural denizens in favor of a paternalistic Mexican state, socialism, and agrarian reform. Now we turn to the ways in which Calles expanded the federal government's control over rural schooling and extended the federal government's influence into the countryside by examining his centralization of primary schooling in Chihuahua.

2

Federalization of
Education in Chihuahua

Between 1924 and 1935, Mexican federal policy makers faced numerous obstacles in their drive to provide religion-free universal primary education for all children. These obstacles ranged from interference by local *caciques* who feared that federal schools would undermine their historical powerbases to pro-religious parents and teachers who disagreed with the constitutional separation of church and state. This chapter about the politics behind the initial centralization of primary education in Chihuahua (the first Mexican state to fall under near complete federal control), during the 1920s and 1930s, aims to analyze the series of initiatives undertaken by the Mexican government to attain power over Chihuahuan schools. These ranged from federal government block grants to state authorities to the creation of a parallel federal school system that competed with state school systems and the consolidation of the state educational system under the federal government's control. Analyzing these programs will illuminate one aspect of the process by which the federal government sought to consolidate its power in post-revolutionary Mexico, create a corporatist state, and promote a common national culture.[1]

As previously noted, Porfirian political leaders had failed, despite much discussion, to extend federal primary education into the countryside, the long-time domain of municipal, state, and private Catholic schools.[2] Mexico's post-revolutionary leaders picked up the challenge and again promoted a centralizing program meant to improve the delivery of education by increasing the federal government's control over rural education. Although the Constitution of 1917 gave municipal governments control over the funding and delivery of primary education, President Obregón, head of the Interior Ministry Calles, and head of the Education Ministry, José Vasconcelos, believed that the only possible way to deliver an adequate primary education was under the auspices of the federal government.[3]

They faced a daunting task. Mexico was "many Mexicos," a patchwork collection of people who were motivated by their "ethnic, regional, ideological, class, and clientelist" allegiances rather than by patriotic feelings toward a nation that often had little to do with their own lives.[4] Obregón and Calles hoped that by tapping into the widespread support for rural education and implementing federally run education for all Mexicans that focused on creating good citizens and workers they could accomplish two mutually compatible goals: stability and economic development in a country that was politically, ethnically, socially, and economically fragmented; and consolidation of their own power base by using schools as vehicles to take the place of existing local and, later, state institutions and construct out of the many regional Mexicos a single, unified nation.[5]

In 1921, Vasconcelos pushed for and obtained changes in the Mexican Constitution that gave the federal government the right to create its own school system as long as it did not interfere with state sovereignty or the states' own schools. The National Congress of Teachers, which had met the previous year, promised to support the federal government's efforts and approved a proposal that backed joint federal-state co-operation. Nonetheless, when federal policy makers raised the issue of centralized federal control over schooling, congress attendees refused to consider it.[6] Since state educators were not willing to give up their local prerogatives, the Education Ministry shifted its focus to the undermining of individual municipality's constitutional rights to control local education. Interestingly, the theft of local power by state and federal *caciques* had been a key impetus in the onset of the revolution in the first place. Article 14 of the Constitution of 1917 addressed this by naming municipalities the base of political and administrative power.[7]

Vasconcelos argued that the constitutional framers had done Mexicans a great disservice by leaving primary education in the hands of municipalities.[8] SEP officials noted that municipal schools were in a "deplorable" condition.[9] To overcome this, Vasconcelos refused to deal with municipal governments, even when these local entities were, by state law, entitled to govern over local education, as was the case in Hidalgo, Durango, and Colima.[10]

By 1923, the federal government was providing educational grants to many of the individual states, with the only requirements being that the states contribute a minimum percentage of the overall educational budget.[11] Education Ministry officials, however, argued that the direct subsidizing of state education was failing because it ignored the "principle of local responsibility."[12] In January of that year, the federal government released a report entitled *Bases para la acción educativo federal*, which reiterated the SEP's goal of advancing a national educational project that did not infringe the rights of local authorities. The Education Ministry argued that, in spite of its recognition of the sovereignty of the individual states, it must remain involved in local and state educational systems. The report noted that it was the SEP's duty to create a unified national culture and to improve the output of Mexico's agricultural sector because the individual states had neither the resources nor a sufficient number of rural schools to advance these projects.[13]

The de la Huerista rebellion in 1923 underlined Obregón's tenuous grasp on power, forcing him to advance a political policy that was, on its face, based on "accommodation not centralization."[14] His regime pursued, in the words of Moisés Sáenz, the educational goal of filling "a real necessity . . . that would not clash with the actions of the local authorities."[15] Despite the regime's apparent weakness, it did manage to remove municipal governments from educational policy-making concerns by simply refusing to recognize their authority.[16]

Early post-revolutionary Chihuahua provides an excellent example of this process. The state had been a hotbed of revolutionary activity because of the severity of *caciquismo* imposed on the municipal governments by Porfirian state oligarchs. As noted in the Introduction, Chihuahuan campesinos had earned their right to local self-rule (and land ownership) by defending their communities against the Apache threat.[17] One rebel announced that their only requirement for putting down their arms was that "no one should interfere with them, nor bother them for anything, nor meddle in their affairs."[18] Revolutionary leaders in the state such as Pascual Orozco and Francisco "Pancho" Villa, recognizing the political desires of their local supporters, backed the free election of local leaders and non-state interference in local matters.[19]

National-level post-revolutionary leaders sought to change that. After the revolution, Chihuahua's economy lay devastated. Its agricultural, transportation, commerce, mining, and communications networks were in ruins. The leftovers of revolutionary bands still roamed the countryside, and about three-quarters of Chihuahua's livestock herds had been lost during the revolution.[20] Furthermore, severe droughts hit the state, destroying the corn, wheat, and bean harvests in 1920, 1921, and 1922. The lack of agricultural production produced a shrinking tax base that led to perennial budget shortages. De la Huerista military action between December 1923 and spring 1924 further disrupted the state economy. As a result, the state government was always behind in paying its employees, including its teachers.[21]

General Ignacio C. Enríquez, a close ally of Obregón, was the Governor of Chihuahua (1920–24). Enríquez, who in 1916 as a revolutionary general had returned estates confiscated by revolutionary forces back to their original owners, did not believe in the viability of ejidos. He spent the first several years of his administration stabilizing the social and economic situation in Chihuahua. He pushed for U.S. investment to shore up the economy and refused (in spite of his alliance with Obregón) to implement federal anticlerical legislation, which he saw as divisive.[22] To address the state's financial problems, Enríquez turned to the federal government for help. In 1922, the federal government agreed to subsidize the state's educational system. Specifically, the SEP agreed to pay 50 per cent of state teachers' salaries. Additionally, they promised not to interfere in the state's running of state schools. Finally, both parties conceded that they had based their agreement on a "transitory" economic situation and would immediately cease once the state had regained control over its budget problems.[23]

By dealing with the state governor as the only official representative of the state, the federal government, through the Education Ministry, actually undermined the position of municipal governments as local power brokers. As we shall see, these initial attempts by Obregón and Calles to gain a political and educational space within Chihuahua to advance their revolutionary project of ideological unification were only the first timid steps.

In 1923, the Chihuahuan mining sector rebounded. Coupled with increased pressure by campesinos, Enríquez made an abrupt about-face on his earlier policy and carried out the first land reform in the history of the state.[24] Obregón and then Calles mirrored Chihuahuan state policy at the national level as they measurably increased the pace of land redistribution in rural areas to respond to campesino demands.[25] The educational picture in the country remained dire.

Shortly after Calles became president and Jesús Antonio Almeida (1924–27) became governor of Chihuahua, nearly two-thirds (65.1%) of Chihuahans were functionally illiterate. While state schools educated the highest numbers of students (32,493) and spent the highest percentage of its state budget on education in Mexico, the federal government had only an ephemeral presence in the state. Only 3,515 students attended federal schools (offering classes that advanced federal educational policies and ideologies meant to produce better and more productive Mexican citizens), and less than half of the state's school age population (42.3%) had access to government schools, either state or federal.[26] Many of the federal schools that did exist lacked completed buildings and had to hold classes in the shade of trees or in temporary structures.[27] While Chihuahua was doing better than many other places in Mexico, Calles vowed to improve the situation.

He decided to create an educational system that was parallel to and independent of the individual state school systems. This federal educational expansion would not only provide Mexicans who lived where there were no schools with a chance to learn, but would also allow the federal government to further penetrate the domain of the individual states and local communities. He ordered an increase in the number of schools by 1,000 in each year of his presidency.[28]

Federal school expansion certainly served the purpose of providing greater access to schooling for the campesinos who stood at the center of Calles' dreams of economic progress. To avoid backlash from state educational authorities, the Education Ministry vowed not to open any schools within three kilometers of already existing state schools.[29] Nonetheless, the SEP often based its placement of these new schools more on political criteria than on educational need, and thus provided Calles' regime with additional power bases in the countryside where the federal government's control was weakest.[30]

There was no organic law that laid out what the SEP's prerogatives were, and one official figured that 60 per cent of the acts taken by the Education Ministry were against existing law.[31] Nonetheless, in the absence of explicit restrictions the SEP moved to take command of available political spaces. Calles' move to create a parallel educational system was the next logical step in the power consolidation process that Obregón had begun. Whereas Obregón focused on using the expansion of education into the countryside to overcome the political independence of municipal authorities, Calles' parallel school system addressed the control that the individual states had over primary education.

Calles began this process by annulling all the existing educational contracts that Obregón, Vasconcelos, and the leaders of the individual states had previously reached.[32] He then appointed a single director of federal education for each state who would report directly to the head of the newly created Rural Schools Department.[33] As these new directors took charge of the parallel federal school systems created in each of the states, the federal government completely halted the subsidization of state primary schooling.

Federal school inspectors then traveled across the countryside asking communities to donate or construct a local school building. As noted earlier, if locals promised to provide a school building, the Education Ministry, in turn, promised to send a trained teacher with school materials and books to the community to begin the government's education project.[34]

In contradiction to their promises not to interfere in state and municipal education, the SEP also looked favorably on parents of children attending municipal and state primary schools who petitioned the federal government to take over control of their schools.[35] They also pushed to place non-religious private schools under federal control in areas where the federal government was having trouble asserting its influence.[36] Overall, one of the major difficulties the federal schools encountered was in gaining the co-operation of the local populace.[37] To allow for the peaceful entry of teachers into local communities the Education Ministry strictly prohibited teachers from intervening in any way in local politics.[38] The Education Ministry could only claim that its cultural project was neutral and apolitical – though it is hard to believe that they actually believed it themselves – because its creators advocated a school curriculum that was "rational" and "scientific."

Puig announced that "politics do not interest us here in the SEP ... the patriotic function of the [SEP] is only educational and social."[39] Yet, the Education Ministry advanced a program that consistently placed itself in the thick of local politics by doing things like organizing community members into Education Committees and Mother's Societies in order to strengthen the federal government's claims vis-à-vis local officials. These community activities stressed the advancement of the rights of common people and their constitutional obligations to Mexico and its federal government. Furthermore, inspectors and teachers focused on including children in these activities so that they could mold them into proper citizens and future supporters of the federal government.[40] In practice, the running of these committees was seldom democratic or apolitical. Inspectors often changed the composition of these groups in an ad hoc manner when they were unhappy with the results of local educational initiatives. On other occasions, teachers refused to allow indigenous people (or failed to consider them as possible candidates) to sit on these governing bodies in ethnically mixed communities.[41] Despite these drawbacks, collective actions like these served the dual purpose of further undermining local authority and advancing the federal government's education project.

The supposed apolitical nature of the SEP's federal parallel school system also did not match Calles' own beliefs or actions. Calles was no lover of democracy or even fair democratic competition. His biographer Jürgen Buchenau argues that Calles "envisioned a political system in which the [future] ruling party dominated through electoral triumph, if possible, and fraud, if necessary."[42] In Chihuahua, Calles and Obregón tried to convince Enríquez to run for another term as governor.[43] When that failed, Calles recognized Enríquez's pick for the next governor, Almeida. Almeida, unlike his predecessor, worked diligently to establish an independent political base in Chihuahua (and regularly intervened in local politics himself, installing his relatives as municipal presidents in Ciudad Juárez and Ciudad Chihuahua) until the military zone commander Marcelo Caraveo overthrew him in 1927. Though there is no smoking gun to prove that Calles directed or approved the coup against Almeida, he did remove 25 governors from office between 1925 and 1927, and there is circumstantial evidence that Calles at least knew about the coup beforehand.[44]

As the federal government built its parallel school system across Mexico, Governor Almeida resisted as much as politically feasible the redistribution of agricultural lands in Chihuahua and federal interference in state affairs. Only the communities of the original colonists in Galeana, Casas Grandes, Namiquipa, and Las Cruces who had earned their citizenship by defending the frontier against the Apaches won major land concessions. Importantly, these areas were outside the areas of Almeida's major political support in western Chihuahua. At the same time, Calles' leading worker's union, the *Confederación Regional Obrera Mexicana* (CROM) failed to gain much traction in Chihuahua.[45] As Mark Wasserman notes, Almeida was the "last independent political boss in Chihuahua," and his downfall in 1927 would usher in closer state-federal coordination of policy.[46]

Calles' promotion of a parallel school system brought with it some problems that plagued federal policy makers. First, as soon as the federal government proceeded to advance its own school system and cut state schools systems off from funding, it lost the ability to influence the nature of education advanced by the states. Policy makers complained that there was little or no coordination between federal and state education.[47] Second, federal policy makers protested that for every school they opened the states were closing one of their own in order to save money. This may have been an unfair complaint since the number of state and municipal schools was double that of federal schools in 1928.[48] Nonetheless, states and municipalities severely under-funded their schools (as did the federal government). State governments were providing about 40 per cent of overall combined educational budgets across the nation, but this total ranged widely from a low of about 10 per cent in Durango to highs of over 50 per cent in Sonora and Chihuahua. The Education Ministry wanted states to spend at least as much on their state school system as the federal government was spending on its own system (i.e., 50 per cent each), arguing that it was impossible to enforce obligatory school attendance requirements where there were no schools.[49]

Top education officials came to realize early on that if the Education Ministry wanted to implement an ideologically consistent educational program, only a single unified education system run by the federal government would suffice.[50] Aaron Sáenz argued that the "school should be the base of our national consolidation, the genesis of our culture."[51] To expand further the federal government's reach across the countryside the SEP advanced a program of circuit schools in 1928. The federal government would fund a central rural school run by a fully trained teacher who, in turn, would oversee a series of local schools that the members of nearby communities would sustain.

Within two years, this program allowed the federal government to expand its control over 2,491 additional schools with 58,380 students.[52] Still, the federal government did not have as much control over the country as it would have liked. If parents did not choose to send their children to a federal school, the federal government could not force the issue.[53] The Minister of Education in 1929, Ezequiel Padilla, argued that "one of the unforeseen effects of the federalization of education was its deplorable interpretation ... in the majority of states ... [as] local authorities left unfulfilled their responsibility to attend to the education of the masses." He reminded everyone that "during the armed struggle, the Revolution is the campaign; in times of peace, the Revolution is the school!"[54] Although the federal government had doubled the amount of its educational budget aimed at rural primary schooling over the previous three years, by 1931 the SEP was ready to further tighten its grip over the control of primary rural education in Mexico and put the revolution back on course.[55]

The ascent of Narcisso Bassols to the post of Education Minister in 1931 coincided with political turmoil in Chihuahua. At the root of much of the chaos was the eventual governor, a close ally of Calles, a political outsider in Chihuahua, and a person closely connected to gambling interests in Ciudad Juárez – General Rodrigo Quevedo (July 1932 – 1936). Governor Andrés Ortiz (September 1930 – November 1931) lost the support of Calles when he backed his godparent President Emilio Portes Gil in a dispute with Calles. It also did not help that Ortiz was Catholic and a supporter of the Knights of Columbus. Calles ordered Quevedo to appear before the Chihuahuan legislature and demand Ortiz's resignation, which Ortiz proffered three days later. Calles selected Colonel Robert Fierro (November 1931 – July 1932) to take Ortiz's place as governor, but only to give Quevedo more time to establish himself in Chihuahua. Quevedo's rise to power in Chihuahua mirrored Calles' attempts, through the *Partico Nacional Revolucionario* (PNR) and its state affiliate, the

Partido Revolucionario Chihuahuense (PRCH), to consolidate political control over state government.[56] It also mirrored Calles' and Bassols' attempts to do the same in the field of education.

Bassols undertook the most radical steps to centralize power over the educational system in Mexico during the Maximato. During his tenure, Bassols managed to centralize control over the circuit schools created over the previous couple of years and the schools sustained by private entrepreneurs according to Article 123 of the Constitution of 1917. Also under Bassols' watch a number of individual teachers' unions came together to form the *Confederación Mexicana de Maestros* (CMM) in 1932. This was a precursor of the syndicalization and centralization of teachers under President Cárdenas.[57] Finally, the implementation of anti-religious socialist pedagogy in the same year led to the further politicization of teachers.

The circuit schools that were originally created in 1928 to expand the federal government's reach into the countryside during a time when the government was facing a financial and budgetary crisis proved too much of a success for the liking of SEP bureaucrats. Local communities reacted with enthusiasm to the idea of being able to control their own schools and choose their own teachers. The continued intervention of parents in running circuit schools led Bassols to centralize control over them. In the process, the federal government came to own approximately 2,500 school buildings that provided additional strategic political spaces for advancing its political and social goals in the countryside.

Prior to Bassols' tenure as Minister of Education the federal government had found it against its best interests to enforce provisions of the Constitution meant to make owners of large haciendas, mines, and plantations build local schools and pay the salaries of federal teachers for their workers.[58] When he took over the SEP, however, Bassols was determined to force the owners to provide primary schooling regulated by the federal government if their business was located three or more kilometers from the nearest federal primary school and if there were more than 20 children in the area. More importantly, for the first time congress also gave the Education Ministry the ability to impose sanctions and fines against business owners who refused to comply with the new regulations.[59]

Despite the new tools in his arsenal, Bassols still had a tough fight on his hands. There was no guarantee a business owner would comply with the regulations without a long legal battle. For example, the owner of the Compañía Maderera de Chihiuahua, S.A. refused to sustain a federal school, arguing that the inhabitants who lived around the company had lived there before the company opened its doors for business, thus making it the government's responsibility to provide them with an education. They even took the SEP to court, suing to avoid paying the 60 pesos monthly necessary to employ a teacher. The company finally relented under federal and state pressure in 1935. Other business owners claimed that even though they had several hundred people in their employ, their workers did not have enough children to warrant a federal school. In some areas, workers with children petitioned the federal government not to force the owner of the company to abide by the new rules for fear that the owner would fire them and replace them with childless workers.[60] In the end, Bassols' implementation of Article 123 proved to be a half-victory but still another step in expanded federal government control of Mexican countryside.

Bassols' promotion of socialist pedagogy demanded that teachers socialize the children under their care by including them in campaigns meant to advance the "productivist, hygienic, redistributive, and ideological goals" of the revolution.[61] These goals were anti-religious, and in Chihuahua, pro-Quevedo. However, the federal government simultaneously charged teachers with advancing its politicsand prohibited them from engaging in politics. The federal government advanced its position in one of its official publications, *El Maestro Rural*, arguing that "teachers should not act as politicians" because they represented the social and political advancement of the entire community that they were serving, not just one party or faction of it. The SEP asked teachers to promote the principles of "modern science … without prejudices."[62] Yet, Quevedo himself was radically anticlerical and a fervent supporter of socialist education. He successfully pushed to rename localities with religious names to pro-revolutionary ones, changing, for example, Santa Isabel to General Trías.[63] Thus, the federal government was asking rural teachers to advance the federal and state government's political program as if it were a neutral and non-political solution to the very political problems in the Mexican countryside.

More than any other factor, the anti-religious tenets of the federal government's socialist education program elicited the greatest resistance in Chihuahua. Especially troublesome for many Catholic parents was the introduction of sexually integrated schools, a proposition that Quevedo unleashed a propaganda campaign to support. In Camargo, the change from unisex schools to coed schools resulted in a series of public protests. Jesús Coello, the local SEP inspector, claimed that the protestors were led by the local municipal president, a former teacher who was a priest, the rich, a number of *beatas* (religious women), and a cabal of politicians.[64] Salvador Varela, the head of federal education in Chihuahua, correctly noted, however, that the opponents of coeducational schooling were upset because they considered coeducation immoral and felt that the government had not consulted them before making changes.[65] Despite the contradictions inherent in asking teachers to advance a political program while asking them to remain politically neutral, the federal government pushed through constitutional changes in 1934 allowing for the official adoption of its socialist education platform.[66]

It was during Bassols' tenure as Minister of Education that Chihuahua's state government once again began to run into budget shortages. The world Depression radically undermined the state's economy beginning in 1929. The sudden drop in the demand for minerals put an estimated 20,000 Chihuahuans out of work by 1932. Coupled with poor harvests in 1929 and 1930, U.S. officials repatriated "voluntarily" some 500,000 Mexicans and people of Mexican descent. Governor Fierro responded by slashing the salaries of state employees by 10 to 20 per cent in 1932.[67] He also turned to the federal government for help.

Just prior to leaving office in 1932, Fierro made a proposal to the federal government that echoed the agreement that state politicians had hammered out with the federal government in 1922. Noting that the state could not even afford the back pay already owed to its teachers, he proposed that the federal government take over 100 state primary schools. He asked the federal government to pay these teachers at least 54.74 pesos monthly plus all the back pay that the state owed them. Furthermore, Fierro insisted that the federal government had to accept all the state teachers, regardless of their training, along with the schools. The state, in turn, promised to continue running the remainder of its primary schools. Like a decade earlier, Fierro demanded that the state have the right to take back control of state schools under federal supervision when the state's budget situation improved.[68]

The SEP's response to Fierro's proposal was quite unlike the response that it had given a decade earlier. The Education Ministry categorically denied that if it chose to take over state schools it would have to accept the state teachers with them. SEP officials noted that if the state teachers did not meet federal government standards, they would replace them with teachers who did. Furthermore, the Education Ministry agreed to take over only twenty-nine rural schools, and only those that were located in areas of importance for the federal government; namely six rural schools located on the U.S.-Mexico border and twenty-three located in areas with a high concentration of indigenous people.[69] Perhaps federal officials were simply waiting for Fierro's interim term as governor to end so that they could deal with the pro-Calles Quevedo. In any case, there is no actual evidence that Fierro agreed to these terms, but the exchange of proposals nonetheless demonstrates the increasing ability of the Education Ministry to set the terms upon which it would be willing to help state officials.

A year later, with Quevedo in place, Chihuahuan officials again approached the federal government for help with its budgetary problems. On July 24, 1933, Governor Quevedo asked his legislature to approve the federal takeover of state primary schools in order to advance the goal of school uniformity.[70] In response, the state legislature authorized the federal government takeover of the state's primary school system.[71] In August 1933, the state of Chihuahua and the SEP officially signed an accord, and all the state's primary schools came under the control of the federal government.

The accord stipulated that all of Chihuahua's primary schools would adopt the federal government's official education program; the federal government would come to own all of the school buildings and materials previously owned by the state; and the state would subsidize the federal government's running of primary schools in the state. The Education Ministry, on the other hand, agreed to continue maintaining the 293 state schools already in existence and promised to spend at least 538,248 pesos annually on primary schooling in Chihuahua. They also agreed to keep Quevedo informed of the amount and nature of future annual budget expenditures; he would later ask the SEP to increase its funding of boarding schools in the Sierra Tarahumara. Finally, the accord gave the Education Ministry final decision-making power on teacher placement and pay. The federal government would pay state teachers the same as federal teachers. If the governor and Chihuahua's legislature agreed that the SEP had not fulfilled its contractual obligations after one year, then the governor could ask that the state take back control of the schools.[72] The important shift from Fierro's request that the federal government subsidize state schools to Quevedo agreeing to subsidize federal schools probably reflected two realities: Chihuahua's economy had begun to rebound from the Depression and Quevedo was not only an ally of Calles, but also wholeheartedly supported the Education Ministry's ideological project.

Rafael Ramírez, the head of federal rural schools, instructed federal inspectors to take an inventory of state schools and teachers. He was concerned because only days after the pact had been signed he was informed that the state had inflated figures and had only 205 rural schools that were actually functioning.[73] He told inspectors that for the moment all state teachers should be kept on to maintain continuity, but that those without titles, diplomas, or a sixth-grade education would be replaced by federally trained teachers as soon as feasible.[74]

At the time of the federal take over 73.3 per cent (713 of 973) of state teachers were earning (when they were being paid) about the same or less than the federal minimum wage for teachers of 54.74 pesos per month.[75] This would prove pivotal as federal teachers and federalized state teachers, who were paid on a regular basis and were much better paid overall than their counterparts in other states, would become one of the most important interest groups in favor of the centralization of education in the coming decades.

The initial survey of state schools showed that, by federal standards, the majority of state school buildings were inadequate. Schools were often poorly organized and divided by gender; many locations had separate schools for boys and girls. Federal officials worried that there were too many female teachers, about a 9:1 ratio. In addition, many state teachers were poorly trained. Finally, some state teachers had been employed for 30 to 40 years, making it unlikely that they would be willing to adopt the SEP socialist pedagogy.[76]

Salvador Varela promised to take care of these matters. He immediately enforced coeducational schooling, which led to problems from religious parents. He also attempted to hire more male teachers and pledged to phase out teachers who had been in service for many years, replacing them with better-trained, younger teachers.[77] Varela also took an additional step by naming Inés Estrada as his special assistant in charge of overseeing the smooth transfer of state schools to federal control. After an initial survey of the situation, she produced a report that noted several things. Estrada pointed out Quevedo's association with Calles, which could prove beneficial in a permanent federal takeover of Chihuahua's schools. She also noted that many teachers attained their positions through political and family connections, which was important to think about before replacing them. Other problems included poorly trained rural teachers and low pay.

Her solution – one that the Education Ministry would adopt quite successfully – was to turn the state's teachers into allies of the federal school system. She argued that in order to do so the federal government would have to train the teachers correctly, raise teacher salaries to their proper level, and, most importantly, guarantee punctual pay.[78]

Upon being dispatched to take an inventory of state schools, federal inspectors worked with both teachers and local communities to prepare them for the changes their communities were about to undergo. Some inspectors took note of conditions in schools and lobbied for better wages for teachers. Others found poorly trained teachers and reported that improvements in that area were necessary.[79]

The Education Ministry also discovered, much to its chagrin, that some state rural teachers were closely linked with local Catholic churches. This relationship was bound to cause some problems in local community politics and in some instances did so. For example, SEP officials placed teacher Tito Terrazas M. in San Lorenzo and gave him an old state teacher, Dolores Trevizo G., as an assistant. Shortly thereafter, the assistant teacher complained that Terrazas was immoral and was working her too hard. Miguel Ceballos Durán, the education inspector, investigated the charges and found that Trevizo was working closely with a local priest named Aguirre. Furthermore, Ceballos declared that Trevizo fully supported the role of the church in the local community, was a religious fanatic, and her uncle was running a pro-church, anti-school campaign. Upon deeper investigation, the Ceballos also discovered that state officials had originally opened the school at the behest of the local postmaster, an adherent of the local priest with political connections. Moreover, Trevizo's uncle owned the school building and the state was paying rent.[80]

In August 1935, Governor Quevedo decided either to take back control of the schools that he had ceded to the federal government or to use the threat of doing so as a gambit to extract further concessions from the federal government. The federal government first discovered that Quevedo was planning to petition Chihuahua's legislature for a redaction of the agreement through a newspaper article written by Chihuahua's General Secretary of Government, Professor Manuel López Dávila. The article claimed that the SEP had failed to maintain the minimum number of schools as stipulated in the agreement.[81] The Education Ministry immediately protested.[82]

Several days later Quevedo officially informed the SEP that Chihuahua was preparing to recover its primary schools because the state had previously notified the federal government on three occasions of their failure to comply with the compact. The federal government had failed to rectify the situation.[83] The Education Ministry quickly pulled together its case, amassing statistics that showed that the federal government was now maintaining 333 former state primary schools staffed with 1,076 teachers.[84] The governor responded that since the state was still subsidizing all 333 former state schools (329 rural schools and four Tarahumara boarding schools), the state should be able to run them.[85] By the end of August, however, Quevedo seemed to have changed his mind. He assured the SEP that the newspaper articles written by López Dávila reflected only Dávila's personal view and not that of the state government itself.[86] With that, the SEP hoped that the issue would die.

On September 10, however, Quevedo informed the Education Ministry that he had sent a proposal to the state legislature asking it to vote to take back control of the state's former primary schools. He promised that the legislature would decide within a week.[87] On September 24, Quevedo came clean. He told SEP officials that on August 14 he had signed an order to end federal control over state schools. The three unresolved complaints were: (1) Bassols had promised him that the federal government would hire an additional 80 teachers, but had hired only 45; (2) the federal government had yet to raise the wages of local teachers as much as promised; and (3) the SEP had yet to provide all the materials and furniture needed in former state primary schools. Nonetheless, he assured the Education Ministry that if it were willing to comply with his present demands, he would drop the issue.[88]

It appears, however, that the real reason that Quevedo dropped the issue was due to the pressure from former state teachers. Despite Quevedo's complaints that the SEP had failed to raise teacher salaries as much as promised, the Education Ministry did make teachers' salaries uniform and ensured that they received their pay punctually. The members of the *Instituto de Preparación y Mejoramiento de Maestros de Chihuahua* (Institute of Preparation and Betterment of Chihuahuan Teachers) approached the governor and asked him to renew the agreement. He complied. Nevertheless, he used the disagreement to pressure the SEP to comply fully with its original promises.[89] The Education Ministry had found a winning formula and used it, with the pressure of local teachers, to advance federal control over state schools in Coahuila, Colima, Nayarit, Morelos, and Tlaxcala during this same period.[90]

The *Plan Sexenal* of the PNR is a historical case of double speak.[91] Published in 1934, it promoted the goal of greater coordination between the federal government and state and municipal authorities in the field of education while denying that the federal government was interested in increased centralization or control over primary education, saying that the federal government "neither aspires to the federalization nor centralization or control of education" and that "the action of the federal government and that of the states and municipalities should be coordinated."[92]

Despite its assurances to the contrary, the SEP immediately pushed to implement further accords between the federal government, saying that these agreements would give the Education Ministry "technical and administrative management of primary schools." In addition, to reaching agreements similar to that previously reached with Chihuahua, the federal government wanted to expand its control in the countryside by providing funding for 12,000 additional schools over the next six years.[93] Bassols reiterated that the SEP's goal was merely to increase co-operation between the federal government and state and local authorities and that this was "without a doubt" the ideal "of all the teachers of the Republic."[94]

In 1935, the Education Ministry reached an agreement with the state of Queretaro that mimicked almost word for word the previous agreement that the federal government signed with Chihuahua.[95] Nonetheless, the SEP did face some obstacles in its centralization program. The politicians and policy makers in charge of education in Veracruz, one of the first states to implement socialist education pedagogy, agreed to work with the Education Ministry as much as was feasible, but refused to sign any official agreement that might undermine that state's control over its own education system. Not surprisingly, the PNR moved to co-opt Veracruz's policy makers, naming Gonzalo Vázquez Vela and Gabriel Lucio, the men in charge of education in Veracruz, as SEP's new Minister and Sub-Minister of Education. It then became their task to advance the Education Ministry's goal of educational centralization.[96]

Between 1935 and 1939, the SEP managed to sign additional agreements with San Luis Potosí, Michoacán, and Aguascalientes. They also took the various federal teachers' unions then existing, the *Federación Nacional del Magisterio* (FNM), the *Confederación Nacional de Organizaciones Magisteriales* (CNOM), the *Confederación nacional de Trabajadores de la Educación* (CNTE), the *Federación Mexicana de Trabajadores de la Eduación*, and the aforementioned CMM, and created a single national union out of them: the *Sindicato de Trabajadores de la Eduación de la República Mexicana* (STERM). In 1939, the leaders of this union, seeking to increase their bargaining power (with the support of the SEP) by increasing the number of federal teachers, launched a campaign in favor of the complete centralization of primary education through the absorption of state schools and personnel. By 1940, eight more states had signed agreements that handed over much of their power over primary education.[97]

The presence of a national teachers' union during the Cárdenas administration and after proved to be one of the centerpieces of the near completion of the centralization of control over primary schooling by the federal government. It is ironic that the growing strength of the teachers' union – the *Sindicato Nacional de Trabajadores de la Educación* (SNTE) took the place of the STERM in 1943 – would lead to the PRI's initial attempts to decentralize educational services in Mexico.[98] Only later, under the pressure of conforming to the neo-liberal economic programs of the International Monetary Fund and the World Bank and the international ideals of electoral democracy, would the federal government seek to have the individual Mexican states become responsible for the funding of primary education while the federal government maintained control of the actual content and delivery of these services.

This chapter has traced the centralization of primary education by the Mexican federal government between 1920 and 1940. Even before the Mexican Revolution, federal officials were concerned that neither states nor municipalities were capable of providing primary education adequate to Mexico's needs. It was not until after the Mexican Revolution, however, that officials took major steps in centralizing primary education under the auspices of the federal government (in spite of the fact that the Constitution of 1917 gave control over primary education to the municipal governments). Vasconcelos used the power of the newly created SEP to subsidize state-run primary schooling, and in doing so took the first steps in undermining municipal control over local education. Under the auspices of Puig, Sáenz, and Padilla, the federal government annulled all the existing contracts between the federal and state governments that subsidized state education. In their place, they created a parallel federal primary school system, which reached its peak with the creation of circuit schools. Bassols further centralized federal government control over primary schooling by federalizing the circuit schools created by his predecessors, implementing policies in support of Article 123 of the Constitution of 1917, and, most importantly, attempting to centralize federal control over the grassroots unions created by local teachers. Bassols' drive to centralize federal government control over schooling reached its climax with the federalization of primary schools in Chihuahua and Queretaro in 1935. The centralization of federal schooling reached its climax with the further federalization of primary schools during the presidency of Cárdenas and the creation of the SNTE under president Miguel Ávila Camacho (1940–46) in 1943. By tracing the evolution of federal government centralization over primary education, this chapter has attempted to provide an initial step in understanding the process by which post-revolutionary leaders worked to gain control over a fractured nation, ultimately resulting in the creation of a clientelistic one-party state. Now we turn to the federal government's attempts create one Mexico from many through its *indigenista* program of the Mexicanization of indigenous people along Mexico's northern frontier.

3

The Tarahumara

Stephen Lewis, following Alan Knight, correctly argues that indigenismo was an "elitist, non-Indian construct."[1] Seen from the northern frontier point of view, the march of modernization and progress was in some ways inevitable. Those indigenous people who sided with the Yoris and modernization were redeemable. Those who did not would be (and needed to be) swept aside to make their land and resources available to those who would properly use it.[2] Indigenismo was, in one sense, the attempt by elite policy makers and politicians to formulate a plan to overcome the historic oppression that indigenous people had suffered at the hands of white and mestizo Mexicans in order to offer them a bridge to modernity, progress, rationality, and a scientifically approved way of life, even if it ended up sweeping most, but not all, of their culture and way of life aside in the process.[3]

The extension of education to the indigenous (and rural people in general) served a dual purpose. As Alexander Dawson and Claudio Lomnitz correctly argue, most indigenistas and educators did not view rural dwellers, including indigenous people, as being "ready for citizenship"; instead, they were seen as mere "proto-citizens" who were in need of "state tutelage" before they would be capable of attaining the comprehensive duties, responsibilities, and rights of full citizenship.[4] Along these lines, Obregón and Calles had no faith in the ability of communal landowners, small landholders, or indigenous people to direct their own agrarian development.[5] Policy makers saw them as sickly, backwards, and exploited. Likewise, most educators infantilized campesinos and "denied them knowledge, culture, and rationality" and looked down upon indigenous people as "decadent and deformed by oppression."[6] Nonetheless, the Education Ministry viewed the "rescue" of indigenous people as the linchpin of the material and social welfare of the country.[7] Finally, elites hoped that indigenismo might grant legitimacy to a political regime lacking support in rural Mexico.[8]

As previously noted, policy makers thought that rural schools could end indigenous groups' rural isolation and exploitation in order to make the best use of whatever positive qualities were "latent" in Indian culture.[9] Puig, for example, outlined his approach to *indigenismo* by noting that the truth about Mexico's indigenous population lay somewhere between the positive physical and spiritual characteristics attributed to them by their supporters and the negative characteristics of docility attributed to them by skeptics.[10] In spite of Puig's "positive" view on the educability of Indians, he still thought that the only way to "save" them was to modernize them by incorporating them into mainstream Mexican society.[11] Nonetheless, this was an advancement over the nineteenth century's liberal theories on the role of Indians in Mexico, which had traditionally held that Indians were racially backwards and an impediment to modernization and progress. During the Porfiriato, the Mexican government had responded to these theories with a variety of policies ranging from forced assimilation to extradition to outright murder.[12]

Unlike its predecessor, the new *indigenismo* held that the reason for Indians' backwardness was their history of exploitation at the hands of whites and *mestizos*. Moreover, these *indigenistas* argued that given a proper education, Indians were redeemable.[13] Although Alexander Dawson has argued that some indigenistas held up indigenous people as role models for the future construction of the ideal Mexican citizen and state, policy makers generally reserved the role model status for indigenous groups for those sedentary groups with a glorious pre-Columbian past such as the Aztecs and the Maya.[14] Even then, dominant society often ascribed the positive cultural values of these redeemable Indians to them with little or no indigenous input.[15] On the other hand, for those groups living on the fringe of the Mexican nation like the Tarahumara, Seri, and Tohono O'odham, many *indigenistas* believed that complete assimilation through *mestizaje* was the only possible course of action.[16]

All *indigenismos* are local and varied. This was especially true in the 1920s; the federal government and the Education Ministry had extremely limited resources and their footprint in the Mexican countryside was more ephemeral than real. In the following chapters I will explore how the local, state, and federal officials tapped into, interpreted, and applied *indigenismo* and made use of the SEP to advance their own indigenous assimilation programs vis-à-vis the Tarahumara in Chihuahua, the Seri in Sonora, and Tohono O'odham in the Arizona-Sonora borderlands in the 1920s and the first half of the 1930s.[17] I will also explore the ways in which indigenous people actively made use of the Education Ministry to try to advance their own aims. In each case, indigenous people were interested in harnessing the federal government in an attempt to protect their access to and ownership over land and other social, economic, and cultural resources. Local caciques, ranchers, and state officials, however, were often far more interested in protecting local non-indigenous property rights, maintaining close supervision over indigenous people, and restricting their migratory movement through both coercion and co-optation.

The following chapters explore the ways in which each of these indigenous groups were empowered by what Alexander Dawson has called the "mediating role" that many of their leaders adopted by "allowing the state into local communities in exchange for certain concessions." Dawson argues that this mediating role permitted indigenous people "to challenge the terms of their own domination," certainly an important hedge against state power.[18] Although this mediating role did not come to full fruition until the late 1930s and the organization of Congresos Regionales Indígenas under the Cárdenas administration, during the Calles years local power holders, indigenous or not, took on the mediating role on behalf of, and sometimes against, the best interests of the indigenous group they represented. In some areas, this fits the later pattern that Dawson has illustrated whereby the SEP allowed local elites to "monopolize power with the consent of federal officials, as long as they supported federal officials on certain key issues."[19] In others, contestation over power by local elites was unresolved enough (and the federal government's reach fleeting enough) that local elites could not monopolize power and the federal government was of little help to local elites. Finally, these chapters will analyze why local, state, and federal officials failed in their attempts to assimilate the indigenous groups even though the Indians' leaders expressed a desire to take part in the assimilation program. Once again, this mirrors Dawson's finding that national programs "resonated on a local level only as much as they met local needs."[20] Hence, in the end, these indigenous groups abandoned the government as much as the government abandoned them.

In a 1927 account of the condition of the Tarahumara, education inspector José Macias Padilla argued that the problems the SEP needed to address in order to implement successfully their education program in the Sierra Tarahumara of Chihuahua were enormous. He noted that many Tarahumara were enduring conditions akin to slavery at the hands of local mestizos. He reported that the indigenous people often received only a miniscule amount of liquor, soap, or salt for an entire day's work. The lack of good roads, the hostility of the climate, the sterility of the land, and the distance that tribal members lived from one another also posed serious problems. Macillas suggested that instead of trying to congregate the Tarahumara into Spanish-style settlements – a formula that had seldom been effective over the preceding 300 years – the Education Ministry should form a troupe of traveling teachers to instruct the Tarahumara throughout their seasonal migrations.[21] His superiors ignored his suggestion. Three years after the SEP's initial penetration into the Sierra Tarahumara, education inspectors were just beginning to comprehend the difficulties that blocked their proposed indigenous education program and the Herculean effort that would be necessary to transform the region.

The name Tarahumara – they call themselves Rarámuri – means something akin to 'foot racer' after their affinity for long-distance running. The 1930 census found 25,726 Tarahumara, only 11,170 of whom spoke Spanish, living in the southwestern third of the state of Chihuahua, though their propensity for secrecy and their common practice of hiding from non-Tarahumara suggests that the number was probably higher.[22] Their homeland, the Sierra Tarahumara, is in the Sierra Madre Mountains; huge canyons ranging from 3,000 to 6,000 feet in depth cut the terrain into small isolated sections. The Tarahumara's dual economy consisted of maize agriculture and goat and sheep herding. Each nuclear family functioned "as an autonomous social and economic unit" for much of the year, migrating from the highlands to canyon caves in the winter and then back to their agricultural plots at higher altitudes in late spring and summer.[23] They lived in *rancherías* with (usually) from two to five households scattered some distance from each other. It was at the ranchería level that the Tarahumara had the obligation to engage in reciprocity, sharing their goods with their neighbors and relatives in exchange for their neighbors' assistance in some task such as the planting or harvesting of a crop. These obligations were usually undertaken in the context of a *tesgüinada*, a *tesgüino* or corn beer drinking party.[24] Legal affairs were managed at the pueblo level, which was usually centered on the site of an old Jesuit church. A pueblo generally had legal jurisdiction over all of the rancherías in a radius of 25 kilometers. Each pueblo had a series of native officials with Spanish names, the most important of which was gobernador, whose job it was to "regulate behavior, adjudicate disputes, punish offenders, and organize and carry out the pueblo-wide religious ceremonials."[25] The Tarahumara were further divided into two lopsided groups: those who had been "Christianized" were known as baptized ones or *bautizados* while those refusing baptism were known as gentiles or *cimarones*. The gentiles, about 3 per cent of Tarahumara, were the most conservative, most likely to flee outsiders, and least likely to be exposed to Education Ministry officials.[26]

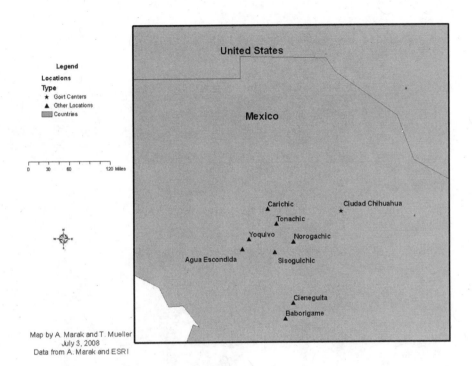

Legend
Locations
Type
★ Govt Centers
▲ Other Locations
▨ Countries

United States

Mexico

0   30   60   120 Miles

Carichic ▲   Ciudad Chihuahua ★
        ▲ Tonachic

Yoquivo   Norogachic
        ▲   ▲
Agua Escondida   ▲
              Sisoguichic

              Cieneguita
                   ▲
              Baborigame
                   ▲

Map by A. Marak and T. Mueller
        July 3, 2008
Data from A. Marak and ESRI

CULTURAL MISSION MEMBERS MEET WITH TARAHUMARA ELDERS IN THE SIERRA TARAHUMARA. PHOTO COURTESY OF FIDIECOMISO ARCHIVOS PLUTARCO ELÍAS CALLES Y FERNANDO TORREBLANCA.

Macias' report on conditions and accompanying suggestions certainly outlined some of the major problems that educators would face, but it had several shortcomings. First, Macias, like many of his colleagues, failed to realize that the Tarahumara did not live great distances from one another for cultural reasons alone. The hostility of the climate and the sterility of the land necessitated that they do so. Thus, unless the Mexican government moved the Tarahumara to better lands outside of the Sierra Tarahumara, an action they never contemplated, schooling alone could not modify their migratory lifestyle or their preference for widely dispersed settlements. To congregate them into tighter, more centralized communities would have subjected them to abject poverty and starvation.

Second, the federal government had little real control over the area. The federal government was in many ways clueless about the Sierra Tarahumara. They sent out a delegation of engineers in 1923 in hopes of better understanding local conditions.[27] In order to consolidate their political position at the national level, Presidents Obregón and Calles had to devolve much of the political control of the country to state and local actors.[28] In the Sierra Tarahumara, state and local officials appointed police and militia members. These officials charged with enforcing national, state, and local laws were usually mestizos and seldom had the best interests of the Tarahumara in mind. In fact, they often served to undermine at the local level the very programs – such as education – espoused by the federal government that would have served to improve the economic and social conditions faced by the Tarahumara. This chapter explores the policies the Education Ministry tried to implement in the Sierra Tarahumara and the problems it faced in doing so.

The SEP's response to Macias' dilemma was to request voluntary co-operation between rich and poor and between whites, mestizos, and indigenous peoples. Puig's toothless promotion of schools as "centers of social cohesion" also epitomized this approach. In the school, he argued, people from different social, ethnic, and economic backgrounds would come together to find their common interests.[29] Of course, this glossed over the quite real possibility that locals might further oppress and take advantage of the Tarahumara through schools. It also ignored the fact that the rich had other options, such as private schools.[30] Aside from Puig's tepid response, Macias' superiors were not predisposed to act on his report. The Education Ministry's dedication to creating a class of U.S.-style yeoman farmers through federal primary schools removed from consideration the adoption of radical educational approaches such as traveling schools.

Perhaps it was the Tarahumara's abject poverty or their relatively large population that caused so many people from all levels of Mexican society to take an active role in their welfare.[31] Whatever the cause, among the Tarahumara the Education Ministry would put forth its greatest effort in all of Mexico, using the number of special schools set aside specifically for the Tarahumara as a measure in their attempts to convince them to adhere to the customs and mores of modern Mexican society. Of course, not everyone looked kindly upon the SEP's efforts. Noted historian Frank Tannenbaum found in his tour of Mexico in the early 1930s that many whites and mestizos living near the Tarahumara were adamantly opposed to educational efforts for the Tarahumara because they feared that once the Education Ministry was finished with them, the latter would no longer submit themselves to the harsh working conditions often imposed upon them.[32] Despite much local opposition (as well as more limited local support), the SEP went ahead with its program, at first timidly and then later, with the help of some members of the Tarahumara, vigorously.

During the first couple of years of Calles' presidency, the federal rural school system rarely touched the lives of the Tarahumara. That does not mean, however, that the Tarahumara had no schools. Until 1925, state authorities in Chihuahua had run a number of *misiones de civilización indígena* that gave instruction to approximately 600 Tarahumara children. Nevertheless, due to budget considerations, state officials closed them.[33] In the absence of federal and state schools, some municipal authorities and the Jesuits, who had been in contact with the Tarahumara since 1607, provided schools. Macias viewed the Jesuits as the main culprits with respect to Tarahumara superstition and backwardness and argued that if the Education Ministry turned old Jesuit convents and churches into government schools, then the Tarahumara would adopt the customs that the government espoused, much as they had done when the Jesuits arrived.[34] Macias misunderstood the Tarahumara. He was right that they had adopted the façade of Spanish legal offices such as gobernador and that they had restructured their pueblos and rancherías around Jesuit missions, but he was wrong to assume that the Tarahumara had internalized Roman Catholic or Jesuit values. Baptized Tarahumara undergo two forms of baptism. Fire baptism is done only among the Tarahumara and confirms their "membership in the Tarahumara community," while the Christian water baptism is used as a means of making ties of coparentage or *compandrazgo* with members of the non-Tarahumara community. Frances M. Slaney notes that the Tarahumara do not assume that undergoing Christian baptism will result in "cultural breakdown or assimilation into white culture."[35] Olivia Arrieta further emphasizes that the Tarahumara have been masters at taking "external impositions" and changing them rather than being changed by them. For example, even though they adopted the Spanish legal nomenclature of gobernador, since Tarahumara society has no place in it for the "direct authority of a single individual" the gobernador is viewed as a mediator and moral guide whose job it is to arrive at community decisions by consensus.[36] Hence, external appearances of assimilation actually served as a means of cultural resistance. The Tarahumara might find some aspects of the Education Ministry's program to their benefit, much as they did with Christian baptism, but their adoption of the program did not signal their acceptance of it on the same terms as SEP officials.

To begin the process of turning Jesuit convents into government schools, officials claimed that religious officials unconstitutionally forced the Tarahumara to pay taxes to sustain these schools.[37] They would not be successful until 1927. In the meantime, religious and municipal authorities were not capable of providing the type of education that many mestizos demanded for the Tarahumara. For example, Indalecio Sandoval, the head of the *Liga de Protección para la Raza Indígena* in Chihuahua, petitioned the SEP to construct enough schools in the Sierra Tarahumara so that they could be "civilized."[38] The residents of other communities – namely Choquita, Guacayvo, Cuiteco, Monterde, and Basogachic – asked the Education Ministry to construct *escuelas de civilización indígena* on the model of the old state schools.[39] Nicolás Pérez, a diputado in the Mexican Congress, offered to donate a school building for the Tarahumara.[40] The *Delegados de la Alta y Baja Tarahumara* asked that the federal government separate Tarahumara children from their parents and place them in schools to civilize them.[41] The rhetoric of "civilizing" the Tarahumara also suggested that while many mestizos meant well in their overtures for improving the Indians' livelihood, they considered Tarahumara identity as expendable and unimportant and Tarahumara children in need of deculturalization. The idea of separating Tarahumara children from their families as a means of civilizing them was not new. Governor Enrique C. Creel (1904–6) had suggested that state officials place indigenous children in the homes of middle- and upper-class non-Indian families as servants in order to assimilate them, a common practice in the United States.[42] Although Chihuahua never put Creel's policy into place, it clearly signaled that any assimilation of the Tarahumara into mainstream Mexican society would be on an unequal basis.

The Education Ministry responded to these suggestions by sending missionaries to examine the situation in more detail. Gustavo Jarquín, one of those missionaries, correctly pointed out that the Tarahumara retained their culture by marrying endogamously, though his suggestion that it was because Tarahumara men were too jealous of their wives and daughters to allow them to sleep with whites or mestizos probably says more about Jarquín than the Tarahumara. He noted that both men and women had long hair, that they rarely bathed, and that they lived in caves. Interestingly, Jarquín's claim that the Tarahumara lived in caves suggests how little time he actually spent with the Tarahumara and how little he came to understand them. He filed his report in January, but had he arrived prior to the winter, he would have known that the Tarahumara also lived in single-room homes constructed of wood and stone during the much of the year. While he failed to note the Tarahumara transhumance agricultural and herding strategy, he did note that when crops were poor, the Tarahumara tapped into the seasonal labor markets in northern and central Chihuahua. Jarquín characterized the Tarahumara as "docile, respectful, severe, jealous, sentimental, and lovers of music." He suggested that the Education Ministry establish boarding schools throughout the region because five days a week would not be enough to teach the children everything they needed to know, and in any case, during the two days that they were away from school, Jarquín was sure, they would forget everything. He also asked (a suggestion that the SEP would ignore until 1933) that the Education Ministry send only the best teachers (*educadores verdaderos*) to the region to incorporate "our Indian tribes into Modern Civilization."[43]

Another missionary, Carlos Basauri, who spent most of 1925 and 1926 among the Tarahumara, proposed constructing boarding schools in the three municipalities of Sisoguíchic, Norogáchic, and Tónachic, where the Jesuits were already operating, plus a regular rural school in Carichic where there were an estimated 40 or 50 Tarahumara children.[44] Basauri probably saw the Jesuits as a threat but he may also have seen their previous work among the Tarahumara as a base upon which to build. By September 1926, however, the SEP had successfully opened only two schools for the Tarahumara.[45] The Education Ministry encountered myriad problems in its efforts, including federal schools built near state schools, teachers incapable of performing their duties, and abuse of power by local officials.[46] In response to the problems, Delfino Bazán, the head of

CULTURAL MISSION MEMBERS POSE WITH TARAHUMARA ELDERS IN CREEL, CHI-
HUAHUA. PHOTO COURTESY OF FIDIECOMISO ARCHIVOS PLUTARCO ELÍAS CALLES Y
FERNANDO TORREBLANCA.

eel

federal education in Chihuahua, asked the SEP for funds to open Tarahumara boarding schools in Sisoguíchic and Carichic. He planned to make use of the old Jesuit buildings in the area, but first he needed permission from the federal government to acquire them. He also asked for the expulsion of the Jesuits in the area – especially Juan Navarro in Carichic, who was running a Tarahumara boarding school, and Trinidad Legarda, who was the head teacher in another Jesuit-run school, La Máquina – because they were allegedly influencing, exploiting, and abusing the Tarahumara.[47] Bazán even proposed closing three rural schools in Huacaréachic, Huehuachérare, and Tehueríchic in order to have enough funds to open a single boarding school in the area.[48]

Despite Bazán's willingness to sacrifice a number of rural schools for Tarahumara boarding schools, Education Ministry officials in Mexico City informed him that it would be impossible to create boarding schools in the region because of a lack of resources.[49] Bazán then requested that in lieu of boarding schools, the SEP should authorize him to create *escuelas de concentración* in Carichic, Yoquivo, and Baborigame. Instead of the federal government paying to feed and clothe Tarahumara children, mestizos would take the children into their homes and provide for them.[50] The Education Ministry put Juan B. Salazar and Salvador Varela, both future heads of federal education in Chihuahua, in charge of organizing these new schools. Because all the local inspectors believed that separating Tarahumara children from their parents to deculturize them was the best way to educate and acculturate the Tarahumara and because *escuelas de concentración* encouraged such, SEP officials decided to test this approach. As a pilot project they opened the first federally run boarding school in Yoquivo in October 1926.[51] In other areas, like Sisoguíchic, where both Bazán and local residents had unsuccessfully petitioned the SEP to create boarding schools, they opened regular rural schools in their stead.[52]

Despite the loud clamor for more Tarahumara schools, inspectors and teachers at first showed little patience or persistence. Bazán, for instance, summarized the predominant view of the educational officials working in the Sierra Tarahumara, reporting that the Tarahumara "eat primitively; live in caves; go about half naked; possess an autonomous government; pursue a livelihood of robbery; their sexual relations are purely biological; they drink alcohol to excess; they are superstitious … [and] their most hated enemy *is the mestizo*, who looks to exploit them like a hunted animal."[53]

Given such a stark depiction of otherness, it is not hard to understand how difficult it would prove to be for inspectors to overcome their prejudices. Also, in the summer of 1927 when the Tarahumara were threatened with starvation and were forced to migrate in search of work and food, the Education Ministry closed a number of schools because of low attendance, thus making it impossible for those Tarahumara children who did not migrate to continue their studies. Moreover, because locals had to invest their sweat labor into schools to make them functional rather than having schools directly invest back into the community, the SEP missed an excellent opportunity to provide relief supplies to the Tarahumara through the schools, which might have won many Tarahumara over to their cause. Many of these schools would first reopen a year later only after the economy improved.[54]

The fall of 1927 saw a continued struggle by SEP officials to deal with what they perceived as the Tarahumara problem. The Education Ministry dispatched inspector Macias to the Sierra Tarahumara to study the situation. He reported on the dire need for federal schools. As he pointed out in his report, the formation of a troupe of traveling teachers to instruct the Tarahumara could prove beneficial. Instead of forcing the Tarahumara to accommodate themselves to a mestizo lifestyle, the company of traveling teachers would migrate along with a given group of Tarahumara, providing them with schooling for about two months, before moving on to work with a different group.

Macias' efforts among the Tarahumara proved daunting at first. In all but one settlement that he visited, the Tarahumara failed to attend the meetings he called to solicit their opinions about the schools. This is hardly surprising given that historically the Tarahumara have used avoidance of outsiders, especially mestizos, as a means of avoiding both acculturation and oppression, going so far as to "voluntarily abandon fertile agricultural fields if a mestizo community [was] established too close to them."[55] In Santa Rosa, however, where there were both Tepehuanas and Tarahumaras, Macias encountered a school that he thought should serve as a model for other schools in the area. There he found that the students had undergone a "marvelous transition" – they were now washing themselves daily and wearing pants, shirts, blouses, and skirts. We should be wary of Macias' report, however, since the Tarahumara are known for adopting outside cultural influences but then transforming them to fit internal cultural understandings.[56] Given Macias' cursory inspection, he could not have gained a deep appreciation of the Tarahumara's understanding of their own cultural transformation. In spite of this outward success, he concluded that, overall, the problems that the Education Ministry needed to overcome in the region were huge.[57]

Escuela en Creel

Construida por Tarahumaras

SCHOOL BUILDING CONSTRUCTED BY TARAHUMARA IN CREEL, CHIHUAHUA. PHOTO COURTESY OF FIDIECOMISO ARCHIVOS PLUTARCO ELÍAS CALLES Y FERNANDO TORREBLANCA.

Another inspector in the region, Efrén Ramírez, argued that the root of the problem was that the Tarahumara were "savages," a view many SEP inspectors adopted. Their social organization, according to this observer, was completely rudimentary and without the normal affection associated with "civilized" society. As soon as a child was old enough to travel a good distance from home, her parents left the child unsupervised and exposed to grave dangers. Ramírez's depiction of Tarahumara society is reminiscent of that of famed University of Chicago anthropologist Robert Zingg's claims that much of Tarahumara society was "spurious" and served no function. Zingg, who traveled to the Sierra Tarahumara in 1930, went so far as to claim that even the Tarahumara knew that their seasonal migration was counterproductive because their winter caves were uncomfortable and did not meet western hygiene standards.[58] So it was with Ramírez's comments on the fact that in Tarahumara culture children were given adult responsibilities at a much earlier age than in Mexican society.

Ramírez noted that even erecting federal schools next to extant Tarahumara churches did not work because most families lived at least ten kilometers from central community meeting places, and as soon as food became scarce, they stopped coming into town, thus abandoning schools and, presumably, churches. He suggested that the Tarahumara could overcome all these problems if the Education Ministry built dormitories, kitchens, and dining rooms into the schools of the region. He further advised the SEP to hire only male teachers with wives to work in the region so that while the husband was leading classes, "the wife of the teacher ..., [could] lend her services to attend to the domestic education of the students and to prepare their food for them."[59] Ramírez proposed that the wives be paid one peso per day for their work, about half the average salary for a federal rural schoolteacher.

In the meantime, the Education Ministry received a number of complaints about both state and federally run schools in the Sierra Tarahumara, including problems with incompetent teachers and a lack of good teachers.[60] Both state and federal authorities were having problems attracting teachers to work in the Sierra Tarahumara. In February 1928, SEP officials in Mexico City complained that 14 of the federal government's 21 teaching vacancies in Chihuahua were located in Tarahumara schools. They asked government officials to remedy the situation and ensure a more equitable distribution of teachers.[61]

In 1929, the Education Ministry had some success in other areas though. Salvador Varela reported that the local Tarahumara had greeted the circuit schools surrounding Polanco, which were community financed but federally run, with great enthusiasm. Moreover, in Agua Escondida, local inhabitants agreed to pay for a portion of the teacher's salary if the federal government would establish a school there in place of the private school.[62]

In both Nabogame and Turuáchic, however, mestizo authorities refused to work with the Education Ministry to help provide local Tarahumara children with education.[63] It is unclear whether this situation was a matter of apathy or a calculated decision. In La Gaita, the teacher, María Refugio Chávez, quit after a mestizo man raped her and the Police Commissioner in the community refused to arrest the suspect. In Tenoriva, Baborigame, and Santa Rosa, only about half of the usual Tarahumara children attended school because of food shortages.[64] Instead of attending school, children foraged for food to help their families.

Despite the widespread hunger that the Tarahumara were suffering throughout the region, inspectors still discovered tribal members using the little corn they had to make tesgüino (corn beer) rather than meals. In an attempt to bend Tarahumara culture to the promotion of Mexican patriotism, one inspector asked federal officials to declare the drinking of tesgüino illegal for the Tarahumara except during Semana Santa (Holy Week) and on September 16 (Mexican Independence Day) and May 15 (Saint Isidro's Day).[65] Another noted ironically that the failure of the Tarahumaras' corn crop had actually reduced their tesgüino abuse to manageable levels.[66] The inspectors clearly neither understood the centrality of tesgüino or tesgüinadas to Tarahumara culture nor the nature of tesgüino consumption. Because tesgüino cannot be stored for long and is low in alcohol content, there are, according to anthropologist John Kennedy, no Tarahumara alcoholics (other than those who adopt mainstream society and the distilled alcohol consumption that comes with it). In addition, the Tarahumara spent the vast majority of their time in relative isolation, seeing only other members of their immediate family on a daily basis. The Tarahumara hosted about 95 per cent of their tesgüinadas in order to undertake co-operative labor or religious rites. Since most Tarahumara were likely to flee from contact with mestizos unless the Tarahumara were at a gathering, inspectors were more likely to run into Tarahumara when they were drinking corn beer. Although the Education Ministry had put new emphasis in 1929 on fighting the abuse of alcohol, in the Sierra Tarahumara tesgüino "abuse" was not a major issue even as its use was widespread. While it was true that parents often pulled their children from school to watch after fields and herds while they attended corn beer parties, had SEP officials harnessed tesgüinadas rather than trying to eliminate them, they may have been more successful in convincing the Tarahumara to send their children to federal schools.[67]

The rise of Salvador Varela from inspector in the Sierra Tarahumara to head of federal education in Chihuahua occurred in 1930. With his promotion came the first concerted effort by Education Ministry officials to address the continuing problems in the region. Varela began that year by asking SEP officials in Mexico City to provide him with the budgetary resources for 150 additional teachers so that he could do his job properly.[68] The Education Ministry did not respond to his request, probably because the Depression shrank the agency's budget.[69]

As a result, the lack of good teachers (or in many cases, teachers) continued to be a major concern. For example, The SEP closed schools in Otóvachic and Papajícjic when their teachers left and administrators could not find new teachers to replace them.[70] A circuit school set up in the ranchería of San Antonio best epitomizes the problems faced by the Education Ministry in placing good teachers in the schools in the Sierra Tarahumara and demonstrates what can happen with nepotistic appointments. In March 1930, inspector Abelardo de la Rosa visited the school. The school's teacher, Macrina Yañez, had yet to finish the necessary schooling to qualify. Nevertheless, her uncle, Primitivo Holguín, the head of circuit school and a good friend of Salvador Varela, placed Yañez anyway. Faced with these circumstances and no readily available candidates to take her place, de la Rosa merely suggested that Yañez spend her free time catching up on her studies.[71]

When de la Rosa returned in October, he found that the majority of the local inhabitants were sending their children to other schools or not bothering to send their children at all because the teacher was so poorly prepared. De la Rosa asked the Education Ministry to replace Yañez with a new teacher. Nonetheless, when he returned in January 1931, he found Yañez still on the job. He decided to give her, as well as all of her remaining students, an exam to test their knowledge. He discovered that several of Yañez's students were better prepared to teach than she was. De la Rosa was convinced that over the last year neither Yañez nor her uncle had done anything to improve her teaching ability. He again asked the director of federal education to remove her from her post. It was May 1932 before the SEP found a new teacher to take her place.[72]

The "abuse" of tesgüino continued to be a major concern of the Education Ministry as well. A report entitled "Superstitions, Prejudices, and the Dominant Traditions in the Southwest Zone of Chihuahua" noted that the

Tarahumara even used tesgüino as a regular part of their repertoire in dancing, witchcraft, and medicine. Since Education Ministry officials wanted to eliminate dancing and witchcraft and replace them with modern medicine and science, they concluded that a major program aimed at completely changing Tarahumara society would be necessary to eradicate the vice.[73] Furthermore, a 1929 presidential decree by Portes Gil made it obligatory for all inspectors and teachers to organize anti-alcohol campaigns in every community where there was a school.[74] Although those in charge of implementing the circular often preferred to interpret it as demanding only that they speak out against the use of alcohol, it was clear to educational inspectors that the use of tesgüino was unacceptable.[75]

In fact, when SEP officials investigated they discovered that many inspectors were drinking in cantinas and playing billiards when they were supposed to be traveling to schools in their inspection zone. Yet Education Ministry officials could hardly blame those inspectors who did try to eradicate the use of alcohol among the Tarahumara for failing (even if it were possible to do so) when many municipal authorities were making a living off the fermentation and sale of tesgüino.[76] Inspector Ramón Villanueva tried to combat alcohol abuse among the Tarahumara as well as police alcohol sales. In Agua Fría he showed the Tarahumara how to make "*pitole* [*sic*] *morado*" (*pinole*, toasted maize) and reported that they found it to their liking.[77] They probably found it to their liking because they had been toasting maize long before SEP officials arrived. In the school Mesa de la Reforma in the municipality of Guadalupe y Calvo, Villanueva tried to develop a sports program to combat alcohol consumption and noted a high level of enthusiasm on the part of the Tarahumara.[78] Nonetheless, this ignored the fact that the Tarahumara engaged in their own sports, especially a running game that incorporated the kicking of a wooden ball over long distances, and still incorporated tesgüino into their culture. Perhaps more importantly, SEP records show that mestizos also combined liberal alcohol use with sports, especially baseball.[79] Inspector de la Rosa viewed the use of tesgüino as a cultural matter and thought that if he could teach the Tarahumara to love tortillas, then they would stop using their corn to make alcohol. In hopes of enforcing the change, he asked mestizos to prevent the Tarahumara from drinking.[80]

Nearly everyone who worked in the region continued to believe that the only method of transforming the Tarahumara was to open additional boarding schools.[81] Inspectors complained that they spent most of their time unsuccessfully trying to convince Tarahumara parents of the benefits of sending their children to school.[82] Even worse, Villanueva noted that the Tarahumara in Chinatú were attending school on a regular basis, but it had done little to change their habits. They were still going hungry and their parents still drank tesgüino. As a result, he argued that if the SEP could not change the school into a boarding school, then they should shut it down to avoid wasting valuable resources.[83]

Some teachers, such as Simeón González, transformed their schools into boarding schools on their own initiative, hoping to secure Education Ministry support after the fact. To convince his superiors of his sincerity, González created a thick set of rules for his boarding school that read like military regulations for boot camp. González told his local inspector that there were four main reasons the Tarahumara generally failed to send their children to school: the "nearly chronic epidemics that attack their community"; the misery that they suffered as a result of the "little maize that they raise," the majority of which they immediately turned into tesgüino; the ingrained prejudice that they had against sending their children to school; and the obstructions placed in their way by mestizos when they had managed to overcome the first three.[84]

González hoped that his boarding school could overcome these barriers to Tarahumara school attendance. But only two months after its unofficial conversion into a boarding school, Villanueva informed SEP officials that the school was failing due to a lack of support on the part of the community members who "promise to comply but do not do so." Villanueva instructed González to gather the community members together to inform them that if they did not lend their assistance to the boarding school, the Education Ministry would close it.[85] From the records, it is hard to tell if the resistance to the boarding school was Tarahumara or mestizo, though it was probably both.

Even the boarding school that was functioning in Yoquivo was facing hardship. In addition to the problems already mentioned with one of its teachers, inspector de la Rosa reported that the school was not meeting minimal Education Ministry standards. It both failed to celebrate patriotic festivals and failed to hold the required social meetings on a regular basis.[86] Meanwhile, Salvador Varela – desiring to focus the transformative powers of the school on Tarahumara youth, especially young males, wanted all Tarahumara attending the school to be between the ages of 14 and 20. When Varela tried to kick out 17 students not meeting the criteria, governor Almada intervened and convinced SEP officials to allow them to stay on.[87]

In 1931, with the introduction of socialist action pedagogy on the national level, inspectors and teachers began to focus more on overcoming the often con-flictive relationship between mestizos and Tarahumaras.[88] Inspectors took on the role of mediator to help resolve problems between the two groups. Also in 1931, inspectors started linking more strongly the Tarahumaras' use of tesgüino and their almost perpetual lack of food. Some inspectors, after realizing the futility of trying to eliminate tesgüino completely, adopted the same strategy as the Jesuits before them and shifted their focus instead to limiting it.

Other inspectors focused instead on trying to achieve economic progress within Tarahumara communities to overcome "alcoholism" and poverty. In Las Lajas, for example, J. Miguel Ceballos D. told community members that if they made ample use of the school and its resources – which, of course, they were to provide – they would no longer need to migrate in search of work.[89] In Agua Escondida the teacher, Primitivo Holguín, tried using the teaching of modern agricultural techniques to overcome the region's poverty. The community ini-tially planted carrots, radishes, and a variety of legumes for local consumption, as well as white mulberry trees to produce silk. Later, they expanded their crops to potatoes, corn, lettuce, cauliflower, chiles, tomatoes, and fruit trees. They even began manufacturing wool and tanning hides. The school became such a success that inspectors singled it out on a trip through the region by Narciso Bassols in 1932.[90] Agua Escondida, however, was a rare exception. Throughout much of the Sierra Tarahumara, the Tarahumara lived such a miserable exis-tence that they reportedly often went several days between meals.[91]

In 1932, there was again a renewed clamor for the use of boarding schools to integrate the Tarahumara into the mainstream of Mexican society. The two existing boarding schools in Yoquivo and Cieneguita were in dire economic straits after severe crop failures in 1931. The SEP reorganized the boarding school in Cieneguita to save money, and the school's director asked for dona-tions of food and clothing so that hunger would not drive students away from the school.[92] The teacher sent the students home in the evenings to save resources, thus undermining the entire idea of separating children from their parents. In late 1931, the Education Ministry closed the boarding schools because of a lack of resources, including a debt of 744 pesos to a local businessperson.[93] Varela vowed to revive both boarding schools, in addition to opening another one in Ciudad Chihuahua – which never got out of the planning stage – modeled on the Casa del Estudiante Indígena in Mexico City.[94]

Despite the tight economic situation of the present boarding schools, federal educators at many different levels reached the conclusion that additional boarding schools were the only viable remaining alternative.[95] Varela argued that they were necessary to overcome caciquismo and the exploitation of the Tarahumara by mestizos.[96] Inspectors like José Vázquez Luna argued that without additional boarding schools, teachers could not advance the situation of the Tarahumara.[97] Varela and Rafael Ramírez, the head of the department of rural education, then began to investigate the feasibility of additional boarding schools in the Sierra Tarahumara. They asked Odorico García, a federal teacher in the area, to look into the matter and make suggestions for the re-establishment and augmentation of boarding schools for the Tarahumara.

García suggested a complete overhaul of the approach to indigenous education in the region. First, he argued that if the Education Ministry expected the Tarahumara to accept the changes that the federal government was advocating, then Tarahumara leaders would have to have a role in carrying them out. The failure over the previous decade showed that the SEP could not just impose its will. Specifically, García advocated appointing Ignacio León, a Tarahumara teacher and graduate of the Casa in Mexico City, as the head of all Tarahumara education. While the SEP did not name León as the head of Tarahumara education, he did accept the position of director of the boarding school at Tónachic. This was perhaps the single most important innovation that the Education Ministry adopted in the Sierra Tarahumara. As we will see, after a difficult start León would go on to run a successful boarding school and act as a mediator between the Tarahumara and the federal government.[98]

Furthermore, García proposed that each municipal government have at least one Tarahumara representative in order to counteract the continued persecution of the group by whites and mestizos. As for the boarding schools themselves, García thought that the SEP should establish them in Sisoguíchic and Tónachic. Each boarding school needed to have only one director, to avoid the infighting that had led to their collapse in the past, along with eight to ten of the best teachers that the Education Ministry could get to ensure the quality of instruction. Moreover, García believed that it was imperative that each boarding school have dorms and focus on teaching morals, proper customs, and industrial crafts so that the schools would eventually become economically self-sufficient.[99] Varela, being familiar with the area from his days as a teacher, then suggested to Ramírez that the SEP establish boarding schools in Tónachic, where the inhabitants were of "pure Indian blood," and in Cieneguita.[100] The

Education Ministry approved the schools and they officially began functioning in January 1933.[101]

García's suggestion that the SEP needed to do something definitive to overcome the persecution of the Tarahumara at the hands of whites and mestizos got at the crux of the problem. The fact that the inspectors and teachers raised the issue repeatedly suggests that while many members of the Education Ministry were cognizant of the root of their failure in the region, there was little they could do about it. Varela complained to his superiors that local caciques, police commissioners, and municipal presidents often forced the Tarahumara into virtual slavery. He noted incidents where those charged with protecting the Tarahumara made them act as domestic servants, cut firewood, and hand over their crops without compensation. Varela argued that the SEP was powerless to effect meaningful change without having "elements of public force" at their disposal.[102] This underlines the ephemeral nature of the state's penetration into the countryside in post-revolutionary Mexico. Nevertheless, it also reinforces, at least prior to 1932, its paternalism and ethnocentrism. Prior to García's report, no members of the Education Ministry had considered using Tarahumara pressure to open up access to political channels in mestizo-run communities. It was clear that most SEP officials believed that the Tarahumara did not know what was best for them and that these decisions were best left in SEP hands. The dilemma over educating and empowering the Tarahumara but not trusting them mirrored the struggle in the United States over the proper place of Indian students. Ethnohistorian Wilbert Ahern notes that educated Indians faced the dual dilemma of "suspicion from other tribespeople [and] hesitations and resistance from white staff," fueled by "racism, prejudice ... or a drive for control."[103] This underscored the main problem with assimilation: whites and mestizos on both sides of the border were hostile to Indians who did not know their proper place.

Despite the renewed emphasis placed on boarding schools in 1932, their re-inauguration in 1933 did not go smoothly. The SEP completely abandoned the boarding schools and the majority of regular rural schools in the Sierra Tarahumara because the area had been without the services of a permanent inspector for more than a year. The new inspector, J. Humberto Paniagua, was sure that teaching the Tarahumara basic trades such as farming, carpentry, shoemaking, blacksmithing, and tailoring would best assimilate them into Mexican society.[104] Finally, on March 11, 1933, the Education Ministry opened the boarding school in Cieneguita, now called a *centro de educación*, with 35

En Creel

TARAHUMARA CHILDREN NEAR RAIL DEPOT IN CREEL, CHIHUAHUA. PHOTO COUR-
TESY OF FIDIECOMISO ARCHIVOS PLUTARCO ELÍAS CALLES Y FERNANDO TORRE-
BLANCA.

students. Paniagua planned to increase attendance to 60 students when more Tarahumara returned from their seasonal migration.[105]

In April and May, the SEP began construction of a number of buildings around the centro de educación in Tónachic. The future members of small agricultural colonies (*pequeñas colonias agrícolas*) that the government planned to form out of the surrounding Tarahumara in hopes of giving them agricultural training would put the buildings to use. In Cieneguita the students planted potatoes and prepared their fields for maize and beans. They also purchased 90 goats. Finally, the teachers organized the children into *tribus de exploradores* (Boy Scout troops) in an attempt to integrate them into Mexican society.

The inspector also put reinforced grillwork around the windows of the boarding school to prevent the children from escaping at night and returning to stay with their families.[106] What Paniagua failed to recognize was that the Education Ministry, by forcibly trying to civilize the Tarahumara and liberate them from mestizo oppression, was, as historian Engracia Loyo has correctly argued, "submitting them to a new tyranny, the imposition of a foreign culture."[107] The repeated attempts by Tarahumara children to escape from the boarding schools underlined the fact that the Education Ministry only found it possible to "civilize" Tarahumara children by coercing them and treating them as prisoners in their own land. Nevertheless, the oppression that the Tarahumara suffered at the hands of local mestizos was self-interested and calculated; that which they suffered at the hands of the SEP, for whatever it was worth, was meant to improve their lives.

Despite these obstacles, the SEP pressed forward with its civilization campaign in the Sierra Tarahumara, but by November and December 1933, the schools had made little if any progress. Several teachers had pay problems and left to straighten them out, forcing the closure of the tailor and carpentry workshops. After a full year the schools had only managed to build a chicken coop, make 35 pairs of shoes, 1,000 pieces of soap, and form a 48-member marching band and a 12-person orchestra.[108] At the end of the Maximato, Jacinto Maldonado, the new director of federal education in Chihuahua, noted the sorry condition in which the boarding schools for the Tarahumara remained. The buildings were dilapidated, and the dorms lacked mattresses, beds, and sheets, forcing the majority of the children to sleep on the floor. The "desertion of students" continued to be a major problem. Maldonado summed it all up by noting that the conditions in the centros de educación were no different from the generally prevailing conditions in the remainder of the Sierra Tarahumara.[109]

The task that the Education Ministry set out for itself in 1924 – to integrate the Tarahumara into mainstream Mexican society – was nearly impossible. By the end of the Maximato, only 280 of the estimated 8,000 Tarahumara children in the Sierra Tarahumara were attending boarding schools. In the remainder of the region, Salvador Varela guessed that only 5 per cent of all Tarahumara children were attending school due to their oppression at the hands of mestizos and whites. It did not take SEP officials long to recognize that they lacked the resources to overcome the social and economic problems that lay at the roots of the oppression of the Tarahumara. When Delfino Bazán asked for 1,600 new schools and Salvador Varela asked for an additional 150 teachers for the region, they were advocating budget expenditures that they surely knew their superiors in Mexico City would not approve. Moreover, when Odorico García argued in favor of sharing political power with the Tarahumara at the local level, and when Varela pleaded to be given the means of enforcing those laws that already existed in favor of the Tarahumara, they were clearly illuminating the powerlessness of the federal government in the face of local realities. None of this is surprising.

What is surprising is that after a decade of interaction with the Tarahumara, many Education Ministry officials and inspectors still had no accurate concept of the plight of the Tarahumara. Moral and cultural issues, in the minds of many SEP employees, overshadowed the structural and economic causes of Tarahumara poverty. Odorico García's suggestion that the Education Ministry redeem the Tarahumara by empowering them and harnessing their efforts was the first break in this approach. When the SEP named Ignacio León as the head of the boarding school in Tónachich, it took its first step in allowing the Tarahumara to take a leading role in their own redemption and elevation. Conditions improved under president Cárdenas. Dawson notes that León and his wife, by gaining the co-operation of local Tarahumara communities, trained "several generations of teachers" who would later work in the Sierra Tarahumara by the early 1940s. Between 1940 and 1945, León would use his position as a teacher, community leader, and bilingual spokesperson to act as a mediator between local Tarahumara communities and the federal government. In doing so, he managed to promote the deepening of pueblo level democracy and local elections "without outside interference."[110]

In spite of these timid first steps, a meeting in Estación Creel in 1934 between Mexican officials and the "little governors" of several Tarahumara communities perhaps best epitomizes the Maximato's failure to bring meaningful change to the Sierra Tarahumara. At the meeting, Tarahumara officials continually stressed the need to address the theft of their land and resources by mestizos and whites. Government officials, on the other hand, thought that these issues were secondary to the need to gain the support of the Tarahumara leaders for building additional schools in the region.[111] Mexican and Tarahumara officials made little progress on either set of issues. Ultimately, the federal government's failure to understand the needs of the Tarahumara or to further empower the Tarahumara to pursue their own liberation and redemption left the fate of tribal members mostly in the voracious hands of the region's mestizo and white capitalists, businessmen, and landlords.

4

The Seri

When rancher and Seri benefactor Robert Thompson petitioned Mexico's *Secretaría de Educación Pública* (SEP) to establish a primary school for tribal members, he claimed to do so for the sake of humanity and because the Seri were living in "physical and moral misery" that could only end through their integration with the rest of Mexican society.[1] Thompson's adoption of *indigenismo*'s commonly articulated causes of the "Indian problem" – isolation and cultural backwardness – was an early indicator of the post-revolutionary government's ability to create what Mary Kay Vaughan has called "a common language for consent and protest" and served to tie a local Indian land and resource "problem" to the newly created federal government and its bureaucracy.[2] That it did so through the auspices of a U.S. rancher and his American associates less than a decade after the end of a revolution that contained a strong strain of revolutionary nationalism was unprecedented.

When 'missionaries' from the SEP went into the countryside to spread the word about Mexico's new rural education program and recruit both teachers and students in the early 1920s, the Seri Indians, with a population of around 200, were never directly contacted.[3] Who could have imagined that, instead, federal officials would ask their self-proclaimed benefactor, a local rancher originally from the United States named Robert Thompson, to work on their behalf?[4] Clearly, Education Ministry officials were much more interested in using their limited resources to provide schools for the nearby, and in their view, more troublesome, Yaqui Indians.[5] Nevertheless, the Seri met the basic criteria the SEP was looking for in a redeemable indigenous group. They were both isolated and exploited. In a case of exaggeration and self-promotion that nonetheless mirrored how the Seri were viewed by mainstream Mexican society, anthropologist W.J. McGee argued that the Seri were "so savage and treacherous that they remain nearly unknown" and that their ethics prevented them from having "conjugal relation with alien people."[6] Ironically, by tapping Thompson and his associates as mediators between the Seri and the Sonoran government and the Mexican government, Education Ministry officials would place the Seri in the hands of an indigenismo much more closely tied to attitudes and practices of the borderlands region and the United States. In the process, they undermined some of the very tenets of early indigenismo in Mexico, which sought to weave together a single Mexico from the many existing Mexicos through integrating indigenous people into mainstream society.

The Seri lived along a 4-mile-wide and 70-mile-long band of coastal desert on the Sonoran coast west of Hermosillo stretching from Kino Bay to Desemboque and on Tiburón Island. In addition to Tiburón Island, the Seri regularly had camps at Bahía Kino and Puerto Libertad in addition to rancherías in Pozo Coyote, Las Estrellas, and San Francisco de Costa Rica. Although the coastal strip is a desert, the bay provides a natural trap for large fish and is the breeding ground for the Pacific green turtle, which, combined with the fish, made up about two-thirds of the Seri diet. Men did the fishing and occasionally hunted small game both on the mainland and on Alcatraz and other small islands. Women and children collected mollusks as well as the fruit of succulents.[7]

The Seri had lived through two major extermination campaigns. In 1748, when the Seri complained to the Spanish government about the expropriation of their land by the inhabitants of the new presidio in Pitic (present-day Hermosillo), Spanish forces arrested 80 families and deported the women to Guatemala.[8] This resulted in nearly 20 years of warfare in which the Spanish government tried literally to exterminate the Seri. During the 1850s, a group of ranchers and cowboys tired of what they viewed as the Seris' constant theft of their livestock undertook the other, "private" campaign. They killed an estimated half of the Seri for what tribal members viewed as a legitimate use of cattle maintained on their ancestral lands.

Military campaigns meant to assimilate, or failing that, to exterminate the Seri continued during the Porfiriato. Government officials complained, however, that "because of their character and customs [the Seri] could never be transformed into useful citizens and workers."[9] The perpetual cycle of Seri raids followed by Spanish and then Mexican retaliation continued into the early part of the twentieth century, forcing the Seri closer and closer to the coast and Tiburón Island.[10] In 1904, when the Seri allied themselves with several Yaqui who were at war with the government, Governor Ramon Corral responded by sending the military to guard all of the sources of fresh water in the Seri homeland. Thirst drove the Seri to settle for peace on the condition that they limit themselves to Tiburón Island and Bahía Kino.[11]

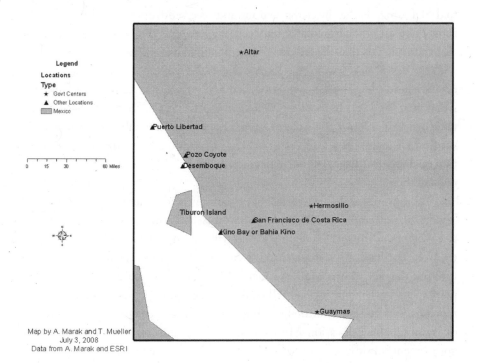

Map by A. Marak and T. Mueller
July 3, 2008
Data from A. Marak and ESRI

By 1923, when Robert Thompson[12] stepped forward offering to work on their behalf, a number of Seri had become hangers-on at local cattle ranches as well as in the burgeoning fishing industry located in Kino Bay.[13] Thompson told Fernando F. Dworak, State Director of Education in Sonora (1926–32) and Federal Director of Education in Sonora (1932–35), that he had dealt and traveled with the Seri for many years because they lived close to his ranch.[14] He told SEP officials that he had asked for and received from state authorities the right to be an official mediator between the Seri and the rest of society.[15] He told state officials that the federal government had named him official mediator with the Seri.[16] In actuality, the *Secretaría de Gobernación* had named him to this position, and then Thompson approached SEP officials when the first Cultural Mission arrived in Hermosillo, Sonora in 1924.[17] He proclaimed that he had taken on this role for the sake of humanity, as local ranchers had persecuted the Seri for many years for livestock theft. He was concerned that this persecution made them "disposed to flee from civilization," making it more difficult to redeem them.[18]

Thompson's probable motives were complicated. There is no doubt that Thompson's attempts to convince the Seri to settle down and become productive workers in the local economy would have saved him and his fellow ranchers from the loss of livestock through Seri hunting and the trouble of trying to track the Seri down after the fact.[19] In addition, if the Seri established a permanent settlement, it very well could have opened up more coastal land for ranchers. Furthermore, although Thompson had no pedagogical background or training, the Education Ministry paid him handsomely even as the state government subsidized most of his expenses. He also used his position to secure paid employment and lucrative contracts for his brother and business associates. He was an unlikely champion of the Seri's education and welfare. Nonetheless, Thompson was not the first local rancher to befriend and hire the Seri: Pascual Encinas, owner of the Rancho de San Francisco de Costa Rica, had done so by 1850, and his son Pablo did so in the late 1890s.[20] Thompson and the Seri were neighbors and probably met and got to know one another through work. His fascination with the Seri was not unusual. Indians had been entertainment curiosities since at least the 1890s in the United States and Mexico. The rise of indigenismo in Mexico also placed indigenous people at the center of the government's nation-building efforts, something that Thompson clearly did not fail to notice.[21] However, his relationship with the Seri must have been based on more than just fascination as he underwent a lot of hardship during the years in which he attempted to assimilate the Seri into mainstream Mexican society. Finally, photos taken in the early 1930s show Thompson still with the Seri even after their troubling times together in the 1920s.[22]

Although Thompson championed himself as the Seri's commissioned agent in 1923, there is clear evidence that he was already acting as a cultural broker on their behalf in 1922 when he introduced them to Edward H. Davis, an agent from the Museum of the American Indian (now the George Gustav Heye Center, part of the Smithsonian National Museum of the American Indian), who arrived in "Seriland" to bargain for artifacts.[23] The Seri were also in contact with state officials prior to Thompson's intervention. For example, state officials administered vaccinations in 1921 to the Seri; the Seri annually reported to state officials whom they had selected as "gobernador primero" and "segundo comandante" in 1922; and state officials had responded to a Seri petition by giving them a state-owned canoe in 1922 (they had bargained for another with Davis) and paying Juan Tomás, their governor, 25 pesos in 1923 simply for agreeing to work with the state.[24] Herein lays the first clue as to why state officials may have felt comfortable allowing Thompson to act as the Seri's agent. Government payments to indigenous leaders much more clearly reflect the common practices of the U.S. Bureau of Indian Affairs (BIA) – where they hired Indian judges, police, and students returning from off-reservation boarding schools in hopes of co-opting Indian leadership in addition to gaining some leverage in local governance – than those of the SEP.[25]

In December 1923, Robert Thompson reported that he, a SEP official, and his brother Luis had begun teaching the Seri sustainable farming at Palo Alto, about 30 kilometers east of Tiburón Island. Thompson testified that local ranchers had asked him to prevent the Seri from leaving the camp to hunt and gather, but that, given their customs and traditions and his limited resources, it was impossible to do so. More importantly, local ranchers had threatened to kill both the Seri and the Thompsons if they were found hunting deer on rancher land; in response, the Seri were preparing to defend themselves. Interestingly, Thompson noted that Antonio Moreno, a local rancher, had complained that the Seri had killed several deer on his land while the Thompsons were with them. Thompson argued that this was not possible because whenever the Seri left their camp, the Thompsons went with them; though he admitted that it was hard to keep an eye on them because he needed to stay on horseback to keep up with Seri, and they often went places where horses could not. Furthermore, the Seri refused to stop hunting on state-owned land without explicit official orders. Robert Thompson asked Sonora's Governor Alejo Bay (1923–27) to intervene and arrange an accord between the local ranchers and the Seri, reminding him not to automatically take the side of the ranchers because the Seri were not always in the wrong.[26] Bay declined to get involved until such a time as either Thompson or the SEP could provide a solution to the difficulties that Thompson had described.[27]

The letters between Thompson and Bay are interesting for a couple of reasons. First, the fact that the Seri did not hunt on private land when the Thompsons were with them (or at least made sure to lose the Thompsons before they did so) suggests that they were well aware of ranchers' claims to land ownership, even if they did not agree with them. The fact that the Seri refused to stop hunting on state-owned land until such a time as state officials explicitly ordered it reinforces this. Secondly, Bay's refusal to intervene in the situation, together with Robert Thompson's plea that the governor consider the possibility that the Seri were not always in the wrong, unsurprisingly implies that the status quo favored the ranchers.

In 1924, state officials accepted Francisco Molina in the salaried position of second in command of the Seri, granting him and anyone accompanying him the freedom to travel unimpeded throughout the state. Governor Bay noted that he had officially notified both civil and military officials of his decision. This highlights two important points. First, unlike in the United States, neither the Education Ministry nor the state government had the power to select which member of the tribe would receive a government salary. While BIA officials took into account local feelings when they selected Indian judges and police, local superintendents were the ultimate arbiters. The Seri, on the other hand, selected their leaders through consensus and then reported the results to state officials. Sonoran officials, in spite of the fact that they spent a fair amount on education and worked closely with the federal government, had less leverage over indigenous affairs than their BIA counterparts.[28] The federal government also had little leverage. When Puig tried to recruit two "full-blooded" Seri for the Casa in Mexico City, the Seri failed to comply.[29] Second, the fact that Molina needed governmental dispensation to travel freely throughout Sonora meant that his fellow Seri (other than their governor) did not have this same freedom. This also mimicked similar paternalistic U.S. practices where Native Americans often needed passes furnished to them by BIA officials to leave their reservations. The lack of any other documentation in 1924 hints that, other than the monitoring of Seri "passes," the Seri and local ranchers had at least arrived at a temporary truce.[30]

The truce ended in less than six months. The Seri got the attention of state officials by killing 11 head of cattle on local rancher Eliseo Davila's Rancho Santa María in early February. The cattle were owned by an assortment of local ranchers, all of whom the Thompsons and the police chief of Siete Cerros, Luis Felix, called by the title of "don," indicating their high social status. Davila and the other ranchers, Antonio G. Morales, Ignacio L Romero, and Ignacio A. Navarro, demanded restitution of $120 pesos for their livestock. In a surprising move, Governor Bay promptly paid them from state coffers without asking the Seri for reimbursement.[31] Bay responded by contacting Robert Thompson, explaining that he could not permit the Seri to continue killing ranchers' cattle because it might escalate to bloodshed. The governor demanded that the Seri turn in all of their rifles except five (which they could use for hunting), suggesting that if they did not do it willingly, the state government would do it forcibly.[32] Of course, the Seri could continue to "hunt" ranchers' cattle with five rifles, but to do so would put them at an extreme disadvantage should local ranchers retaliate as they had promised to do. Nonetheless, the governor's decision to step in and advocate on behalf of the Seri suggests a true concern for their welfare.

Thompson, his brother Luis, and Luis Felix met with the Seri in Pozo Verde to convince the Seri to turn in their rifles and stop "robbing livestock." The Seri, distrustful of the government, retired with Luis to Rada Ballena on Tiburón Island to discuss their decision. The day-long conference of 35 Seri families under the leadership of Governor Juan Tomás and Francisco Molina agreed to turn in their arms in exchange for five rifles of the same caliber and brand. Tomás agreed to distribute the rifles and punish any Seri who misused them. The Seri, however, demanded concessions in return. First, they wanted state officials to understand that the Seri who met at Rada Ballena had not taken part in the livestock raid that had precipitated state intervention. Second, they insisted that the state pay them for the rifles that they turned in. Third, they stipulated that the state would need to promise not to prevent them from buying ammunition for the five rifles. Fourth, they requested that the state provide them with wood, nails, paint, and other materials necessary to construct four canoes so that they could focus on fishing rather than hunting. They asked Governor Bay to respond to their demands in two days in Santa Cruz, where the rifle and materials exchange would take place. If the governor was willing to meet their demands, then they would promise to "pursue an honorable liveli-hood."[33]

Governor Bay did not respond by the Seri's deadline, and Thompson told him that the Seri, fearing an ambush, had retreated to Tiburón Island.[34] Pascual Blanco, a tribal member, sent a note to Governor Bay through Luis Thompson and Chico Romero (a future leader of the Seri) with a peace offering of a rifle. Blanco asked that Bay not consider the Seri retreat to Tiburón Island as an end to negotiations. Blanco described the Seri's condition in desperate terms, say-ing that the women and children had no clothes and the men no pants. Blanco assured Bay that the Seri were industrious and had never meant to deceive him. If the government was willing to send them wood and blankets, they would stop poaching cattle. He told Bay that the men had gone to Pozo de Paña to fashion bows and arrows for hunting and posed the government no threat.[35] It is difficult to know exactly how much influence the Thompsons had on the Seri's negotiation with the state, especially in their critique of Seri poverty and livelihood, but this exchange does highlight a few important themes. There are indications that the state had used prearranged meetings as a setup for attack-ing the Seri in the past. Furthermore, perhaps also based on past practice, they anticipated the state's attempt to limit their ability to hunt by restricting their access to ammunition. There is some evidence to suggest that having rifles was more important as a tool for self-defense than as a means for hunting, since the Seri were experts with bow and arrows and were even adept at hunting deer without weapons.[36] Interestingly, the Seri presented their crafting of bows and arrows as a move to de-escalate the possibility of hostilities with ranchers and state authorities, but not an end to their hunting. In their deliberations with state officials, the Seri cast themselves in the accepted language of "civilization," and it is here that the Thompsons probably had the most influence. Although the Seri clearly understood that state officials frowned on their hunting ranch-ers' cattle, hunting in general still remained an honorable male occupation. Furthermore, the description of the Seri children without clothes and the men without pants as an indication of severe poverty was a non-Seri concept, since Seri men did not generally wear pants, and Seri children usually went naked. There is little at this stage to suggest that the Thompsons had convinced the Seri to adopt western dress. Finally, it is worth noting that in spite of their posi-tion of weakness (hiding on Tiburón Island in fear of a renewed extermination campaign), the Seri drove a hard bargain.

Bay responded by calling Robert Thompson to his office to make arrangements for providing the Seri with provisions and the rest of the things that they had requested in exchange for their rifles.[37] After meeting with Governor Bay, Thompson outlined the steps that he thought would be necessary to turn the weapons exchange program into a success. First, he suggested that state officials give the Seri Remington 25 x 70s, which, because their ammunition was hard to get, would make it difficult for the Seri to purchase ammo from local ranchers, fishermen, and miners as they normally did. Second, state officials would need to let local authorities in Guaymas and Altar know that the Seri were restricted from purchasing both weapons and ammunition. Third, state officials would give deserving Seri passports, allowing them to leave Tiburón Island and Bahia Kino. Not only would this provide the Seri with an incentive to conform and help local ranchers distinguish those Seri who had agreed to the program from renegades, but it would also give Thompson leverage over the Seri since he would play a pivotal role in distributing ammunition and providing passports. Finally, Thompson suggested that Bay should tell them that if they did not turn in their arms, then the governor would send out the army.[38] Interestingly, when Thompson made these suggestions he clearly adopted the indigenista concept of the "proto-citizen" that I discussed in the previous chapter. Only those Seri accepting "state tutelage" and agreeing to conform (or at least promising to begin the transition) to the norms of mainstream society would be granted full citizenship rights; those who refused would be considered renegades and savages deserving to be exterminated.

Thompson petitioned the governor for the right to take a census so that he could give the Seri passports. In addition, he asked Bay to pay for gasoline, oil, and 50 pesos for provisions for himself, a friend, and guides, so that he could visit the Seri.[39] Governor Bay approved Thompson's trip, sent a letter to the Seri (through Thompson) threatening to send out the army if they did not turn in their weapons, and then notified local authorities in Guaymas, Puerto de Guaymas, Altar, Pitiquito, and Caborca not to sell either arms or ammunition to the Seri.[40] While, strictly speaking, Governor Bay's actions met the requirements set forth by the Seri in their petition to the state, it is clear that when the Seri asked that the government make sure that they had ammunition available to continue their hunting, the Seri had not planned on Thompson selecting an obscure caliber weapon so that state officials could leave the Seri defenseless against local ranchers and place their ability to hunt at the feet of state officials.

Two months later Governor Bay sent Robert Thompson to Tiburón Island to inform the Seri that he thought that the best way for the Seri to avoid future issues with local ranchers was "that the Seri not leave the Island, that is to say, that they not come to the mainland."[41] Luis Felix and Robert Thompson returned to Tiburón Island a month later to witness their election of new tribal leaders – Manuel Avila as governor and Francisco Romero as vice-governor – and to get the Seri leadership to promise not "to leave the island and to dedicate themselves to work." The Seri agreed to the new stipulations.[42] This agreement followed conventions of Governor Corral's 1904 agreement with the Seri. However, the policy was again more akin to the U.S. policy of Indian removal and placement on reservations than Mexican assimilationist indigenismo. SEP officials viewed the isolation of indigenous people as the root cause of their oppression. Sonoran officials, meanwhile, believed that unless the Seri isolated themselves from most of mainstream society, local ranchers would oppress if not exterminate them. When the United States adopted its reservation policy in the 1860s and 1870s, "[t]here was almost unanimous agreement among the whites that this was the [N]ative American's best hope of survival." In both the United States and in Sonora, officials rightly feared that indigenous people's interactions with non-Indians were more often detrimental than helpful.[43] Officials wanted to expose indigenous people to the proper elements of mainstream society, in other words, only those people approved by the government and thought to have the best interests of Indians at heart.

When Thompson returned to Hermosillo, he also handed in the arms that the Seri had agreed to exchange. The state's head of purchasing noted that all of the rifles were almost completely deteriorated and were a mixture of different calibers.[44] State officials gave the Seri four (instead of five) new rifles and 80 rounds of ammunition.[45] Given the condition of the Seri's original-weapons and the difficulty in finding ammunition for the different calibers, the Seri could hardly have been the fierce fighting force that local ranchers made them out to be. Instead, the exchange highlights the Seri's ability to advance their interests through negotiation with the state even as the state gained greater control over the Seri's movements and, in the process, opened up some of the Seri's ancestral lands to further incursions by ranchers.

August 4, 1925 would mark a turning point in Seri-Sonoran relations. On this day, the Seri and government of Sonora entered into a legal compact. The Seri agreed to a series of stipulations: (1) they would turn in all their hidden rifles; (2) they would live on Tiburón Island, stay away from mainland ranches, and only pass to the mainland (which they had to do unarmed) with government permission; (3) they would collect water from natural springs in Tecomate, La Cruz, La Higuera, El Carrizo, and Pozo de Peña instead of just at Agua Chiquita; (4) the Seri's governor would ensure that the Seri worked every day to provide for their families and ensure that they had money to buy clothes and medicine because the state government could not continue giving them provisions; (5) the Seri's governor would punish tribal members who were lazy, robbed cattle, damaged other fishermen's boats or ranchers' homesteads by sending them to Hermosillo to be punished by state authorities; and (6) the Seri would limit themselves to five rifles and would not use the rifles to kill cattle or horses. In return, state officials would not allow non-tribal members to go to Tiburón Island without the governor's permission, and in these cases, the Chief of Police would notify the Seri's governor. Furthermore, Robert Thompson would act as a mediator between the Seri and any non-tribal members going to Tiburón Island.[46]

Sonora's Secretary of State wrote a letter to the Seri's governor, Manuel Davila, putting the compact in non-technical language. He told him to keep his people in line, make sure that they worked daily, make sure that the Seri cleaned themselves, make sure the children went to school, prevent his people from going to the mainland without permission, inform the state government every time that a boat landed on Tiburón Island, punish tribal members who did not obey the compact (or failing that, send them to state officials for punishment), and, in general, promote good customs among his people.[47] It bears repeating the both the compact and the Secretary of State's follow-up letter saw the Seri as "proto-citizens" in need of "state tutelage" before they would be ready for inclusion into mainstream Mexican society. It is also worth noting that the legal compact in many ways mirrored that of a U.S. Indian reservation, which Imre Sutton defines as "tribal lands held in trust and protected by federal immunity" and Thompson himself fulfilling the same function as the Indian Agents, who originally served without formal pay but had their expenses reimbursed.[48] Of course, in Sonora the state government offered the Seri guarantees, not the federal government. Nonetheless, due to the geographic isolation of Tiburón Island and its unsuitability for either farming or cattle, the Sonoran government would not face the same difficulties in keeping non-Indians off Indian lands that the BIA did in the United States.

The Education Ministry's broader involvement into the attempted assimilation of the Seri began in November 1926 with the establishment of a rural primary school in the pueblo of Carrizal located in Kino Bay. Although Thompson had reported setting up a school for the Seri in Palo Alto in December 1923, the Seri's move back to Tiburón Island probably prevented it from ever functioning. A Spanish flu epidemic struck the Seri in 1926 and diphtheria would later strike them in 1927. Perhaps the federal government moved in because of the epidemic, but it is as likely that the epidemics afflicted the Seri because of greater contact with the outside world coupled with their forced confinement on Tiburón Island.[49] At any rate, it is worth noting that Carrizal was located on the mainland, and thus, without the permission of Thompson or other government officials, would have constituted a violation of the compact. Although the SEP had been involved in a limited way early on – at least in contacting Robert Thompson in 1923 or 1924 when Cultural Missions arrived in Sonora – November 1926 marked the transfer of Seri oversight and coordination from state officials to federal officials. In some ways this transfer of authority had little impact on the ground since Robert Thompson was still the Seri's mediator and Fernando F. Dworak, the State Director of Education in Sonora, acted as their liaison (probably because of his close personal ties with Plutarco Elías Calles) with the Education Ministry. One thing that the state government did continue to do was to pay tribal leaders in exchange for enforcing the compact. In fact, the payments to tribal members expanded beyond those to the Seri's chief and second in command to include a police officer, just as on U.S. reservations.[50]

The Seri had only twelve children attending the school on a regular basis, which by law was not enough to establish, let alone maintain, a primary school.[51] Dworak, however, was determined to provide all of the necessary resources to make the assimilation of the Seri successful. He asked Education Ministry officials to be lenient about enforcing attendance limits on the Seri because the "physical and moral misery" that they lived in demanded that the government give them special attention. SEP officials agreed.[52]

The assimilation project on the mainland began with a focus on trying to convince the Seri to give up their isolated hunting and gathering and instead settle down as farmers under rancher Thompson's oversight. Dworak asked state officials to donate ten sacks of wheat so that Thompson could use the mules and plows that he loaned to the Seri to raise crops to feed the tribe. In response, he was authorized 60 pesos monthly to introduce industry to the Seri.[53] Interestingly, shortly after the SEP approved Thompson's relatively lucrative salary, several Seri showed up at the 'Cruz Galvez' School for Girls in

Hermosillo begging for clothes. The Seri explained that the government had donated clothes to them in the past, but had failed to do so this year.[54]

Dworak followed up by ordering Thompson to take the fish that the Seri caught and sell it on their behalf on the open market in order to procure more funds for the new Seri settlement. This alone, Dworak warned, would not be enough to make them give up their nomadic lifestyle. He argued, directly counter to the compact, that the Seri could not be allowed to return to Tiburón Island, where they often hid from government officials, if the SEP were to successfully undertake their "moral conquest and their acquisition of work habits and their individual social security."[55] In his attempts to convince his superiors of the need for additional funds, Dworak adopted the very same vision for the Seri that Puig had asked SEP officials to eschew in exchange for a more nuanced and balanced view of the Indians. For example, Dworak described the Seri as living

> [e]ntirely in the primitive age: naked or half-naked ... skin tattooed with bright vegetable colors ... they live by hunting with arrows and by fishing with poor and primitive equipment ... they do not have houses, living in caves ... they live by ... [eating] meat that is scarcely cooked. Their actual industry consists in making a special type of baskets and sometimes, skinning pelicans; the pottery is entirely rudimentary ... they are docile ... they are inoffensive.[56]

Of course, his description (in addition the being factually inaccurate – the Seri did not live in caves, for example) of the Seri ignored the tensions between local ranchers and the Seri. Ranchers would hardly have described the Seri as "docile" and "inoffensive." Taking no notice of the long history of previous failed attempts to "civilize" the Seri and the reservations that Sonoran officials and Thompson had about exposing the Seri to certain elements of mainstream Mexican society, Dworak concluded that the school "would be the center of a peaceful conquest"

In December 1926, Thompson secured a contract with Carlos C. García and Jesús A. Ramírez for the Seri's fish catch. García and Ramírez agreed to pay three-and-a-half *centavos de plata* per kilo for the catch, unless they were unable to be present on the beach when the fish were fresh, in which case they agreed to buy the fish salted at the going market price. Thompson also convinced the prospective buyers to advance 100 pesos to Thompson on behalf of the Seri to insure their compliance with the contract.[57] SEP officials figured that the contractors would eventually sell the fish for 15 centavos de plata in Hermosillo, but thought that the price was acceptable given the amount of ice that the buyers would have to buy in order to get it there.[58] The fact that Dworak felt the need to explain the vast price discrepancy between what the buyers were willing to pay the Seri and what they could sell the catch for suggests that Thompson's deal on behalf of the Seri may not have been very lucrative for the Indians.

At this time, Thompson used the accomplishments that his first several months among the Seri had produced to push the SEP for more resources. He wrote Dworak, telling him that he was having a difficult time living some 35 leagues from civilization with a bunch of Indians that "are like children." In spite of this, he noted that the Seri had harvested a crop of garbanzo beans, built 8 houses with earthen roofs, and constructed a road 30 kilometers long connecting the shore across from Tiburón Island with the main highway to Hermosillo. Thompson had also convinced half of the Seri men to cut their hair short and proudly announced that there had been no reported thefts of livestock since he had been with them. He then threatened to quit unless Dworak granted him an assistant, allowed him to simplify the curriculum for the Seri, and gave him additional funds to buy food for the tribe.[59]

The demand to simplify the curriculum for the Seri, coupled with the nature of the projects that Thompson was successful at, suggests that Thompson's lack of a pedagogical background, coupled with his ranching skills, may have hampered his ability in the classroom but gave him the necessary insight to advance the agricultural aspects of the assimilation program.[60] This did fit well with one of the SEP's major goals: the re-creation of the Mexican countryside through agricultural modernization.[61]

In February 1927 the SEP acceded to Thompson's demands, agreeing to pay him 150 pesos monthly – three times the average teacher's salary – and his brother, Luis, 75 pesos monthly (it was raised to 90 pesos only a month later) to act as his assistant. The SEP also agreed to pay the Governor of the Seri, Francisco Romero, 25 pesos monthly for allowing his people to go to school and the "indio" Herrera 15 pesos monthly to enforce school attendance, even as the state government was paying him the same amount.[62] The Education Ministry's payoff of local leaders is unparalleled; it is remarkable that Dworak convinced his superiors to adopt this policy, which as I noted earlier, was a common practice in the United States but unheard of elsewhere in Mexico. In most communities, the SEP entrusted local municipal officials with enforcing attendance. The hiring of Herrera might be explained by the fact that Carrizal was a pueblo, not a municipality; thus, there were no available municipal authorities near the school, necessitating the adoption of a unique strategy for ensuring school attendance. Nonetheless, this does not explain their paying of Romero or the adoption of the overall strategy of payments in the first place. A much more likely explanation is that Thompson, being familiar with the approach from north of the border, convinced Dworak and others to adopt this system.

At the time that the SEP agreed to Thompson's demands, the Seri lived in two separate groups: about half at Carrizal in Kino Bay and the other half 80 kilometers to the north at Pozo Coyote. Thompson and his brother had gone north to work with the group in Pozo Coyote, where they used a thatched hut as a temporary school building. The only equipment that the Thompson brothers had at their disposal to teach the Seri included a few rustic wooden benches, two tables, a chalkboard, and a map of Mexico. Dworak informed his superiors that there was a better school building in Carrizal, but it was necessary for the Thompsons and the school to follow the tribe in its migratory pattern, even allowing the Seri to miss school when they were on fishing expeditions, if they held out any hope of future success. As we have seen, the Education Ministry rejected a similar proposal in the Sierra Tarahumara. In any case, the idea would be short-lived.

To both Thompson and Dworak, the Seri were slowly gaining "a superior grade of civilization." They had come to accept the necessary devotion to work long hours in order to sustain themselves through agriculture, even if miserably. Some of the Seri had even adopted the custom of bathing themselves; still others were speaking a little Spanish, and the majority of them had given up "theft" as a means of survival. Dworak believed that the next logical step would be to establish a permanent school in a fixed place where there were enough resources to permit the Seris to live off their own agricultural production, a daunting task in a desert. The school would have to be located in the middle of their fishing and hunting zones so that men would be able to go alone, rather than in conjunction with their entire families as was their custom.[63]

Later in February, Dworak went to visit the Thompson brothers and Romero. The Thompsons, Romero, and three hunters escorted Dworak into a land "that very few white people are familiar with due to fear of the Seris." Dworak's depiction of the Seri's isolation turned the indigenista causal link between white oppression, indigenous isolation, and indigenous backwardness on its head, implicitly blaming the ferocity of the Seri for their own lack of civilization. It also contradicted his earlier depiction of the Seri as "docile" and "inoffensive."[64]

The Thompsons, Romero, and Dworak decided to build a permanent school at Pozo Peña, 20 kilometers inland along the littoral of the Canal de Infiernillo near San Miguel Point. They planned to move the members of the tribe slowly to Pozo Peña over the course of a month. Dworak instructed them to build a school, a meeting hall, and most importantly, a road suitable for automobile traffic. The road, following Education Ministry logic, would help to integrate the Seri both culturally and economically with the rest of Sonora.[65]

Dworak insisted that all Seri children must attend school and that women would no longer accompany their husbands on hunting and fishing trips. Instead, they would spend their time weaving baskets and doing other crafts.[66] The Seri would sell these crafts along with excess agricultural production and fish to help sustain them in their new settlement. The settlement of the Seri in a fixed location, the intrusion of a road for automobiles, the realignment of the Seri's accepted gender practices, and their work for profit rather than subsistence would mark, if successful, a major transition in Seri cultural practices, conforming more closely to that of mainstream Mexican society and delivering them from their status as "proto-citizens."

Romero agreed to return with Dworak to Hermosillo, where the medical staff at the local hospital examined him, he learned how to sign his name, he donned Western clothing, and in general, spent several days eating whatever food he could get his hands on. Dworak was surprised to note, however, that Romero did not drink alcohol (although, as noted below, many members of the Seri did), an activity that SEP officials often blamed for the backwardness of other indigenous groups, as we have seen with the Tarahumara, as well as campesinos.[67]

After a couple of days of this hospitable treatment (which perhaps acted as sort of a bribe), Romero professed adherence to the educational program that Dworak outlined. In exchange for his monthly salary, Romero agreed to help the Thompsons discipline the Seri and enforce school attendance. He returned home laden with numerous goods for his family that he and Dworak had purchased with his monthly salary.[68] Like the BIA, the SEP had gained at least some leverage over tribal affairs through the dispensation of salaries to key tribal members.

Romero's trip so favorably disposed Dworak that he petitioned the SEP to provide each member of the Seri with 5 pesos monthly to help them with their living expenses during their resettlement period.[69] The Education Ministry, probably fearing corruption, refused to consider the request until local officials undertook an official census, something that Thompson had claimed to do some years earlier.[70] Although there is no direct evidence, the timing of Dworak's letter to the SEP makes it likely that Dworak and Romero discussed this option during their stay in Hermosillo. Furthermore, Romero's purchase of materials and goods produced by mainstream Mexican society suggests the possibility that the lure of cash disbursements, rather than an enthrallment with contemporary Mexican culture, was the real incentive behind the Seri's willingness to accept the SEP's program.

In the meantime, Dworak sent specific instructions to the Thompson brothers that lay out with seeming scientific exactitude how he wanted them to proceed. The Seri would clear a 300 by 300 meter square at Pozo Peña and would construct their new pueblo around a 115 by 115 meter plaza. The Seri's conformity to uniform, scientific standards following the Spanish model for their pueblo would be only the first step in their "advancement from barbarity to civilization," from "proto-citizenship" to "citizenship." Dworak also instructed the Seri to begin immediate construction of the road connecting Pozo Peña with both the Canal de Infiernillo and the highway to Hermosillo so that they could more easily sell their crafts. Furthermore, Herrera would not only enforce school attendance, but also cleanliness. He was to make sure that "the populace had clean houses and streets" and was to accustom "the Indians to use outhouses with deep pits so that the patios were clean." The SEP viewed cleanliness and sanitation as a major benchmark of civilization.[71] Of course, poverty was a significant barrier to the fulfillment of hygiene and cleanliness campaigns.[72] Finally, reinforcing the idea that the Seri were little more than children who needed constant supervision, Dworak cautioned Robert Thompson that when he needed to buy provisions, he should send his brother so that the Seris were "never left, for now, entirely alone."[73]

In July 1927, Thompson wrote a sparkling report on his accomplishments. He said that when he first made contact with the Seri, locals knew them as "idlers, thieves, and assassins." In fact, when Thompson lived some distance from the Seri he heard and read much about their "robberies [and] assaults," but he believed that locals "created fables ... full of deaths, treasures, robberies, and cannibalism." When Thompson moved to the region, however, he used "different weapons than those that until [then] had been used against them: I treated them with care and I made friends with them; I cured them and defended them and, in this manner, I was able to attain their confidence." From living with them, Thompson noted that 75 per cent of the livestock thefts attributed to the Seri were misplaced. Instead, from their first years the Seri taught their children to pick berries and gather wild food. The adults spent the majority of their time fishing and hunting. He also discovered that the Seri refused to work on local haciendas, not because they were lazy, but rather because in the past local ranchers had treated them poorly, underpaid them or just did not pay them at all. They had been subject to kidnapping and sent to the Yucatán. Similarly, they refused to build houses and settle down for fear of persecution.[74] Thompson's portrayal of the plight of the Seri fit perfectly with his understanding of his role; namely, as an intermediary, akin to a BIA Indian agent, whose job it was to protect the Seri from damaging outside interactions even as he worked to slowly integrate them into Mexican society.

Thompson attempted to show to Education Ministry officials that his ability to gain the Seri's trust would eventually lead to their redemption. For example, he noted that after he had gained their confidence, the Seris agreed to turn over their firearms. In addition, although they still enjoyed dancing, gambling, and drinking corn beer, he had taught them to raise wheat, garbanzos, frijoles, and rice. Also, the Seri built ten wooden canoes (to replace their more customary though less technologically advanced reed boats), constructed 40 kilometers of road, began the construction of adobe houses, and complied with the fishing contract that Thompson had signed on their behalf. Furthermore, Thompson's associate Edward H. Davis had begun selling Seri-made baskets in California.[75] The Seri were well along the road to redemption.

Thompson warned, however, that "the ideas, customs, and superstitions that these Indians have are very backward and it is not a work of the moment to remove them and change them ... it will require patience and abnegation or a reserve [i.e., a U.S.-style Indian reservation] where the government completely sustains them and I will discipline them rapidly."[76] Thompson's call for a U.S.-style reservation with complete government subsidization of the Seri with him at its head once again underlines his American understanding of the purposes of indigenismo. Given Dworak's lifelong work in Sonora, and the state's long ties to the United States, Sonorans were often known as the "Yankees of Mexico," it is not all that surprising that Dworak backed Thompson's proposal.[77]

Only a month after providing the SEP with a sterling review of his work, Thompson claimed that the Seri were on the brink of starvation and that they would either die of malnutrition or would rebel against him if he forced them to stay in Pozo Peña. He tendered his resignation.[78] It is possible that they were in the midst of the diphtheria epidemic.[79] Nonetheless, this turn of events demonstrated that the Seri transformation would neither be swift nor easy and further convinced Thompson that his insistence on the necessity for a U.S.-style reservation was correct.

Along with his resignation, Thompson outlined the Seri's economic difficulties and, once again, requested that the federal government provide him with additional financial resources. He argued that the hides and baskets that he was selling on the Seri's behalf were not enough to make up for the low price that the Seri were receiving for their fish (which, ironically, he was selling for them at a predetermined, below-market fixed price). Even Thompson's slaughtering of some of his own livestock failed to stem the tide. The only food source that the Seri had left was the ocean. Ironically, as the settlement and attempt to farm failed, hunger forced the Seri to revert to their old "habits," many of them slipping away from Pozo Peña to other locations where they could collect edible seaweed and fish.

Thompson said that in order to make the settlement project work the government would have to provide every Seri adult and child over six years of age with 15 pesos per month (raising his previous request of 5 pesos per Seri per month, which SEP officials had already denied). In addition, they would have to come up with "two plows, shovels, hoes, axes, machetes, rakes, and four mules" as well as the "two common carts" that it had earlier promised to provide to the tribe. Dworak noted that in addition to the above problems, Thompson's "small" salary coupled with the isolation of the tribe made it difficult for him to buy food from nearby ranches. He suggested that the SEP approve Thompson's request.[80] The SEP refused.

In September 1927, Thompson, having rescinded his resignation (and having avoided both starvation and rebellion), arrived in Guaymas with eight members of the tribe, including Francisco Romero. They described their arrival in "civilization" as a miracle given the number of armed encounters that they had faced on their journey. Dworak allowed Romero to stay in his home and even took him to the cinema. Dworak then visited local authorities, asking them to make a collection of "fishhooks, harpoons ... spoons, hand axes, clothes, and provision" for the Seri. Dworak next visited the Chief of Military Operations in Guaymas and Sonora's new Governor, General Fausto Topete (1927–29), to see if he would donate one of the boats owned by the "rebel Yaquis" so that the Seri could undertake an expedition in the coming fishing season and bring their catch directly to market, thus avoiding the middleman.[81]

Eight months later, in May 1928, Dworak arranged another meeting with the Seri. Dworak wanted to explain to Romero and the rest of the tribe that the canoes that they were fishing in were not suitable for running a true fishing industry. In fact, Dworak had finally arranged for the Seri to receive the boat donated by General Topete, though they would have to pay a considerable sum to make it seaworthy. This boat would prove to be perhaps the biggest curse that Dworak could have laid upon the Seri. In addition to discussing the boat deal with Romero, Dworak's wife donated a collection of used clothing to the Seri.[82]

Meanwhile, Thompson was still hard at work trying to find a way to raise enough money so that the Seri could be convinced to settle down permanently. Once again he turned to his associate Davis, whom Thompson described as "a protector of the American Indians and . . . a friend of Mexico; a complete, true, and disinterested friend" of the Seri.[83] Davis, who had been working with Native Americans in Mesa Grande, California, for over 20 years as well as on behalf of the Museum of the American Indian in New York City since 1922, styled himself as a "White Chief."[84] His relationship with the Seri was a paternalistic one. He argued that they were

> [a] link with a past, primeval age of nature in America, for these are a strange and primitive people, a people whose lives and habits assign them to the initial place in the scale of cultural development among American Indians, and hence to the lowest recognized phase of savagery.[85]

He also made the unbelievable claim that "Seri mothers commonly have too much milk and frequently relieve themselves by suckling an orphaned puppy or sometimes even a baby pig."[86]

Davis had an offer that might solve the Seri money problem, one that best illustrates the influence of U.S. culture (though not BIA policy in this case) on Thompson. Davis proposed taking 25 Seri with him to "a special place near Hollywood" where they would put on a six- to eight-week exhibition. They would be dressed exactly as they now lived, in "dried pelican skins, painted as they still were one year ago, and occupied with their habitual occupations."[87] Davis agreed to pay for their transportation and living expenses while they were in the United States. His goal would be to earn enough money for the Seri so that they could "buy abundant clothes, agricultural implements, axes, etc." The only catch was that "naturally, a portion of what the exhibition produced would be left in favor of the businessman [Davis] who would have to spend so many hundreds of dollars in taking them, sustaining them, and fixing up their special place. The rest would be for the Seris."[88] In order for the exhibition to draw large enough crowds to ensure profitability, the Seri would have to give up all of the perceived advances, such as dressing in Western-style clothes and cutting their hair, which they had attained under Thompson. The show clearly drew on the long and profitable history of staging Native Americans in the Buffalo Bill Wild West Show and other living museums. These grew out of two important events: the defeat of Native Americans by the U.S. Army and the gathering of everyday Americans to Indian villages to watch dances and other performances, often for an entry fee.[89] Davis himself was no newcomer to these venues, having used his home in Mesa Grande as an exposition grounds, charging locals to see Native Americans who came to visit.[90]

Dworak was in favor of sending the Seri to "Hollywood." He argued that the SEP had already exhausted all other available means of economically improving their plight, and if Thompson was allowed to take them to Hollywood, they would earn enough money to purchase a gas-powered engine for their new boat. The record is clear in regards to Davis, Thompson, and Dworak's motives, but why did the Seri agree to an exhibition, which in some ways was the equivalent of putting them on display in a zoo? Historian Louis S. Warren argues that although these exhibitions in the United States further reinforced the dominant society's racist and eugenics-influenced beliefs of its own superiority by tapping into "the public longing for noble savages as true, uncorrupted, honest primitives fading before the onslaught of modern, industrial commerce," they provided a number of advantages to Native Americans. First, the work paid well, much better than jobs on the reservation, the only other option for many. Second, much of the work was enjoyable. In the Seri's case, it must have been much more appealing than clearing trees for roads and permanent settlements. Finally, and perhaps most importantly, it provided them with a venue to maintain and practice important aspects of their culture in a context in which outsiders might also come to appreciate and cherish them as well.[91]

Davis argued that the Seri would need to be dressed exactly as they were then, but that is a misnomer if we are to believe Thompson's reports. Many Seri had adopted modern dress and hairstyles at Thompson's insistence. Now, under cover of the exhibition, officials might allow them to revert to their own culture's dress, practices, and mannerisms, and Davis would pay them for it.

Underscoring the clash between the U.S.-inspired approach of Dworak, Thompson, and Davis and the SEP's indigenismo, it took only two weeks for the Education Ministry to respond negatively to the request. They ordered Dworak to do everything in his power to impede Thompson and Davis in their attempts to take the Seri to "Hollywood." The exhibition never took place.[92]

Shortly thereafter, an epidemic struck the Seri, perhaps because of their visit to Guaymas. The majority once again fled their settlement. That was only the beginning of their problems. In July 1928, a hurricane hit Thompson and the Seri while they were transporting firewood, damaging their boat. Thompson reported that it would require either 250 pesos or an engine to make the boat seaworthy. Failing that, he was sure that the Seri would be "left condemned to misery."[93] Thompson put 85 pesos down to secure a loan of the 485 pesos necessary to fix up the ship's sails. Nevertheless, he was unable to convince anyone to lend him enough to buy an engine. Nonetheless, the costs of the boat were beginning to add up. The Seri had originally paid 900 pesos to make the ship seaworthy, bringing the grand total of future earnings that the Seri would need to pay off their debts to 1,300 pesos. Given that the average salary for working-class folks was somewhere between 1.50 to 2.00 pesos daily, the Seri would have had to put in somewhere between 650 and 867 full days of paid labor to pay off the debt. Of course, given their isolation, this was highly unlikely. In response, Dworak asked the SEP to cover the 400 remaining pesos from the Seri's most recent bill, considering that "this tribe has never been helped as have the Yaqui in spite of the enormous damages" that the Yaquis had caused.[94]

The SEP refused to cover the Seri's expenses. Therefore, Dworak asked the *Oficina de Caza y Pesca* (Wildlife Office) to give the Seri a special tax break on the sale of "Burra" deer that they normally caught on specially organized hunts. While waiting for an answer, Thompson rearmed the Seri in hopes that they could use their much-touted hunting skills to raise money to pay off their debts. Dworak purchased four rifles for the Seri and convinced locals to loan them an additional 30, clearly suggesting that few people still viewed the Seri as a serious menace.[95] Eleven days later, the Wildlife Office informed Dworak that the Seri could not hunt tax-free, arguing that if the government did not begin to take radical measures, the species would be driven to extinction.[96] Taxes on the hunting of Burra meant that only those who could hunt for leisure could afford to hunt. This fit in well with the assumption that hunting out of necessity was primitive and backward while hunting for leisure was a middle-class pursuit.

In January 1929, seeing no other alternative and demonstrating his commitment to their redemption, Dworak paid to have the Seri's boat repaired out of his own pocket. While repairmen fixed the boat, he allowed Romero and four other Seri to stay at his house, paying for all their needs. Finally, he gave them 15 days' worth of provisions and clothes for their children.[97]

A week later tragedy struck. Thompson reported the Seri had run aground and destroyed their newly repaired boat. Thompson had gone with several Seri to pick up some state-donated breeding mules. On their return trip, they had run out of food and water and went ashore to forage. When Thompson returned from foraging, he found that the Seri he had left on the boat had run it ashore.

Dworak argued that this even put the SEP in "a very difficult position to remedy this savage tribe." According to Dworak, the SEP had been in the process of convincing the Seri to abandon those places lacking in natural resources and had managed to get the Seri to overcome their fear of interacting with whites. Once again, Dworak asked the government to subsidize the Seris, requesting 25 centavos daily for each of the tribe's children so that they could eat corn and beans. He concluded by noting that "the work of this tribe's redemption is really difficult and also requires a special patience ... it is indispensable that the children now grow up with different customs and that they modify their manner of being."[98]

Soon thereafter, the Education Ministry replaced Dworak with Ramón G. Bonfil. Thompson, meanwhile, claimed to have completely lost the faith of the Seri. In any case, Thompson said that the Seri forced him to leave Carrizal, suggesting that tribal members had had enough of his "assistance" for the time being. Bonfil closed the school, arguing "the tribe has emigrated from the place" and was "almost completely dispersed." Since neither the Seri nor any other teacher was interested in re-establishing a school in Carrizal, the SEP stepped away from the Seri.[99] Although it is impossible to know exactly why both Thompson and Bonfil agreed to end the Education Ministry's unique experiment with the Seri, it was not because Bonfil did not believe in the redemption of indigenous people. He would continue to promote indigenous causes as a member of the SEP and the *Departamento de Asuntos Indígenas* (Department of Indian Affairs or DAI) into the early 1940s.[100] A more likely cause was that

Bonfil, as an outsider, did not agree with Thompson's north-of-the-border approach to redeeming the Seri.

The Mexican federal government would not again attempt to integrate the Seri into mainstream Mexican society until 1938, when the newly created DAI encouraged the Seri to organize a fishing co-operative so that they could take advantage of their local habitat. By then, the road that the Seri had helped construct from Hermosillo to Kino Bay had led to the rise of an export-based, mestizo-dominated fishing industry.[101] In the meantime, when the SEP ceased to support Thompson and his work, Thompson immediately turned his attention back to state officials. He reported to Sonora's new Governor, Francisco S. Elías (1929–31), that he and his brother Luis had discovered that the Seri had killed a local rancher's cow near the Canal of Infiernillo. They promised to act as mediators between the Seri and the rancher, Luis Laavedra. They would make sure that the Seri repaid Laavedra and that the Seri's governor, Chico Romero, would punish the person who killed the cow. The Thompsons had begun anew helping the state government to enforce the compact of 1925.[102]

5

The Tohono O'odham

In late May 1928, cattle rancher José X. Pablo, a member of the Papago Good Government League – composed of "Progressive" Papagos who were largely Presbyterian and graduates of BIA boarding schools[1] – and the future provisional chairperson of the Tribal Council in Arizona, approached officials from the SEP, expressing his people's affinity for Mexico and asking them to provide the Tohono O'odham (Desert People) with an alternative to sending their children to U.S. schools:

> [W]e have always been thinking of Mexico, which is our true country. Hopefully someday our government ... will place schools here in the frontier, very close to us so that we will not have to send our children to schools in Tucson or other American schools that are near the border.[2]

Pablo argued further that although the majority of the Tohono O'dham lived on the U.S. side of the border, his people realized that "those lands are really Mexican," as were the Tohono O'odham. He noted too that although U.S. government officials had been working hard to assimilate his people, the Tohono O'odham preferred to adopt Mexican customs.[3]

Pablo had spent the last decade working closely with BIA officials to set aside reservation lands for the Tohono O'odham and to promote BIA allotment, a policy that would distribute communally owned Tohono O'odham lands to individual Indians in hopes of making them vibrant, capitalistic members of the U.S. economy (and, cynically, open up the remainder of Indian lands to non-Indian settlement).[4] Pablo's adoption of a "play-off system" between the agencies of the U.S. and Mexican government was probably an attempt to extend the influence and modernizing vision of the Papago Good Government League south of the border.[5] However, despite the seeming contradiction between Pablo's working with both the BIA and the SEP to assimilate simultaneously the Tohono O'odham into U.S. and Mexican society, his "play-off system" had an underlying logic. First, both governments saw cultural assimilation as a means of economic modernization,[6] the latter being a primary goal of the Papago Good Government League. Second, the Tohono O'odham had historically been able to use the border and the reservation to tap into the modern wage economy without losing their underlying cultural heritage.[7] Third, many Tohono O'odham living north of the border had a stronger cultural attachment to their relatives living south of the border and to popular Catholicism than to U.S. culture.[8] For example, most of the Tohono O'odham continued speaking Spanish and Papago instead of English in their everyday lives in spite of attending Indian day schools in the United States.[9] Fourth, like the Papago Good Government League, many Tohono O'odham south of the border had recently adopted livestock raising as the foundation of their livelihoods. When the U.S. government granted the Tohono O'odham a reservation in 1916, the BIA stepped in to defend reservation lands against outside claims and invested heavily in infrastructure to improve their livestock herds. The Tohono O'odham hoped that by agreeing to the SEP's education program, the Education Ministry would do the same south of the border.[10] Finally, Pablo was a skilled political leader willing to push the limits of accepted practice to advance his agenda.[11]

The Tohono O'odham were thus caught between two nations, the United States and Mexico, and two religions, Presbyterianism and Catholicism,[12] all of whom wanted to assimilate the Tohono O'odham into their particular culture. They were also caught between two worlds, the traditional and the modern. This chapter explores the attempts by members of the Tohono O'odham, allied with the Papago Good Government League, to use the U.S.-Mexican border as leverage in their attempts to gain better schooling in the northern state of Sonora between 1928 and 1935. It also examines the resistance of Tohono O'odham living in Sonora to Mexican assimilation efforts – especially in light of the government sponsored anti-fanaticization campaigns and the land-grabbing tendencies of non-Indian Mexicans – and their rejection of the Papago Good Government League as their representative.

Members of the Papago Good Government League, founded in 1911, lived mostly in and around Tucson and Sells. For example, Pablo, who spoke fluent English and had attended the Presbyterian Mission School for nine years, lived in Tucson.[13] The League was contested by the League of Papago Chiefs (LPC), whose members largely lived in the northern reaches of the Papago Indian Reservation and who practiced a hybrid Sonoran Catholicism centered on an annual pilgrimage to Magdalena, Sonora, to celebrate their patron saint, Saint

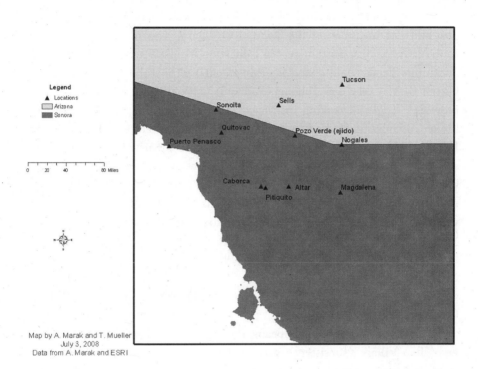

Legend
▲ Locations
☐ Arizona
■ Sonora

Tucson

Sonoita

Sells

Quitovac

Pozo Verde (ejido)

Nogales

Puerto Penasco

Caborca

Altar

Magdalena

Pitiquito

0   20   40   80 Miles

Map by A. Marak and T. Mueller
July 3, 2008
Data from A. Marak and ESRI

Francis Xavier. The LPC opposed allotment and were more likely to maintain the traditional ways of the Tohono O'odham.[14] Some Tohono O'odham living on the Mexican side of the border – the proposed beneficiaries of Pablo's overture to SEP officials – were willing, however, to accept assistance from the Mexican government, but only on their own terms. In the process, they rejected wholesale assimilation into either mainstream Mexican or U.S. society.

After Pablo approached SEP officials, they immediately embraced the possibility of assimilating the Tohono O'odham. Tohono O'odham leaders continually expressed an interest in Education Ministry assistance, but only if Mexican officials could match the investments in the Tohono O'odham made by the BIA. Every day Tohono O'odham had additional demands, such as providing English-speaking instructors, an indication of their prior, though limited, adaptation to the U.S. economy. With the advent of the Indian New Deal in 1934, Xavier Pablo turned his attention to the new U.S.-government-sanctioned Papago Tribal Council. By 1935, with the New Deal's Civilian Conservation Corps – Indian Division providing the Tohono O'odham with new wage earning opportunities, SEP officials abandoned their efforts to convince the Tohono O'odham to assimilate into Mexican society.

The U.S. government created the 2.75-million-acre Papago Reservation in 1916.[15] It covered much of southern Arizona. Just over 12 years later, the Mexican government set aside 7,675 acres in Pozo Verde. Both governments were acting in response to Hispanic and Anglo encroachment onto Tohono O'odham lands.

Prior to the arrival of Europeans, the Tohono O'odham practiced a modified "Two-Village" subsistence pattern through seasonal migration between winter villages located near mountain springs (*tinajas*) and temporary summer desert settlements located near the deltas of washes.[16] The extended family was the basis of Tohono O'odham society. A council that "based their actions on group discussion and consensus" governed each village, the villages ranging in population from 20 to 300.[17]

Men worked together to build *charcos* (ponds) in summer settlements and they hunted. Women gathered wild plants and processed domesticated plants.[18] The Two-Village system was supplemented through wage labor and cattle raising. By the early twentieth century, men increasingly took part in the local wage economies as mineworkers, ranch hands, and cotton-pickers. Women followed suit by migrating into non-Indian areas to work as domestic servants.[19] Cattle raising and staple crop production was more common in the U.S.-Mexican border region among Tohono O'odham who had attended mission or off-reservation boarding schools. Unlike their American and Mexican counterparts, however, the Tohono O'odham raised cattle communally, village councils naming stockmen to take care of the livestock when they were grazing outside of the summer village. The BIA tapped into local tradition by naming Pablo stockman in 1917.[20] Outside of this region, they raised only limited livestock, focusing on raising or hunting cattle for subsistence and breeding of horses for prestige.[21]

A combination of their social structure and their environment has allowed the Tohono O'odham to avoid wholesale assimilation with outside societies since their first contact with Europeans. Jesuits and Franciscans, arriving as early as 1687, had little long-lasting impact on the Tohono O'odham. Throughout the late nineteenth century, the Tohono O'odham continued to live as if the international boundary between the U.S. and Mexico did not exist.[22]

By the 1870s, however, the Tohono O'odham had integrated work for wages or payment in kind for the Akimel O'odham (or Pimans), who were producing wheat as a staple crop.[23] Shrinking access to their ancestral lands forced many Tohono O'odham into a life of cattle rustling.[24] Increased tensions often culminated in armed conflict. Local mestizos and Tohono O'odham disputed the ownership of some cattle in 1898, resulting in a Tohono O'odham raid on El Plomo, Sonora. A few Tohono O'odham died. The mestizo response to the raid was so intense that a large number of Tohono O'odham, perhaps as many as 800, decided to migrate to the U.S. side of the border in search of a safe haven. This proved to be the first of a series of northward Tohono O'odham migrations and an early example of the ways in which they used the border as a means of defense.

For those Tohono O'odham who chose to remain on the Mexican side of the border, however, their troubles were just beginning. Between 1905 and 1908, the federal government under Porfirio Díaz used soldiers to remove them from their lands in Caborca, Pitiquito, and Altar in order to make room for additional mestizo settlers.[25] In 1911, explorer Carl Lumholtz noted that "the part of the tribe that lives in Sonora is much more disrupted; they have lost most of their lands and are largely servants of the Mexicans, doing efficient work as *vaqueros* (cowboys), miners, etc."[26] The Mexican Revolution (1911–17) led to additional problems.[27] The Tohono O'odham lived near 75 miles of the unfenced, unpatrolled international boundary, and Tohono O'odham cattle made tempting targets for the Mexican forces on the other side. Banditry and intervention by Mexican revolutionary forces forced many Tohono O'odham to

TOHONO O'ODHAM WORKING IN LIVESTOCK YARD IN ARIZONA. PHOTO COURTESY OF
NATIONAL ARCHIVES AND RECORDS ADMINISTRATION, PACIFIC REGION — LAGUNA
NIGUEL.

flee to the U.S. side of the border and resulted in the confiscation of much of their cattle. Although Native Americans would not become U.S. citizens until 1924, the Tohono O'odham who fled to the U.S. during the revolution took advantage of the proximity of the border to turn to the U.S. State Department and the U.S. Vice Consul's Office in Nogales, Arizona, in an attempt to get their cattle back.[28] They also agreed to donate labor to the BIA in constructing a fence along the international boundary line.[29]

The 1920s would continue to be a troublesome time as Sonoran authorities tried to promote economic modernization in the Papaguería, often at the expense of the Tohono O'odham. In 1920, José León, governor of the Tohono O'odham in Sonoita, complained to state officials that Mexicans had taken over "the most ancient of Papago lands in Sonoita" and were using them to plant wheat. In addition, the Mexicans had acquired the land above the local dam and refused to share water with Tohono O'odham. Adolfo de la Huerta directed the local police chief, Reyes O. Carrasco, to "procure a satisfactory solution" to the land and water issue.[30]

In 1921, León again contacted de la Huerta, notifying him that Carrasco had not followed through. León noted that Bartolo Ortega, the non-Indian legal owner of Tohono O'odham ancestral lands in Sonoita, had allowed them access to it and control over dispersing the water for the last 25 years.[31] When the Tohono O'odham settler in charge of dispersing water died, however, Ortega had given control over the land and water to a non-Indian, Jesus Montijo. In response, Carrasco argued that the water dispute was out of his jurisdiction. He had resolved the situation by informing the chief of police in Quitovac to look into the matter. As for the land complaint, he believed that the Tohono O'odham claim of 25 years of access to the land was untrue. In the end, he spoke with Montijo, "satisfactorily fixing the troubles between the Papagos and their neighbors."[32] In other words, he asked Montijo to play nice with the Tohono O'odham.

Access to land and water in the Papaguería was not an isolated issue for the Tohono O'odham. In June 1921, Antonio L. Bustamante, tribal spokesperson in Pozo Verde, complained to de la Huerta that a non-Indian, Lucas Oros, had confiscated a Tohono O'odham well that they had drilled a decade earlier about 25 miles outside of Pozo Verde. Interestingly, Bustamante sent his letter through the Mexican Consulate in San Fernando, Arizona. Bustamante received better news than León. De la Huerta informed Lucas Oros that the well belonged to the Tohono O'odham.[33]

In October 1921, the owner, Jesus M. Zepeda, and president, Mose Drachman, of the San Carlos Cattle Company, both of whom were U.S. citizens and lived in Tucson, responded to complaints that they were putting up fences around Tohono O'odham lands. Zepeda and Drachman noted that in 1913 the then governor of Sonora, José M. Maytorena, had forced them to stop fencing the boundaries, cultivating crops, and making capital improvements on the 17,000 acres owned by the company in the Papaguería. They had complied not because it was legal, but rather because the Mexican Revolution made further investment at the time too risky. Maytorena had named a commission to look into the legality of their land ownership and found that Zepeda had legal copies of the deeds and legitimate titles that clearly demarcated the boundaries of his land. It is likely that the San Carlos Cattle Company's land titles were the result of Baldíos Law of 1883. The law gave the government the necessary "legal cover" to advance one of the main planks of its modernization program, rationalizing the use of supposedly underutilized lands. The government expropriated these lands and then sold them to "mining corporations and cattle ranchers."[34]

Zepeda warned de la Huerta that he would not settle for some "admnistrative resolution" to appease the Tohono O'odham because the lands that he was now refencing were legally his. Drachman added that if the state allowed the Tohono O'dham to maintain their cattle and horses on San Carlos Cattle Company land, it would be to the detriment of everyone in Sonora since the Tohono O'odham did not practice modern cattle-raising techniques, refused to castrate poorly bred horses and bulls, and often killed the company's cattle for subsistence. Instead, they asked state officials to expel the Tohono O'odham squatting on company lands. The governor complied and sent the local police chief to do so.[35] Hence, attempts by the Tohono O'odham to use the power of the Sonoran state to protect access to their ancestral lands had generally resulted in inaction, the status quo, or their expulsion, while their similar attempts to seek governmental interference in the United States had resulted in the creation of a reservation and governmental efforts to retrieve their property.

Bustamante responded to the Tohono O'odham expulsion with an explanation of their right to the land. He noted that in 1886 the Mexican government had given the Tohono O'odham of Pozo Verde official title to only three square miles of land, half-hilly and half-flat, for its 170 indigenous inhabitants. From the start, the designated land was not sufficient. The land shortage was compounded when the Tohono O'odham adopted cattle raising as their main source of economic livelihood. Since no one else occupied the lands surrounding their legally titled land and since these lands "clearly . . . belonged to their ancestors," since "time immemorial," they migrated back onto them, improved them, and therefore "had the right to maintain themselves" on them. Some years later, Zepeda and his company began sinking wells, fencing off the best pasturage, and forcing the Tohono O'odham off their ancestral lands. Not only had Zepeda and his company completely encircled them in Pozo Verde, but they were also acquiring vast tracks of the Papaguería on the U.S. side of the border as well. Bustamante feared that he intended to confiscate all of their ancestral lands on both sides of the border and force them into starvation. Others could use the 'play-off system' as well.

Tapping into well-understood concepts of frontier citizenship, Bustamante reminded state officials that many of the older Tohono O'odham had played an integral role in fighting off the Apache threat in the nineteenth century and establishing peace in Sonora. He affirmed that the Tohono O'odham had "always been industrious and lovers of peace" but pointed out that given Zepeda's provocation and the fact that justice was on their side, they might be forced to respond.[36] De la Huerta responded by referring their case to the National Agrarian Commission with the recommendation that they keep their ancestral lands.[37]

A year later, the San Carlos Cattle Company was still making use of Tohono O'odham ancestral lands, and the Tohono O'odham turned to the Local Agrarian Commission in hopes of winning restitution of enough land to sustain themselves.[38] A year after that Tohono O'odham leaders again pressed state and local officials for land restitution and asked them to locate the Tohono O'odham land titles that predated those granted to the San Carlos Cattle Company. Again, local and state officials informed the Tohono O'odham that they were working on their behalf. In fact, however, both local and state officials had simply referred the case to the federal government and were awaiting a decision.[39] Meanwhile, Bustamante, perhaps suffering from a leadership crisis in Pozo Verde due to the lack of a resolution over the land issues, asked the state officials to oversee a local tribal election, which he hoped would result in the "renovation" of his powers.[40] The Tohono O'odham would need to be patient in their pursuit of justice.

In 1925, Bustamante presented his credentials to Sonoran Governor Alejo Bay and petitioned money to go to Altar, a municipal seat in northeast Sonora, perhaps to look for the Tohono O'odam land titles.[41] Nonetheless, local, state, and federal officials did not intervene on the Tohono O'odham's behalf. By 1927, non-Indians had succeeded in confiscating Tohono O'odham lands in Sonoita and there was still no resolution over the land dispute in Pozo Verde.[42]

In late May 1928, a year after Mexicans confiscated Tohono O'odham lands in Sonoita and shortly after President Calles created the Pozo Verde ejido for the Tohono O'odham, Pablo met with SEP officials to ask for more schools for his people.[43] Remembering that the BIA had begun investing heavily immediately after the establishment of the reservation on the U.S. side of the border, he probably thought that the Mexican government would do the same after the establishment of the ejido south of the border. When Pablo, acting as a spokesperson for the Tohono O'odham living on the Mexican side of the border, told Dworak, as outlined at the beginning of this chapter, that his people had always had much stronger cultural connections to Mexico than the United States, one can only wonder what Dworak thought about an English- and Papago-speaking Tohono O'odham spokesperson advocating for improved Spanish language schooling for his people. This does not mean, however, that Pablo was misleading Dworak. As previously noted, many Tohono O'odham had stronger cultural connections to Sonora and its popular Catholicism than they did to the United States. Furthermore, Pablo's earlier travels in Sonora suggest that he had many social connections in the state and probably had the support of those for whom he was advocating, though it is open to question whether his supporters were Catholics.[44]

In any case, Dworak explained to Pablo that the SEP was already trying to provide education to the Tohono O'odham through the Casa in Mexico City. Pablo replied that the Tohono O'odham had several children in the Casa, but it did little for the rest of his people.[45] He argued, "We want all of our children educated so that ... we will have a strong country that the Americans respect."[46]

The Mexican nationalism and patriotism that the Education Ministry promoted in its schools not only included learning about Mexican independence heroes like Miguel Hidalgo, José Morelos, and Vicente Guerrero as well as more recent revolutionary heroes, but it also insured that children learned a Spanish not corrupted by English and a history that did not glorify George Washington and other U.S. heroes. Inherent in Pablo's argument was an attempt to play to SEP concerns about U.S. cultural imperialism in the border region to strengthen his own hand in dealing with the BIA on the U.S. side of the border. At the same time, he would be able to harness the SEP to the Good

Government League's goals of providing the Tohono O'odham with greater economic opportunities and safeguarding their ancestral lands. From extant documentation, Pablo's approach to the SEP might have been an attempt to expand the Good Government League's constituency to the Mexican side of the border. Bustamante's admission that the Tohono O'odham near Pozo Verde had recently adopted livestock raising and the fact that he wrote some of his letters to Mexican authorities from Arizona also suggest a connection between Pablo and Bustamante. Dworak promised to see what he could do about the situation and reported to his superiors that his surprise at the "elevated concepts of this indigenous Papago."[47]

An initial visit by federal education inspector David Torres Orozco to the Papaguería highlighted the usual cultural changes that the SEP's schooling programs wanted to inculcate in indigenous people: the creation of permanent Spanish-style settlements, an end to seasonal migration, and the adoption of modern agricultural techniques. Torres Orozco noted that the 1,180 Tohono O'odham engaged in agriculture and the raising of small animals were scattered across several settlements – Sonoita, San Francisquito, Pozo Verde, El Carrizo, Veracruz, and El Bajio – and living in apparent misery.

The Education Ministry preferred the more cost-effective approach of administering to larger Spanish-style settlements, but the arid Papaguería precluded such. In addition, the ejido that Calles had ceded to the Tohono O'odham was some distance from the closest town, making it impossible for children to attend school. Torres Orozco also noted that many Tohono O'odham migrated to mines in El Ajo, Arizona to look for work, making them unable to attend school. This was a legitimate concern from the SEP's point of view, since many Tohono O'odham tapped into labor markets outside of their ancestral lands as a means of "resistant adaptation." Finally, Torres Orozco thought that the Tohono O'odham did not rotate crops, planting only wheat and corn. He failed to note, however, that the Tohono O'odham practiced agriculture uniquely adapted to the Sonoran Desert. They planted not only wheat and corn in areas with permanent water sources, but also "squash … cotton, tobacco, gourds, devil's claw, and a host of other useful field-border 'weeds'" in areas of seasonal water availability.[48]

Torres Orozco suggested that the SEP use the Tohono O'odham church as a school to prod them into constructing a new school.[49] Education Ministry anticlericalism, however, served to undermine Tohono O'odham support for the education program. Torres Orozco was only the first of many SEP officials who saw the Tohono O'odham's strong religious beliefs, especially their veneration of Saint Francis Xavier, as a major obstacle to their assimilation into mainstream Mexican society.[50] What Torres Orozco failed to consider was the religious split among the Tohono O'odham. Pablo was probably speaking on behalf of the younger, Protestant members of the indigenous group, while many of the Tohono O'odham that Torres Orozco visited had incorporated the "miraculous aspects of Catholicism … into their cosmology."[51] The SEP goal of eradicating traditional Tohono O'odham religious beliefs, however, precluded their using religion as an incentive for participation. Furthermore, it drove many Tohono O'odham to the U.S., where BIA officials were much more open to their practice of Catholicism as demonstrated by the fact that one member of the BIA staff at the Sells Indian Agency in Arizona, Mary Doyle, was actually Sister Alfrida, a Sister of the San Xavier Mission.

Despite Torres Orozco's crude suggestions (which were not implemented), he understood at least part of the plight of the Tohono O'odham, reporting that the indigenous population in the communities he visited was not fixed because they were often forced to migrate to Arizona for work on the reservation as a result of persecution from local white and mestizo landlords. The Mexican government, he contended, had failed in its duty to protect the Tohono O'odham, usually siding (as they did in 1927) with landlords and not the Indians when confronted with conflicts. Meanwhile, the U.S. government had, through the reservation system, given the Papago "guarantees of life."[52]

Torres Orozco visited the Sells Indian Agency. Pablo showed him the many advantages that the Tohono O'odham had on the U.S. side of the border. Torres Orozco thus got an idea about Tohono O'odham hopes for the Mexican side of the border. The primary teachers in the Tohono O'odham schools on the U.S. side of the border were well paid and the buildings modern.[53] The reservation had a modern hospital. In addition, the United States had given the Tohono O'odham ample land and modern farming equipment. The only problem that the Tohono O'odham had with U.S. schools was that they were coeducational. Perhaps trying to impress Torres Orozco with Tohono O'odham flexibility, Xavier Pablo noted that they had, over time, reluctantly changed their minds and were presently sending the majority of their children to these schools.[54]

Using the seeming paradise on the U.S. side of the border as leverage, Pablo presented his case to the Mexican government:

TOHONO O'ODHAM CONSTRUCTING A BUILDING IN SELLS, ARIZONA. PHOTO COURTESY OF NATIONAL ARCHIVES AND RECORDS ADMINISTRATION, PACIFIC REGION – LAGUNA NIGUEL.

TOHONO O'ODHAM AND BIA OFFICIALS TAKE A BREAK FROM CONSTRUCTION. PHOTO COURTESY OF NATIONAL ARCHIVES AND RECORDS ADMINISTRATION, PACIFIC REGION — LAGUNA NIGUEL.

We do not want schools like those that the [Mexican] government has established for us until now in poorly constructed rooms with bad light and ventilation and without furniture and school equipment, in which they try to give an education to a growing number of children with only a single teacher, who most of the time is poorly paid and is constantly thinking about how to get by in these places so remote, so lacking in communication, and where the cost of living is expensive. Thus, to these schools our children will not go ... and [we want you] to give us teachers that will not only be able to teach us to read and write, but also to love Mexico, to which we are connected by origin, tradition, and customs.[55]

Pablo adopted the SEP's own discourse of pro-Mexican nationalism in combination with a veiled threat to advance his goals. Furthermore, there is little doubt that the Education Ministry teachers assigned to remote Tohono O'odham schools would have agreed with him about their plight. Pablo was sincerely interested in using SEP schools to harness the Mexican government's ability to protect the Tohono O'odham communities and ancestral lands that spanned the U.S.-Mexican border. Earlier, he had argued that the SEP's backing of the Tohono O'odham would create "a strong country that the Americans respect." In Pablo's 'play-off system,' however, the Education Ministry would have to match U.S. investment in the Tohono O'odham. If they did, both the Tohono O'odham and Mexico would benefit. If they did not, the Tohono O'odham would turn their backs on the SEP and undermine its program aimed to counter U.S. cultural imperialism. The Mexican government was in no economic position to comply. Nevertheless, that does not suffice to explain how little they invested in their effort to woo the Tohono O'odham, especially in light of the SEP's focus on promoting Mexican nationalism in the borderlands and their considerably much stronger effort vis-à-vis the Seri. Perhaps the Seri's prior history with state officials or their proximity to Hermosillo was the deciding factor. On the other hand, it is possible that the fact that Pablo did not speak Spanish convinced SEP officials that the Tohono O'odham were much too closely connected to U.S. culture to be 'saved.'

After Torres Orozco's trip to Sells, Dworak determined that the education of the Tohono O'odham would be daunting. Once again, cultural misunderstandings were at the root of the problem. By now, Dworak had come to believe that the Tohono O'odham lived in poverty because they lacked morals. He told

FROM MANY, ONE

his superiors that they would be difficult to educate because they lived in scattered settlements and they were having problems finding teachers willing to live with the Tohono O'odham in the Papaguería. Nonetheless, he promised the SEP that he would personally visit the one Mexican Tohono O'odham school, which was located in Sonoita.[56] There is no record of his trip, and if he did visit, he failed to educate himself about the historical impact – the Two-Village system and migratory "resistant adaptation" – that living in the Papaguería had had on Tohono O'odham culture. Instead, he gave up.

In 1929, Bustamante approached an Education Ministry inspector in Pozo Verde. He reiterated the Tohono O'odham's willingness to co-operate with the SEP. Like Pablo, Bustamante asked the Education Ministry to provide good teachers and school buildings so that Tohono O'odham parents would not have to send their children to Tucson to go to school. The inspector, Gustavo A. Serrano, argued that given local Tohono O'odham land ownership, the SEP could transform them into "good" Mexicans producing for the market. However, given the lack of resources and irrigation, it would require a 10,000- or 20,000-peso investment in schooling and agricultural improvements.[57] Such an educational and agricultural investment, minus its anticlerical aspects, is exactly what the Tohono O'odham were looking for; there is little doubt that this suggestion originated with Bustamante, as inspectors almost never proposed such large expenditures. In the U.S. region of the Papaguería where the Papago Good Government League dominated, the Tohono O'odham had used their organizing capabilities to gain BIA, Franciscan, and Presbyterian support for education, land, access to water, and other resources to develop a local economy based on cattle raising and staple crop production for market.[58]

Once again, however, the failure of Education Ministry officials to understand Tohono O'odham culture undermined their collaborative efforts. Serrano described the Tohono O'odham as "traditionally peaceful and probably more civilized than the average tribe" in Mexico, but also one lacking in industry, doing just enough to satisfy their needs. Serrano misinterpreted Tohono O'odham migratory practices and collaboration with the BIA as first steps in the complete acculturation of the Tohono O'odham into U.S. culture, arguing that the "Indians are living in the frontier and with intimate relations with their North American relatives ... [and] little by little they are separating themselves from our country in order to incorporate themselves into the civilization of their neighbor."[59]

TOHONO O'ODHAM CHILDREN GATHERING OUTSIDE OF THE BIA OFFICES IN SELLS, ARIZONA. PHOTO COURTESY OF NATIONAL ARCHIVES AND RECORDS ADMINISTRATION, PACIFIC REGION — LAGUNA NIGUEL.

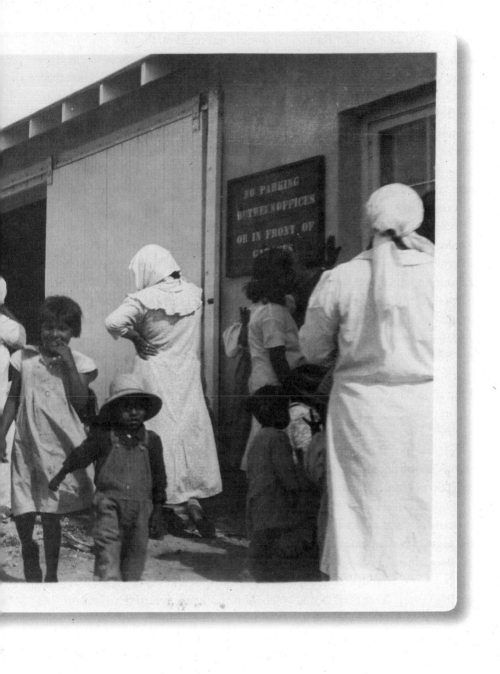

Serrano's supervisor, Ramón G. Bonfil, was tepid on the idea of providing such a high level of the government's scarce educational resources to the Tohono O'odham (just as he had cut off aid to the Seri). He correctly argued that Serrano was making his first trip to the area as an inspector and did not know the Tohono O'odham very well. Bonfil also noted that there already was a rural primary school in Pozo Verde to which the Tohono O'odham sent only four or five of their children on a regular basis. The school, however, was located quite some distance from the Tohono O'odham's ejido and lacked a building, furniture, and educational materials – all issues about which the Tohono O'odham had complained.

Both Bonfil and Serrano correctly surmised that the Tohono O'odham would not co-operate with the SEP until the government paid for and constructed a school for them. The Tohono O'odham had repeatedly asked the Education Ministry to provide them good schools and materials, and the SEP had failed to do so. Furthermore, it was unlikely that the Tohono O'odham would donate their time and effort to such a project when they could send their children to better-furnished schools in the U.S. In spite of the fact that it was the SEP's general policy not to provide rural schooling to those communities that had not already donated or constructed a building first, Bonfil asked the Education Ministry to build a school for the Tohono O'odham because "it is of vital importance for our country to eliminate the peaceful conquest of the north."[60] However, again the SEP failed to follow through.

It was not until February 1932 that the SEP once more tried to address the issue of Tohono O'odham schooling, sending a cadre of state and federal officials to "conquer four indigenous people" for the Casa. The group, headed by Diputado Fernando P. Serrano and Inspector Ramón R. Reyes, met with Bustamante and asked him if he would be willing to send four children to the Casa.[61] Bustamante refused, noting that there was no reason to send their children all the way to Mexico City when they could simply send them across the border to attend BIA schools. Nevertheless, he did express his interest in setting up a federal rural primary school in Sonora, promising to inform the inspector on his next trip through the area about the number of children who might attend such a school.[62]

In December 1932, Vicente Ochoa, the police commissioner in Pozo Verde, asked the SEP to allow his associate, Ulrico Villegas, to establish a rural primary school in the pueblo.[63] Ochoa was with the group that had visited

Bustamante in February. Three days later, Inspector Reyes sent Villegas to Pozo Verde to open a school. Numerous problems confronted him.

First, there were only two school-aged children and three families residing in the pueblo. Second, locals told Villegas that it would be impossible for him to live in Pozo Verde and forced him to commute to and from a nearby town. Third, because of the Two-Village system, the majority of the Tohono O'odham was temporarily living in El Bajío, some 40 kilometers away from Pozo Verde. They refused to send their children back to Pozo Verde for schooling until they returned.

Instead, Reyes was inclined to give up. He argued that the SEP could not compete with the numerous benefits that the U.S. government was providing the Tohono O'odham. He wrongly included among these benefits a number of churches that he claimed the U.S. had built for the Tohono O'odham because they "professed the Catholic faith" which made them "overly fanatic." Reyes concluded that since there were only 400 to 500 Tohono O'odham living in Mexico, the majority of whom already spoke English and sent their children to school in the United States, it was not worth the Education Ministry's time or effort to pursue the issue any further.[64]

Reyes' report to the SEP highlighted a number of important issues. First, most of the Tohono O'odham living in the area probably were not comfortable with the SEP, its employees, or its program, especially its anti-fanaticization plank, which aimed to eliminate a central part of Tohono O'odham culture. Second, the SEP was ill-equipped to deal with the Tohono O'odham Two-Village system. Educators refused to go where the Tohono O'odham were, instead asking them to adjust to Mexican culture by permanently settling in one location. In the cases of the Tarahumara and the Seri, government mediators suggested having the schools move seasonally with the students, something that actually occurred with the Seri for a short time. Reyes, on the other hand, suggested government withdrawal. Finally, Education Ministry employees realized that they could not compete with the BIA on economically equal terms. Furthermore, they believed that the BIA had already won the battle to win the hearts and minds of the Tohono O'odham.

Rafael Ramírez, the head of the rural education department, felt differently. Ramírez told Reyes that he needed to undertake an "intense labor" in the Papaguería so that "our pure indigenous people of that aboriginal race would not be influenced as they are now by our North American neighbors, but rather they might adopt an affection for their country ... [and] identify with our means and modes of being." Ramírez opined that the propaganda that the U.S. government was using to attract the Tohono O'odham to their classrooms would "convert them into men without a country and maybe our enemies," and thus it was necessary to get their attention with "the patriotic campaign of their incorporation."[65] Despite Ramírez's remonstration, Reyes initially did nothing with the Tohono O'odham. In fact, Ulrico Villegas, confronted with Tohono O'odham unwillingness to send their children to school in Pozo Verde, refused to work with them. SEP officials suspended his salary.[66]

In February 1933, Reyes returned to the Papaguería, once again encountering Tohono O'odham resistance to the SEP's program. Reyes sought to find graduates of the Casa to offer them jobs as teachers but was unsuccessful.[67] The Tohono O'odham answered Reyes' attempts to establish schools in San Francisquito and Sonoita with at best tepid responses.[68]

Now that Reyes had failed twice to establish a federal rural primary school in the Papaguería, the new head of federal education in Sonora, Elpidio López, decided to take matters into his own hands. Rodolfo Elías Calles (Calles Jr.), Sonora's governor, had personally chosen López to head the state's education program. Calles Jr., while continuing to pay the budget for Sonora's state-run schools, nonetheless turned their supervision over to López, who, in turn, saw his role as one of redemption:

> The Sonoran proletariat awaits the fulfillment of revolutionary laws. It falls to my humble authority to resolve the problem of organizing, orienting, and sustaining the Sonoran proletariat ... and, united with the federal and state governments, to apply the laws to better the lives of those forgotten by the social revolution in this moment of National Reconstruction.[69]

He was in for a shock.

In March 1933, only a month after taking his new position, López went to visit the Tohono O'odham in Pozo Verde, San Francisquito, Sonoita, and Quitobac. López noted in his report that two previous efforts at setting up a school in the region had failed. The Tohono O'odham had told SEP officials that they would only accept a school if the government paid to build and furnish it and if the Education Ministry provided them with a female teacher who spoke

English and Papago. López was ready to accede to these demands and was convinced that he would be able to establish a number of schools in the region.

When he arrived in the region, however, he "suffered one of the greatest disillusionments" of his life. He tracked down Francisco Domínguez, an ex-student of the Casa, and like Reyes, offered him a job as a teacher. However, according to López, Domínguez had reverted to the savage customs of the Tohono O'odham, collecting firewood and selling it in the United States. He again refused to teach for the Education Ministry.[70] The case of Domínguez once again illustrates Tohono O'odham resistant adaptation strategies. SEP officials, like their BIA counterparts, had hoped that students graduating from Indian boarding schools would emerge as completely culturally transformed individuals.[71] Instead, many "returned to the blanket." Domínguez was not interested in becoming a tool for the further assimilation of Tohono O'odham into Mexican culture though he was actively engaged in the region's modern economic system. The loss of Tohono O'odham lands in the 1920s had forced many Tohono O'odham to cut and collect wood (in addition to cotton picking and mine work) for sale in Tucson, earning about $1 per day.[72] Yet, they adapted woodcutting and collecting into Tohono O'odham society on their own terms, undertaking the task communally.[73] On the U.S. side of the border, the Tohono O'odham propensity to accept acculturation on their own terms also led some BIA officials to express their frustration at keeping the Tohono O'odham in school.[74]

In San Fransiquito, López was a bit more successful. The Tohono O'odham agreed to López's choice of teacher and they agreed to allow provisionally the teacher to use one of their homes as a school. López had to guarantee that Calles Jr. would provide the necessary resources for a new school in the pueblo. López told them that he first needed to see how they treated the teacher, and then they would get everything that they asked for "little by little." The Tohono O'odham then rejected the teacher because they had not received a female teacher as promised. This marked the second failure to come to an agreement with the Education Ministry. On both occasions, the Tohono O'odham demanded new furnished schools. When the SEP refused, the Tohono O'odham equivocated, suggesting that they needed a teacher with qualifications and skills that none of the SEP teachers had before they would accept the Education Ministry into their community.

López tried in Sonoita, where the Tohono O'odham agreed to donate a house and a small parcel of land for a school on the condition that the SEP establish a Tohono O'odham-only school. They had had a series of bad experiences when they sent their children to the local rural primary school filled with mestizo children.

López went to talk to Bustamante. In exchange for agreeing to support local educational efforts, López granted him the title of *Vocal del Comité de Educación*. López thus believed that his mission had been a success. He left the Tohono O'odham in the care of a teacher who was "almost an apostle of indigenous education" and thus, "the incorporation of the Papagos would be most rapid." The result, López was sure, would be that the Tohono O'odham "would become Mexican and would be incorporated into our culture."[75] Yet, despite López's feelings of success, he had managed to establish tenuously only one school. More importantly, he had failed to provide the Tohono O'odham with the things that might have convinced them to work with the SEP: government-built and -furnished schools, access to their ancestral lands, and other resources.

Another major factor that certainly undermined López's attempts to establish schools in the region was his own and Calles Jr.'s extreme anticlericalism.[76] Though none of the education inspectors ever said that Calles' defanaticization campaign had a negative impact on their educational efforts, they did note the positive impact that pro-religious policies had on BIA education efforts on the U.S. side of the border. As noted earlier, many Tohono O'odham were devout followers of Catholicism and the cult of St. Francis Xavier, holding annual celebrations in honor of the saint in both Magdalena, Sonora, and at the Church of Saint Francis Xavier near Tucson.[77]

Between 1931 and 1934, Calles and Calles Jr. began implementing their defanaticization campaign in Sonora by expelling those teachers, mostly women, who refused to take vows denouncing the Catholic Church and its beliefs and closing private religious schools.[78] Rodolfo also promised to "take energetic and effective steps to counteract" the work of religious fanatics by "dictating a series of radical dispositions to implant in the schools of the state teaching based on scientific and historical truth that will eliminate all children's religious prejudices."[79] Rodolfo's defanaticization campaign culminated in the 1934 invasion of the Tohono O'odham church in Magdalena by a cadre of teachers. These teachers burned the majority of the church's religious icons, books, and the venerated statue of San Francisco Xavier.[80] Surely, the religious persecution of the Tohono O'odham at the hands of Mexican state and federal education employees convinced many Tohono O'odham that they would be better off sending their children to school in Arizona where they would be free to worship as they saw fit, and where, in fact, Tohono O'odham religious beliefs and education were closely intertwined.

In the end, little seems to have become of the one school that López did manage to establish among the Tohono O'odham. In 1934, an education inspector noted that Bustamante agreed to work with the SEP in carrying out its anti-alcohol campaign. It is unlikely that the inspector knew about the central importance that drinking saguaro cactus wine played in Tohono O'odham cosmology, a ceremonial practice that Bustamante probably oversaw.[81] In any case, no further mention is made of the school itself. Calles Jr.'s economic policies, in addition to his aforementioned religious policies, also played a role in the Tohono O'odham's disinclination to go along with the Sonoran government's half-hearted attempts to integrate the Tohono O'odham when they could just as easily send their children across the border for their schooling. The Tohono O'odham had repeatedly held out the BIA as an example of the type of educational assistance that they were seeking. The BIA had worked closely with members of the Papago Good Government League to set aside Tohono O'odham ancestral lands and to invest in agricultural and educational resources for the Tohono O'odham.

While Calles worked closely with Elpidio López to expand education among the Tohono O'odham, he also undercut their economic livelihood. The construction of a highway between Santa Ana and Sonoita opened the region to national and international markets and brought with it an influx of mestizos to raise livestock. At the same time, both the federal government and Calles passed a series of laws designed to open up abandoned or unworked lands (untitled Indian lands) to new agricultural and livestock production.[82] The BIA, on the other hand, actively worked to protect the Tohono O'odham from land speculators, white livestock owners who wanted to pasture their cattle and horses on the reservation, and local power holders who pushed to divest the tribe of its lands.[83]

Furthermore, when the United States repatriated a large number of Mexicans during the Depression, Calles Jr. established a series of agricultural colonies in and around Tohono O'odham lands.[84] By 1934, with the Great Depression already in full swing, the New Deal's Indian Emergency Conservation Work program ended Tohono O'odham attempts to establish schools on the Mexican side of the border.[85] In 1935, the number of Tohono O'odham children attending school in the United States had risen to 1,100; there were ten mission schools and six government day schools as well as several local public schools and non-reservation boarding schools. Meanwhile, the number of Tohono O'odham children attending school in Mexico had dwindled to almost none.[86] It would not be until June 1939 that the Mexican government again stepped in to defend Tohono O'odham land rights when President Lázaro Cárdenas set aside a small plot of land in Puerto Peñasco.[87]

6

Frontier Schools

Taking advantage of the "voluntary" repatriation of an estimated 500,000 Mexicans from the United States during the Great Depression, the Mexican government set up a series of *escuelas fronterizas* (frontier schools) in the larger cities along the border in January 1930.[1] The mission of these schools, and increasingly of other federal schools near the border, was to take those suspect Mexicans who had just returned from the United States or who had spent their lives along the border and mold them into patriotic Mexicans who would be willing to devote themselves to the economic and social advancement of their mother country. Scholars have amply demonstrated the post-revolutionary government's attempts to promote a unified national culture and patriotism through schools and other public demonstrations.[2] Few scholars have examined the ways in which federal schools defined Mexican culture and patriotism against that of the United States.[3] This chapter highlights one of the federal government's first steps in doing so.

The SEP created frontier schools to provide an alternative for Mexican parents, many of whom (like the Tohono O'odham) were sending their children to better-funded schools on the U.S. side of the border and in the process had constructed increasingly strong social and cultural connections to the United States. Frontier primary schools were different from regular federal primary schools in two ways. First, the federal government promised to better fund the frontier schools, allowing them to offer a much wider array of classes. These schools would act as special feeder schools for borderlands secondary schools, first created in 1925 and expanded in 1930, and prevent graduates of SEP primary schools from crossing the border to continue their education beyond primary school, possibly undoing the acculturation process they had undergone as youngsters. Second, they also placed a special focus on inculcating Mexican nationalism and eliminating Spanglish and other borderlands "corruptions" of Mexican culture.[4] Frontier schools would teach their children Spanish, Mexican songs and hymns, and their nation's history as opposed to English and the U.S.'s Pledge of Allegiance. Most parents were in favor of the increased funding for border schools and the teaching of Mexican patriotism. Nonetheless, they also understood the necessity of learning English to get ahead in the bilingual border economy. Thus, they pushed the Mexican government to hire native English-speaking teachers and to mimic the course offerings of American schools by threatening to keep their children in U.S. schools, partially undermining the original intentions of the federal government and in the process reshaping frontier school curriculum.

Mexican officials wanted somehow to encourage U.S. economic involvement in the border economy but discourage its citizens from cultural and social involvement in a burgeoning economy increasingly dominated by the United States. Border schools attempted to stem U.S. cultural influences, and they failed. This chapter explores this contradiction by providing an institutional sketch of the frontier schools created by the Mexican federal government. It surveys the battle against U.S. cultural and economic imperialism waged by the Mexican government from 1929 to 1935 in Coahuila, Chihuahua, and Sonora and the struggle over the cultural identity of the people living along the border that resulted from it. It begins with a historical outline of the U.S.-Mexican frontier and the events that led up to Calles' adoption of frontier schools as a means of resisting U.S. economic and cultural imperialism. It then examines how frontier schools in each of the different states had different outcomes based on the differing emphases of the local communities.[5] The educational bureaucrats responsible for these schools in Coahuila, Chihuahua, and Sonora adopted different approaches because of the differing cultural legacies of the different states. In addition, the personal idiosyncrasies of educational inspectors in charge of overseeing the schools were also a significant factor in the role that the schools played.

Much like the identities of the people who populated it, the U.S.-Mexican frontier is a historical construction. The present-day border between the two countries is the product of over a century and a half of U.S. economic, cultural, and military imperialism and the resultant contestation and accommodation between Mexicans and Americans and their governments.[6]

The Mexican Revolution (1910–17) did not end the efforts of some prominent U.S. lawmakers at continued intervention into Mexican territory and sovereignty. Toward the end of Mexican President Victoriano Huerta's (1913–14) term in office, President Woodrow Wilson's special agent, John Lind, suggested that the U.S. needed to either intervene in Mexican affairs militarily or economically back Huerta's opponents. Several prominent Mexican politicians, the most

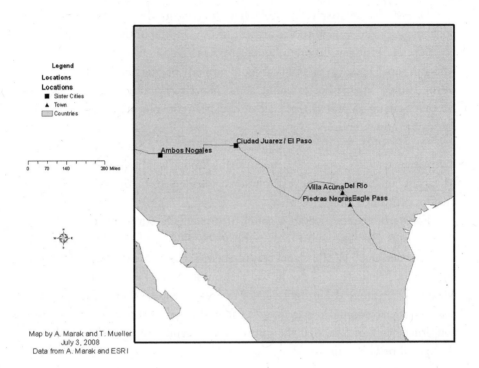

important of whom was Luis Cabrera, supported the proposed U.S. military intervention.[7] Wilson decided to place an economic embargo on Huerta's regime while lifting the embargo against his political enemies, the Constitutionalists. When the United States finally did intervene in the Mexican Revolution by invading Veracruz in April 1914, the vast majority of Mexicans were understandably opposed to it.[8]

Despite the relatively favorable view that most Mexican politicians and policy makers had toward the future role of U.S. capital in the Mexican economy, the end of the revolution did not bring them respite from those Americans who still saw Mexico as a land that more properly belonged under the auspices of the United States. For example, some American politicians, such as New Mexico Senator Albert B. Fall, advocated heavy involvement in Mexico because of his own racism.[9]

Despite the heavy-handed approach that the United States sometimes took in its dealings with Mexico – before, during, and after the Revolution – many Mexicans, including the post-revolutionary leaders from the North, were in favor of continued U.S. investment.[10]

Furthermore, the overall amount of direct U.S. investment rose during the 1920s as Obregón and Calles were in the process of reconstructing their shattered nations.[11] While Calles was interested in increased direct U.S. investment in the Mexican economy, he was determined that incoming capital benefit Mexicans, arguing, "I am fighting not to destroy capital, but rather so that it might work according to our laws."[12] He and his educational ministers were concerned, nonetheless, that the spread of U.S. capitalism would bring with it the spread of U.S. culture. Thus, they paid special attention to the forging of proper Mexicans among borderland dwellers by inculcating Mexican patriotic values through special frontier schools.

In late 1929, the SEP approved a preliminary budget for the "creation of well organized and equipped border schools with the object of impeding Mexican children who might go to the United States to receive their primary education."[13] Originally the Education Ministry proposed opening five schools, four along the U.S.-Mexican border – in Ciudad Juárez, Piedras Negras, Nuevo Leon, and Matamoros – and one along the Mexican-Guatemalan border – in Motozintla.[14] Their top priority, however, was to stem the flow of Mexican children going to the United States, and the frontier school in Motozintla, Chiapas, never actually received funding.[15]

In early 1930, SEP officials acknowledged that they had bungled the job of creating frontier schools by failing to take into account the need to obtain and repair the school buildings within which they would offer the new frontier education. They informed educational inspectors in charge of actually implementing the new frontier school policies that they would have to obtain the moral and material support of local and state officials for the new policies in order to be successful.[16]

By June 1930, the frontier schools were at least nominally functioning. Education Ministry officials reiterated that the frontier schools were an important tool in constructing a "true nation" out of the heterogeneous cultural milieu of contemporary Mexico. In fact, primary schools, in general, they argued, were the key to Mexico's future prosperity.[17] Despite the clear goals of the new frontier schools and the centralized mechanism for policy-making decisions, the actual implementation of frontier school policy would prove to be anything but uniform across the U.S.-Mexican border.

In January 1930, Ramón Méndez, the head of federal education in Coahuila, officially requested that the SEP establish a frontier school in Piedras Negras, across from Eagle Pass, Texas. According to Méndez, the school would "give Mexican children the opportunity to receive a better education and thus counteract the practice of these children going to the United States's schools."[18] The municipal president of Piedras Negras immediately offered his assistance, promising to give the federal government the city's best existing school for the new project. Méndez readily agreed and asked the SEP to establish a separate frontier school in Villa Acuña, across the border from Del Rio, Texas. Even before establishing the school, Méndez noted that if SEP officials wanted the frontier schools to be a success, "it would be very necessary, for example, that the frontier school have some professors that know and teach English; since [Piedras Negras] is contiguous with Eagle Pass, many parents want their children to learn the language and for this reason they send them to the schools of the other country."[19] Local conditions and the desires of local inhabitants were undermining the original aim of creating patriotic Mexicans minus the undue influence of the United States, its language, and its culture that federal policy makers had had in mind for the frontier schools.

In February, Méndez convinced (or so he thought) the governor of Coahuila, Nazario S. Ortiz, to pay the 150 pesos monthly rent for the school building set aside by the municipal president of Piedras Negras. He reiterated that the school would have to teach English classes. In addition, he argued that the school would need a kindergarten and that it would have to offer preparatory classes so students in the fifth and sixth grades would not "abandon Mexico in search of a high school" in the United States.

Interestingly, Méndez informed the Education Ministry that the school had yet to open because it lacked furniture. He did not want to take the furniture from other nearby schools, thereby crippling the delivery of education in already existing schools for the sake of the frontier school. Ortiz had ordered the local construction of the furniture, but Méndez noted (in a twist of irony) that he could acquire the furniture both more quickly and much cheaper if he purchased it in the United States. Hence, we see the second intrusion of U.S. economic imperialism raising its head in only two months, suggesting the strong ties that Méndez and others in frontier Coahuila had with the United States. Finally, Méndez told his superiors that the municipal president of Villa Acuña would now co-operate in setting up a frontier school in his city.[20]

Unsurprisingly, it appears that the municipal president of Piedras Negras and the governor of Coahuila were using the promotion of the frontier school to advance their own personal and political agendas. In January, the municipal president had offered to cede ownership of the city's best existing school so that the federal government could set up a frontier school. Only a month later, however, the head of federal education in Coahuila was not only looking for someone to pay the rent (presumably to the municipal president or one of his associates), but was also looking for furniture so that students could begin to attend the school.

Common sense suggests that the actual building never had been a school (or, at the very least, was no longer functioning as one). Otherwise, it would already have had some furniture and supplies. In May, Rafael Castro, the federal inspector of schools in the border region, complained that the frontier school in Piedras Negras was located in a poor, undersized building for which the SEP had to pay the governor a monthly rent. The size of the school was especially lacking in light of the fact that a large number of federal railroad workers, recently laid off, had settled in Piedras Negras.[21] In any case, the municipal president and the governor rightly viewed the federal government not only as a positive investor in the educational advancement of local citizens, but also as a client to whom they could rent out urban property.[22]

SEP officials agreed to offer kindergarten and English classes at the frontier school as well as any other programs that might provide a social service to the local community. They noted, however, that they could not open a frontier school in Villa Acuña due to budgetary restraints.[23] In response, local educators in Piedras Negras established a sociocultural center where classes in English, dancing, and singing were offered for both primary school students and adults. Patience Schell notes that the offering of *orfeones populares* (public choirs) were an excellent means of promoting school attendance because they were often one of the few venues in which young men and women could spend time with one another in public and gave them "romantic and sexual opportunities."[24] Teachers often viewed them as a means of attracting students to the school in hopes that they would then also take part in additional parts of the curriculum. We can probably assume that the offering of dancing and singing was effective in attracting single men and women (without discounting the draw of English classes). Federal teachers also organized a "tribu de exploradores," based on the model of boy scouts practiced in Britain and the United States.[25] Furthermore, teachers went on a campaign of home visits to teach locals how to live healthier lives and to convince them to co-operate with the frontier school.[26] The intrusiveness of these visits probably won them little support.

By June 1930, the sociocultural center was officially open.[27] The school itself had an enrollment of 113 boys and 98 girls and an actual attendance (during one inspection) of 90 boys and 79 girls.[28] It appears, however, that the lure of U.S. schools far outweighed initial attempts by the federal government to convince Mexicans to attend Mexican schools. Rafael Castro, the federal education inspector, requested that the Piedras Negras' secondary school hand over all the excess school furniture and supplies resulting from low enrollment and attendance so that they could be used in the underfunded primary schools in the area.[29] This suggests that the opening of secondary schools in 1925 did little to change the strategy adopted by many parents whereby they sent their children to Mexican primary schools and only later, when they were ready for secondary school, sent them to the United States.

The next two years of the functioning of the frontier school in Piedras Negras have disappeared from the archival records. Nonetheless, educational inspectors remained busy with other frontier issues along the U.S.-Coahuila border. In 1931 Rafael Castro, while visiting the various schools under his charge, began exhorting Mexicans who lived along the border to protect "our nationals that are being deported from the United States."[30] In addition, the *Comisión Nacional de Irrigación* (National Irrigation Commission), was in the midst of a large project called the *Sistema de Riego No. 6* (Irrigation System No. 6), along the Río Bravo.

The federal government had granted most campesinos in the region provisional ejidos. In 1931 most of the ejidatarios were notified that they would be relocated to San Carlos, Coahuila (the previous site of a hacienda), to make room for newly arriving *colonos*, or colonists.[31] Many of these ejidatarios understandably refused to put forth any further effort to improve the local federal schools that they would soon be forced to abandon.[32] The SEP subsequently shut down some schools as a result.[33]

Castro tried to get the federal government to change the status of the ejidatarios in La Bandera to that of colonos since they had been living there for their entire lives. When he was successful in doing so, he discovered that since colonos were not legally bound to co-operate with federal schools in the same ways that ejidatarios were, the locals refused to work with him further on educational matters. In response, Castro advocated the adoption of sports, other "honest diversions," and the expansion of the local anti-alcohol campaign to eradicate the prominent level of disorder and frequent orgies that he believed both local inhabitants and federal employees working on the irrigation system engaged in.[34]

In addition to being at odds with the local colonos and the irrigation system workers, Castro had a difficult time convincing irrigation officials to donate the five hectares of land demanded by law for primary schools. The local manager of the system continually promised Castro the land, but then refused to turn it over, suggesting that he would again discuss the land with his superiors.[35] In El Tepeyac, Castro discovered that many ejidatarios were illegally renting or had outright sold their lands and were living in nearby Jímenez to take advantage of the cash economy.[36]

In early 1932, federal inspectors tried a new approach to mold the identities of frontier Mexicans. They pushed local communities to purchase radios so that they could listen to the official broadcasts of the *Partido Nacional Revolucionario*, or National Revolutionary Party (PNR).[37] Castro complained, however, that the salary cut he (and the rest of federal employees) received because of the Depression was hampering his ability to purchase radios for all of the schools under his charge.[38] In addition, Coahuila's governor, Nazario S. Ortiz, may have undermined the federal government's attempts to promote patriotism along the border. He believed that while schools did have a role in shaping people's attitudes, the state did not have enough resources to waste valuable school time on festivals, parades, and concerts, a central plank of the Education Ministry's attempts to inculcate a single national culture. Ortiz characterized these events as having a "marked character of exhibitionism" and taking the place of real learning. Nonetheless, he was in step with the SEP in advocating sports leagues, co-operatives, and community-based *cajas de ahorro* (credit unions) to mitigate the severity of the Depression.[39]

In April, President Ortiz Rubio decreed that the sale of liquor within 100 kilometres of the border would henceforth be illegal. Castro worked to convince the local inhabitants to become part of vigilante groups to enforce strict compliance with the new decree. He worked to ensure that every school had a field for baseball so that people would have something constructive to do during their normal drinking hours. Castro was not the first to try organizing the locals against vice. Marcos de León, the head of customs in Villa Acuña, had solicited the closure of a series of cantinas as well as brothels that worked under the cover of hotels located on the Mexican side of the international bridge. The municipal president, however, interceded to prevent their closure, arguing that there was no need to close these "centers of vice." Disingenuously, he argued that since they were aimed at Americans, and Americans came to Villa Acuña to undertake legitimate business that was located in the center of town, not near the international bridge, the cantinas and brothels would go out of business due to lack of clientele. In the end, federal officials overruled the municipal president. Nonetheless, the tepid support for the government's "moralizing campaign" suggests that the health of local businesses was often a higher priority.[40] This time, however, the enforcement of the anti-alcohol decree had a much greater impact in Villa Acuña, where a number of cantinas closed.[41] Not surprisingly, as late as 1934 the campaign against alcohol consumption and the move to close all cantinas near the border had still not been successful. Castro noted that there were no drinking establishments located near frontier schools, but that it would be impossible to close down all the local centers of vice because of their widespread prevalence, and, he should have noted, the resistance of local officials.[42]

In Mira Villa, Castro tried to get the locals to decorate their school and its open-air theater so that they would serve as "cultural propaganda for our federal education system." Another inspector, Abraham Arellano, noted that the poor construction of and lack of furniture in the schools located on the shores of the Río Bravo in San Vicente and Boquillas were an embarrassment to Mexico and asked municipal authorities to lend a helping hand to the federal government's project.[43] This suggests that, for better or worse, education inspectors as well as everyday Mexican citizens measured the Education Ministry's nation-building project against that of the United States. Moreover, like the Tohono O'odham, they often found it wanting.

Castro also tried to convince locals to move closer to the school so that their children would find it easier to attend.[44] This is a surprising request, but one that suggests some important continuities. We have seen that federal inspectors often tried to convince indigenous people to move closer to schools, but these requests were part of a larger campaign to convince indigenous people to adopt a nearly completely new culture. Castro's proposition highlights the fact that he, like many SEP officials, viewed Mexican peasants as little better than their indigenous brethren. In addition, while some cultural aspects of indigenous culture were worth saving (mainly their "natural" artistic skills and their high levels of physical endurance), the same could not be said about campesino culture.

By 1933, the frontier school in Piedras Negras was in deep trouble because of federal mismanagement. The new head of federal education in Coahuila, Maurilio P. Nañez, noted that there had been a sudden influx of students over four days in January so that the school could reach the legal limit of 288 students necessary for keeping on six teachers and assistants. Officials sacked the director of the school, Carlos Morales Sánchez, because he lacked the "active, social, nationalist, and democratic tendencies" necessary to advance the ideology of the Revolution. Federal authorities also noted that Morales Sánchez first began offering night classes for adults at the end of January, probably a final effort to save his job.[45] When the school first opened in 1930 the then head of federal education in Coahuila, Ramón Méndez, had boasted that the frontier school was offering night classes for adults focusing on English, dancing, and singing by the end of the first semester of the school's existence. Clearly, they had had a very short life span.

The new director of the frontier school, Eliseo Ruiz Vadillo, attempted to overcome the school's past difficulties by promoting its work on the local radio station. He asked the president of the local radio station, XETN, to air regularly educational lectures, programs, and works undertaken in school.[46] It was not long, however, before he too ran into difficulties. Two months after taking over the frontier school, the local inspector, Maurilio P. Nañez, discovered that the teacher in charge of the local co-operative, Gilberto Ceja Torres, was embezzling funds.[47] By the end of April, the SEP replaced him with a new director, Fabian García R.[48] García immediately moved to have Ceja Torres fired. He then addressed the conditions of the frontier school. He noted that the majority of the adults they had recruited to attend night classes had already passed the sixth grade. Probably in response to popular adult demand, he pushed to hire typewriting, singing, and choir teachers. Finally, he noted that the school had recently received baseball equipment from the PNR and that it they would put it to good use.[49]

In January 1933, the SEP pushed for the advancement of frontier schooling by arranging for two additional frontier schools, one in Villa Acuña and the other in Piedras Negras. Narciso Bassols notified Coahuila's governor that he would be turning one of the federal primary schools in Villa Acuña into a frontier school.[50] The Education Ministry would staff the new school with six federal teachers and three municipal assistants, capable of instructing 350 primary students.[51] The SEP figured that setting up a frontier school in Villa Acuña (after having been unable to find the resources in the past) was especially important because municipal authorities in Del Río, Texas had established several schools specifically aimed at assimilating Mexican children into U.S. culture.[52] After making the basic arrangements for the frontier school in Villa Acuña, the SEP then turned over its management to the state of Coahuila. By January 1934, work on the Villa Acuña school stopped due to lack of funds. School officials hoped to secure additional funds from the state government to add fifth and sixth grade classrooms and the necessary additional teachers to staff them.[53] When neither the federal nor the state government stepped forward, federal inspector Micaela Zuñiga R. organized a local fundraiser. She hoped that her efforts would provide the school with proper lighting and water.[54]

By the end of the school year in 1935, Zuñiga noted that the implementation of the anti-religious tenets of socialist education advanced by the Bassols had resulted in the creation of numerous locally supported private schools. Local citizens pulled their children from federal schools and placed them in clandestine private schools where they received religious instruction. Even the closure of seven of these private schools had failed to increase attendance at federal schools. Zuñiga tried to convince the inhabitants of Villa Acuña to send their children back to federal schools (and in the process keep parents out of local cantinas) by offering increased sporting events and classes in sewing and knitting. Despite all their efforts, both the federal school and Villa Acuña itself remained in "terrible conditions," demonstrating that the SEP's attempts to overcome the unpopularity of its anti-fanaticization campaign through the offering of expanded courses were seldom successful.[55]

The second frontier school in Piedras Negras opened its doors early in 1933. The school initially lacked electricity and was thus limited to offering day classes. The school's first director, Carlos Flores Fortis, also had problems getting along with the student body. He asked for a two-month leave of absence, and the SEP subsequently replaced him.[56] By March the new director, Mario Matus Micelli, had opened a school store to sell products produced during classes and had arranged electricity for the school. Regular night classes, focusing on sewing and small industries, attracted 80 women.[57]

When school officials tried to offer night classes in basic reading and writing, only ten people showed up. When they expanded the number of classes to include domestic economy, Spanish, math, speech, cultural aesthetics, and singing, an additional 128 people showed up (88 of them women). Again, mixed choir proved to be an excellent recruiting tool. There is no doubt that some adults living in Piedras Negras were still interested in basic literacy courses. The fact that they proved highly unsuccessful and that the Education Ministry replaced them with other classes that found a greater general interest among locals, however, suggests differing needs along the U.S.-Mexican border and the willingness of SEP officials to adjust to popular pressure in order to have an impact in the local community. Nonetheless, even urban schools along the border still advanced Calles' belief that agriculture would be the engine of future Mexican prosperity. In accordance, federal officials forced inspectors to find suitable agricultural lands, often far from the actual location of schools, so that students could learn modern farming techniques even if they would never put them to use.[58]

At the behest of Rafael Castro, municipal officials in Piedras Negras implemented a 2 per cent customs fee in April to pay for the construction of a local high school to provide a Mexican alternative for city residents and as an improvement over the frontier schools. By January 1934, however, municipal officials dropped the 2 per cent custom's fee due to the dismissal of the municipal president, the administrator of customs, and the head of the local post office that coincided with President Cárdenas' assumption of office in Mexico City. In place of the customs fee, the new municipal president offered to donate ten pesos toward the purchase of cultivable land needed by the frontier schools.[59] Local teachers pressed on. In early 1935, federal teachers helped local brick makers form a union that pressed for and received a 1.5-peso daily wage. Despite this success, the frontier schools in Piedras Negras still did not have regular English, music, or typewriting teachers, and attendance was suffering.[60]

At the end of the 1934/35 school year, Castro informed his superiors that if Mexico really wanted to compete against the education being offered in the United States, they would have to open five new schools, each staffed with six regular teachers and two additional teachers to give instruction in English and other special courses. He estimated that these schools would cost up to 400,000 pesos to put into place and an additional 1,500 pesos per month to run effectively. Castro argued that the frontier schools presently located in Piedras Negras and Villa Acuña educated only 10 per cent and 20 per cent respectively of school-aged children in their local communities. The children not attending the frontier schools attended private schools (where many of them received illegal religious instruction) or crossed the border to go to U.S. schools.[61] Castro realized that their task would be a difficult one. Teachers in the United States were earning about $75 per month, more than Mexico's inspectors general. In addition, the United States was running well-funded schools specifically aimed at assimilating Mexican children into U.S. society. Finally, many of the children that did attend Mexican primary schools had to go to the United States. if they wanted to attend secondary or high school. Despite evidence to the contrary, Castro did not believe that rural Mexicans were going to the United States because of better schools. He did not deny, however, that U.S. schools drew many urban Mexicans. Castro's final solution (in addition to the funding of the additional five border schools that he had proposed) was the "absolute suppression of all non-federal schools" to ensure that all Mexican schools were delivering high quality education that could compete with education on the U.S. side of the border.[62] Castro's final solution ignores the fact that, in addition to those who crossed the border to attend secondary and high school, many Mexicans sent their children to the United States because Catholic education was illegal in Mexico. Those who preferred to send their children to clandestine Catholic schools in Mexico would not likely be convinced to send their children to federal primary schools that denigrated Catholics and Catholicism.

In late 1929, the situation along the Chihuahuan section of U.S.-Mexican border, from the point of view of federal educators, was dire. At the center of the problem was Ciudad Juárez. The border city was the most important link between the United States and Mexico and was the location of Mexico's most important custom house.[63] Ciudad Juárez, however, was also the center of smuggling, gambling, prostitution, and contraband.[64]

By 1870, the region had already been the center of a "highly organized" cattle-rustling business.[65] During the Mexican Revolution, it served as a center for weapons smuggling by the various military factions vying for national power. Finally, with the passage of the Eighteenth Amendment (Prohibition) in the United States in January 1919, Ciudad Juárez became the center of a newly flourishing bootlegging and contraband business. By 1929 the main commerce undertaken by Ciudad Juárez's 21,000 inhabitants was distilling alcohol destined to be smuggled north across the border. The city boasted one beer factory and three whiskey distilleries, and U.S. Ambassador James Sheffield complained that Mexico was failing to comply with a 1925 agreement to prevent the exportation of alcohol to the United States.[66] Residents also engaged in running gambling houses. Moreover, while state officials gave lip service to fighting the spread of these industries, the fact that by 1931 gambling was providing the state with over 70 per cent of its overall tax revenue made it political suicide to take any concrete action.[67] A further problem, according to education officials, was that between 50,000 to 55,000 of El Paso's 108,000 inhabitants were Mexican.[68] In the eyes of SEP policy makers, this meant that 50,000 to 55,000 people were in the process of losing their culture.

The advancement of frontier schooling in Ciudad Juárez proved to be an ironic example of one part of the federal government's desire to use education to stamp out the vices associated with the border for moral and cultural reasons while, at the same time, another part of the federal government undermined those very policies by supporting the expansion of gambling and bootlegging for economic and political reasons. Chihuahua Governor Rodrigo Quevedo based his political power on support from Calles, his ruthlessness, and his control of large revenue sources based on border gambling and bootlegging.[69] Calles had played the same double game of advancing morality campaigns while raising revenues by taxing vice industries while governor of Sonora.[70] As we have seen in Chapter 2, Calles used his close political ties with Quevedo to convince him to turn the control of Chihuahua's state primary school system over to the federal government in 1933. In return, Calles did not interfere in Quevedo's illegal border activities.

The state's education director, Salvador Varela, and one of the inspectors assigned to the area, Ramón Espinosa Villanueva, realized that they had nowhere to turn for help in combating these illegal activities because state and local authorities were actively taking part in the contraband trade.[71] At the same time, Quevedo's chief competitors in the gambling and bootlegging industry in Ciudad Juárez, Enrique and Simon Fernández, were donating their monetary and moral support to local federal schools even as federal agents were attempting to shut down their operation.[72] SEP officials commended Enrique on several occasions for donating land, buildings, and supplies to schools located along the border and, in the process, secured the good graces of the local education inspector.[73]

Many of the families (the majority, according to the local inspector) who made use of the schools donated by the Fernández brothers probably engaged in the contraband trade. Almost comically, at the same time that the Fernándezes were cultivating their relationship with local educators, the education inspector, J. Reyes Pimentel, was waging a national anti-alcohol campaign created by President Portes Gil aimed at, among other things, reducing the number of people involved in running alcohol across the border.[74]

Pimentel complained to his superiors that the contraband trade made his job of improving education along the border doubly difficult because many families involved in the business outright refused to co-operate with the schools. Even those families that were inclined to co-operate with school authorities lived scattered across the countryside outside of Ciudad Juárez. He claimed that they did so in order to slip across the border unseen at night.[75] By 1935, the education inspector was convinced that the school's social campaigns and advancement of sports, especially baseball, had undermined the propensity of frontier dwellers for working in the alcohol industry.[76] The repeal of U.S. Prohibition in 1933 and the assassination of Fernández (after one earlier unsuccessful attempt), however, were probably the overriding causes of the industry's diminution.[77]

While the SEP's response to the contraband liquor business played an important role in inhibiting the advancement of frontier schooling in Ciudad Juárez (at least as it was imagined in Mexico City), general apathy and the enticement of better schools on the U.S. side of the border were also problems. When Salvador Varela first advanced the idea of increased funding for frontier schooling in November 1929, he confronted a situation in which about 25 per cent (1,000 of an estimated 4,200) of the children of Ciudad Juárez were crossing the border to attend school in El Paso, Texas. He noted that even the children currently attending primary school in Ciudad Juárez were likely to go to El Paso for industrial, vocational, or English classes after they had graduated. Furthermore, when school inspector Pimentel attempted to involve Mexican parents residing in El Paso in festivities celebrating the anniversary of the Mexican Revolution, they protested vociferously and refused. His attempts to promote increased respect for the Mexican flag and prohibit the use of English words also met with a tepid response. Instead, parents told him that they would consider keeping their children in Mexican schools if the Mexican government could guarantee the establishment of fourth and fifth grade classes in Ciudad Juárez.[78]

In response to the local difficulties, Varela suggested that a former convent that had just been taken over by the federal government be set aside as the future site for a frontier school.[79] In addition, he argued that the teachers hired to staff the new frontier school would have to be from the interior of Mexico because the existing teachers along the border were neither Mexican nor American.[80] In January 1930, the one existing federal primary school in Ciudad Juárez closed to make room for a new and improved frontier school. Varela's call for supposedly culturally pure teachers from Mexico City deserves comment. Education Ministry officials were of two minds about the frontier. As discussed in Chapter 2, inspectors believed that teachers from outside the region lacked the proper understanding of the frontier social construction of citizenship and could not possibly command the respect of locals. Outsiders who (or whose ancestors) had not fought to defend their land against the Apache threat in the nineteenth century or to maintain those rights during the revolution were suspect. At the same time, the region's close connections with Yankee capital and U.S. culture undermined the SEP's ability to recruit teachers in the region who would be able to advance the Education Ministry's program of inculcating a unified national culture. Though archival evidence tells us little about what citizens thought about the program, the fact that parents were less than enthusiastic about celebrating the Mexican Revolution must have been alarming to education inspectors, whose job it was to convince locals (in spite of the evidence to the contrary) that the revolution had been a unifying national event.

Like its counterpart in Piedras Negras, the frontier school in Ciudad Juárez ran into problems. First, when the federal government adopted a socialist pedagogy, parents complained that they were not "in agreement with the new direction" that the school was taking and insisted that the Education Ministry dismiss a number of radical teachers. Failure to do so would result in their pulling their children out of the frontier school and sending them instead to school in El Paso, a clear demonstration of one way in which locals used the border as leverage to realign the SEP's pedagogy more closely with local beliefs.[81]

By 1932, the SEP was in the midst of a court battle over ownership of the school building with the ex-convent's former owner, Señorita Mariana Ochoa.[82] Ochoa had designated the building as a school for the poor, but SEP officials were positive that she was actually using it as a clandestine "Catholic convent" for religious teaching, which had been declared against the law by the Constitution of 1917; SEP officials had begun to enforce the anti-religious measures of the constitution in 1926. In early 1933, the circuit court in Monterrey made a finding in favor of Ochoa, forcing the SEP to appeal the decision to Mexico's Supreme Court on the basis that they had already spent 20,000 pesos to improve the building. In August 1933, the courts finally gave the Education Ministry ownership of the former convent.[83]

While the battle for ownership of the school raged, parents raised 5,800 pesos to buy sewing machines, a radio, a film projector, and an industrial department.[84] Despite the apparent support for the school, parents complained that the school itself was located in Ciudad Juárez's tolerance zone near the international bridge leading to El Paso. They argued that their children were going to school in the same neighborhood where local authorities were promoting prostitution and sadistic public acts – such as prostitutes performing sex acts with burros or having anal sex in public – in order to attract U.S. tourists.[85] Attempts by parents in Ciudad Juárez to use the Education Ministry in hopes of cleaning up the tolerance zone were destined for failure since Governor Quevedo had named his brother Jesús mayor of the city to better control whiskey and narcotic smuggling and legalized gambling. Local citizens were keenly aware that local officials, including policemen and sanitation inspectors, aided the expansion rather than the cessation of vice industries. In addition, they knew that Jesús and his associates were capturing federal and state funds to advance their private interests, including the diversion of $18,000 pesos meant to build a local school, which they used instead to build a mansion for Jesús' brother José.[86]

Parents also complained that many of the teachers lacked a proper education and spent their spare time getting drunk in local cantinas. Once again, they insisted that if the SEP did not promptly address these issues, they would pull their children from the frontier school and send them to El Paso. The SEP responded with an investigation that turned up no concrete faults on the part of the teachers assigned to the school, suggesting perhaps discordance between federal and local ideologies.[87]

In early 1934, a number of parents resisted the educational program promoted by the Education Ministry in Ciudad Juárez, probably in response to the Catholic Church's decree that parents withdraw their children from public schools in Mexico.[88] In addition to the crackdown on religious schooling, parents found the Education Ministry's promotion of sex education particularly troublesome. To overcome the parental objections, SEP officials distributed copies of the textbooks used in class.[89] Scientific or not, the Education Ministry backed away from its insistence that children be exposed to sex education.

Later in 1934, a number of teachers assigned to the frontier school refused to sign a written statement that acknowledged their support of socialist education. Ramón Espinosa Villanueva thought that it was due to the influence of the high number of Catholic priests who had crossed the border into El Paso to establish private religious schools. These same priests, he believed, were behind the demonstrations against sexual (or as the priests called it, "sensual") education. Thus, he asked each of the teachers who had refused to support socialist schooling to renounce their religious beliefs. The teachers refused. The school inspector then initiated a petition campaign with the support of *La Unidad Magisterial* (The Magesterial Unity), the *Bloque Radical de Maestros Socialistas de Ciudad Juárez* (The Radical Block of Socialist Teachers of Ciudad Juárez), and the *Federación de Sociedades de Padres de Family* (The Federation of Parent Societies) to push for the firing of the teachers.[90] Espinosa Villanueva was not without reason. In neighboring Sonora, some of the 35 per cent of teachers whom the state fired on religious grounds crossed into Arizona to open private religiously influenced schools, and many of their borderlands students probably followed them.[91]

In 1935, Espinosa Villanueva asked the SEP for the necessary funding to establish two additional schools in Ciudad Juárez so that Mexican youth would no longer cross the border and acquire "sentiments contrary to the interests of Mexico."[92] A previous trip to El Paso by SEP officials had revealed that the special U.S. school established to assimilate Mexican children into American culture stressed that the United States was the greatest country in the world and had the most powerful navy. The Education Ministry officials noted that the Mexican children attending the school – 2,024 in total, one-third of whom were from Ciudad Juárez – were losing their Spanish to English.[93] Clearly, officials feared that in addition to the corruption of their Spanish, students would also lose their patriotism.

By 1935, SEP officials were beginning to realize that the frontier schools were not doing the job that they had been created to do. In May, Celso Flores Zamora, the head of the Department of Rural Schools, argued, "the rural frontier and primary schools that are presently functioning, until now have not formed the barrier that could impede the passage of our children to the neighboring country in which they look for a betterment that in their own country they can not find."[94] In other words, U.S. schools were more attractive to many borderlands residents.

Espinosa Villanueva believed that the answer lay in the hiring of only male teachers and increased funding; he gave no reasons why locals might prefer male teachers.[95] Another inspector, Jesús Coello, thought that a pro-Spanish campaign where locals were encouraged to take part in festivals and sing songs about the evils of capitalism and religion was the answer.[96] Yet, in many ways, the actions of borderlands Mexicans suggest that it was the U.S. economy for which they most wanted to prepare their children. In fact, the problem was much deeper than that. The struggle between religious and socialist teachers was a factor that constantly undermined the actual delivery of education within the frontier school. Numerous unions called for the forced expulsion of all teachers who refused to denounce their religious views; some teachers feared persecution if they did not join their local socialist teacher's union.[97] While SEP officials chalked it all up to the proximity of the border, the truth was that the border gave religious parents the opportunity to send their children to El Paso to receive a private religious education that was much more to their liking.

Also damaging was the discovery that Espinosa Villanueva and the director of the frontier school in Ciudad Juárez, José Medrano, had been regularly sending false and misleading reports to the SEP. In response, the SEP dispatched its inspector general, Alfonso G. Alanis, to address parental complaints. Alanis found that Medrano attended school irregularly, made personal use of school supplies and resources, hired and fired teachers based on his personal whims (even though the majority of them were unionized), was a local politician of communist affiliation, and did not offer night classes as legally required.[98]

Yet Espinosa Villanueva kept his job. Hoping to reverse the earlier practice set up by Salvador Varela of only hiring teachers from Mexico's interior, Espinosa Villanueva argued that teachers who were not from the border region could not adapt to frontier life and, thus, the Education Ministry should not hire them. Espinosa Villanueva's call for hiring only those from the frontier contradicted that of his previous supervisor, Salvador Varela. Perhaps Varela's focus on the Sierra Tarahumara left him less than completely acquainted with frontier ideals of citizenship. In any case, if the Education Ministry were to follow Espinosa Villanueva's advice, they would seemingly undermine their unifying cultural program by placing in authority teachers acculturated in the borderlands' unique milieu. Furthermore, Espinosa Villanueva's understanding of the obstacles to SEP success ignored the major conflicts created by the advancement of its socialist and anti-religious pedagogy. Merely advocating for equal pay for all teachers, as he did, could not possibly prevent hostility between different factions of teachers.[99] Nonetheless, his proposal that the SEP improve Ciudad Juárez's secondary school so that Mexicans would not be forced to send their children to "gringo universities" where they only learned to think about "the land of [George] Washington" struck at the heart of the problem.[100] Local residents, drawn by better-funded and more comprehensive schooling on the U.S. side of the border might, in time, transfer their allegiance from Mexico to the United States.

Frontier schooling was much less contentious and confrontational in Sonora than in either Coahuila or Chihuahua. Nogales – the site of Sonora's frontier school located across the border from its sister city of the same name in Arizona – had originally been a small outpost established by railroad workers.[101] Ambos Nogales' economic growth occurred in such a manner that they were actually one economically interdependent town "separated only by a street."[102] The fact that many U.S. residents in Nogales learned Spanish while their Mexican counterparts learned English to enhance their business prospects improved relations between Mexicans and Americans. As previously noted, by the time of the Mexican Revolution, locals knew the inhabitants of Sonora as the "Yankees of Mexico" because of their close ties to the United States, and Ambos Nogales epitomized this symbiotic relationship.[103]

In 1928 the SEP set up a primary school for 200 children in Nogales in a vacant building donated (along with 108 double-sided desks) by state authorities.[104] The school, a five-story building that was, according to the school's director Rosalío E. Moreno, poorly ventilated and lit, was located on Avenida Alvaro Obregón.[105] In addition to the regular curriculum, school officials focused on teaching the children how to cross safely the city's busy streets. Accentuating the cross-cultural integration of Ambos Nogales, Moreno complained of poor attendance on both Mexican and U.S. patriotic holidays.[106]

Throughout 1929, Moreno concerned himself with the welfare of the children in the school, trying to convince the families of older children to leave their children in school rather than sending them across the border in search of work.[107] In February, a child came down with meningitis and the Education Ministry officials closed the school. Those exposed to the child were isolated.[108] Illness was not, however, the school's only problem. The Depression forced the federal government to pay teachers only half of their regular salary. In March, three teachers from the border school took their newly reduced salaries and crossed the border to look for work in Arizona, demonstrating that teachers, in addition to everyday citizens, could also use the border to their benefit.[109] Moreno told his superiors that the newly reduced salaries were not "sufficient for [life's] most necessary expenses. I believe that we will not continue working much longer."[110] He then followed his fellow teachers out the door.

The school's new director for the 1929/1930 school year, Alfonso Acosta V., was entrusted with the job of transforming the school from a regular primary into a frontier primary school. In May 1930 he held a meeting with local parents to figure out how they could compete with the "Yankee schools" in Arizona and how best to reach all of the Mexican children who were presently attending school there. Acosta V. figured that 75 per cent of all the children in the Nogales, Arizona, school district were Mexican citizens.[111] There is little indication, however, that the change was anything other than nominal. In fact, in accepting their changed status from primary school to frontier primary school, they did nothing more than discuss how better to serve Mexican children. In deciding to continue working closely with U.S. educational authorities, they made no immediate changes to their existing curriculum or practices.

The 1931/1932 school year brought with it another new director, Agapito Constantino, who implemented policies that likely pushed additional Mexican parents to send their children to school in Arizona. For example, Constantino believed that it was necessary to shame the students who attended his school into changing their behavior. He did so by scheduling a public assembly at the beginning of every school day in which he divided the children into different groups and forced them to stand underneath banners corresponding to their perceived level of punctuality and cleanliness.[112] While the Education Ministry advocated the promotion of proper hygiene and cleanliness, there is no evidence that they espoused the use of shaming students to accomplish it.

Another issue that forced Mexican families to send their children to the United States for schooling was the deplorable condition of Nogales' only secondary school. In 1932, the school was sharing a building with a local primary school. Furthermore, the fact that the primary school graduated only 26 students in 1931 – many of whom would immediately enter the job market – made it nearly impossible to keep the secondary school functioning properly, unless they could attract Mexican students who attended primary school in the United States.[113] Nonetheless, the Education Ministry moved the school to a new location near the frontier primary school on Avenida Alvaro Obregón and put it under the authority of a new director, Angel Alfonso Andrade, who, according to SEP officials, "rescued the school from the toilet."[114] By 1933, SEP deemed the secondary school to be functioning perfectly. By 1934, school officials noted that influential members of Ambos Nogales actively supported it.[115] By acquiescing to existing cross-border co-operation, the Education Ministry undermined the school's original purpose of stemming the tide of U.S. cultural influence on the Mexican side of the border.

The truth is that frontier schooling was not a high priority for Sonoran officials. First, parents in Ambos Nogales seemed inclined to continue supporting the practice of sending the majority of Mexican children across the border to Arizona for their primary and secondary schooling. Second, Calles Jr., the state governor, thought that the best way to improve the situation of Mexicans repatriated during the Depression was to place them on colonies set up by the state on former lands of the Mayo and Yaqui Indians in southern Sonora rather than expand the school system along the border.[116] Third, and most importantly, Calles Jr.'s main preoccupation in the educational field was his role in implementing the government's widespread defanaticization campaign begun in 1931 aimed at removing, for the last time, the influence of the church in Sonora.[117]

The Education Ministry wanted somehow to encourage U.S. economic involvement in the U.S.-Mexican border region while at the same time discouraging Mexican citizens from cultural and social involvement in the burgeoning economy. Frontier schools were the means by which they hoped to stem U.S. cultural imperialism. They failed to do so. Mismanagement, better course offerings, better opportunities to learn English, and better facilities on the U.S. side of the border, as well as access to religious education in the United States, all played roles in the failure of frontier schools.

This chapter has provided a preliminary institutional history of Mexican frontier schools, highlighting the ways in which different local, political, and social environments led to very different conceptions of the roles of frontier schools. Despite a long history of hostility between their states and Texas, SEP officials in Coahuila and Chihuahua were unable to stem the flow of Mexican children to primary schools in the United States. Mismanagement, political struggles between different factions of teachers, and the drive to eliminate religious teaching from federal schools plagued the frontier schools in both states. Nonetheless, inspectors soon realized that they could increase enrollment by providing English and vocational classes, offering coed choir, and lessening the emphasis on festivals, parades, and concerts meant to develop a sense of patriotism. In Sonora, where there was a spirit of co-operation between leading members of Ambos Nogales, the federal government's attempt to create a frontier school led local officials to actively court the support of community members on both sides of the border. In so doing, they avoided the issue of trying to stem the flow of Mexican children to U.S. schools.

Conclusion

Plutarco Elías Calles and his political allies constructed a federal education system to advance their goals of creating a modernizing, economically prosperous, and culturally cohesive Mexico out of the detritus of a war-ravaged country. Education Ministry officials hoped to use a common curriculum to incorporate disparate groups of people, including urban dwellers, peasants, and indigenous groups, into a unified national culture stripped of its Catholic influences. They also promoted parades, concerts, festivals, and other civic rituals[1] in addition to a series of frontier schools to not only inculcate Mexico's borderlands residents with proper Mexican culture, but also to prevent these residents from adopting aspects of U.S.-influenced borderlands culture. The SEP wanted Mexican borderlands residents to learn that Benito Juárez was the father of their country, not George Washington. They wanted Mexican boys to become members of tribus de exploradores, not Boy Scouts. They wanted Mexican children to learn that Mexico deserved their patriotic support, not that the U.S. Navy was the largest and most powerful in the world.

Increased federal control over education was one of the tools that SEP officials used to accomplish their task. The federal government's takeover of the Chihuahuan state primary school system in 1933, the culmination of a long series of federal moves to centralize political power over municipal and state governments, is just one example. The federal government used this opportunity to either retrain or replace teachers not familiar with (or politically against) the SEP's action and socialist pedagogies. These newly trained teachers were the frontline of the Callista modernizing and anticlerical cultural war. The effectiveness, or perhaps radical-ness, of the nation-building project was also heavily dependent on the strength of political ties between the federal and state government. For example, the anticlerical tenets of the cultural program were put into practice only after Plutarco Elías Calles' son Rodolfo took over the governorship in Sonora in 1931. The same pattern holds true in Chihuahua where the anticlerical aspects of the program rose in importance after Rodrigo M. Quevedo became governor in 1932. Finally, the federal government's offer of higher pay to teachers and their subsequent unionization, should not be underestimated as forces that made the federal government's job of centralizing education possible (and desirable from the point of view of teachers).

Vasconcelos began the federal government's centralization program by attacking the autonomy of municipal authorities, refusing to subsidize their educational expenses and officially ignoring them despite the Constitution's formal acceptance of the municipality as the central locus of political power.[2] Calles advanced Vasconcelos' project by discontinuing the subsidization of state primary schools. Instead, he constructed a parallel federal primary school system to compete with the already existing municipal and state schools.[3] By doing so, the federal government was able to use its own employees to work directly with Mexico's campesinos in implementing their post-revolutionary economic and cultural programs. In the process, the federal school system allowed the SEP officials to bypass several layers of possible resistance to their programs and gave them a direct role in the day-to-day lives of Mexican citizens. Finally, the creation of a parallel primary school system also made it possible for the federal government to step in and take over state school systems when state authorities ran into economic difficulties.

Mexico's "proto-citizens," indigenous or campesino, were often eager to work in tandem with SEP officials to promote local education. The state offered full citizenship and all of its concomitant rights, including the right to education, if indigenous people and campesinos were willing to embrace and carry out their duties. As Alexander Dawson notes, along with the duties of citizenship the federal government wanted to promote "'modernization,' national integration, and an expanding corporatist nation-state."[4] Mexicans, in pursuit of social justice and increased economic prosperity, were often prepared to adopt selectively the modernity that the SEP was promoting, but negotiated the terms upon which they were willing to integrate themselves into the national fabric. Other studies of post-revolutionary education suggest that SEP officials were greatly aided in convincing residents to actively take part in the state's modernizing project when they had something to offer, especially when that something was tied to land or employment rights. Elsie Rockwell, Mary Kay Vaughan, and Stephen Lewis have traced the correlation between local support of federal schools and agrarian reform and Article 123 schools in Tlaxcala, southern Sonora, and the ladino sectors of Chiapas. In a negative sense, Puebla also reinforced this correlation. Vaughan discovered that in places where land reform preceded the efforts of the Education Ministry to advance its project, SEP officials garnered little support. Land and labor reform, however, were not the be-all and end-all of support for federal schooling. Lewis found that ladinos in Chiapas continued to support federal schools even after the SEP no longer supported its earlier cultural project, suggesting that education and literacy themselves were valuable commodities among certain constituents.[5]

My research supports the connection between agrarian and, on a lesser level, labor reform (though this may have much to do with my focus on the rural north) and support for federal schools. After the federal government set aside some of Tohono O'odham ancestral lands in 1928, both José X. Pablo and Antonio L. Bustamante agreed to advance the SEP's modernization campaign in exchange for federal investment in the Tohono O'odham and defense of their ancestral lands. Along the coastal desert of the Sonoran coast, access to land and local resources played a central role in Seri willingness to work (through Thompson) with the Education Ministry. The relationship (often negative) between education and land and labor reform was probably strongest in those places where the SEP either had little to offer or lacked the ability to intercede on behalf of locals. In the Chihuahua, Tarahumara tribal leaders explicitly linked their failure to support expanded schooling with the SEP's failure to defend their land and resources from white and mestizo theft. The conditional nature of support for education was mirrored at Coahuila's Irrigation System No. 6, where ejidatarios withdrew their support for federal schooling once SEP officials succeeded in having them reclassified as colonos. Since colonos, unlike ejidatarios, were not legally bound to support the Education Ministry and the colonos of Irrigation System No. 6 had already gotten what they wanted, they had little reason to continue supporting the SEP. Mexicans, however, did not tie all of their support for Education Ministry to the SEP's ability to intercede on their behalf on agrarian and labor matters.[6] Some people backed SEP schools simply because they viewed literacy as a useful tool, others supported its defanaticization campaign, and still others wanted to take advantage of the possibility to meet members of the opposite sex that coed choirs provided them.

When negotiating with the Education Ministry, peasants, indigenous people, and their mediators with the state, adopted a "common language of consent and protest."[7] This does not mean that they agreed with the SEP or even that they wanted to advance the SEP's cultural project. However, as long as citizens accepted certain key aspects of the cultural project, at least rhetorically, they were free to dissent about and negotiate over the particulars. José X. Pablo is perhaps the best example of this. As I have argued earlier, there is reason to believe Pablo's argument, in spite of the fact that he neither spoke Spanish nor practiced traditional Sonoran Catholicism, that many of the Tohono O'odham on both sides of the border more closely identified with Mexico than the United States and were therefore more inclined to approve of important parts (though obviously not the anticlerical aspects) of Calles' modernizing cultural project was sincere. Pablo framed his argument in a way that successfully tapped into the Education Ministry's growing concerns about borderlands residents losing their Mexican culture. The Tohono O'odham had "always been thinking of Mexico," which was their "true country." Even when he critiqued the Education Ministry's past failures to follow through on their pledges of providing the To- hono O'odham with schools, Pablo did so in a way that supported the general outlines of the cultural project, noting that they needed instructors capable of teaching the Tohono O'odham to "love Mexico, to which we are connected by origin, tradition, and customs." Nonetheless, Pablo's real goal of extending U.S. Bureau of Indian Affairs–style schools, infrastructure investments, and pos- sibly even the adoption of a reservation south of the border to protect Tohono O'odham land holdings was neither possible nor supported by many members of the SEP, who preferred that the Tohono O'odham integrate themselves into mainstream Mexican society. Robert Thompson also skillfully employed the common language of consent and dissent on behalf of the Seri. Thompson talked of redeeming the Seri and integrating them into "civilization." He cast the Seri as poor (which they were) because the men and children did not wear pants, even though this was the common practice among the Seri. Like Pablo, however, Thompson and Sonoran officials were more closely attuned to U.S.- style Indian assimilation. The Sonoran policy of "Indian removal" to Tiburón Island and payment of tribal leaders, not to mention the attempt by Thompson and Edward H. Davis (supported by Sonoran officials) to put the Seri on display in the United States to raise money suggests their divergence from Education Ministry assimilation policy. Not only indigenous people and their go-betweens harnessed the language of consent and dissent. Everyday Mexican citizens also quickly learned to do so in order to gain the federal government's response. In Ciudad Juárez, parents tapped into the federal government's fears that border- lands children would lose their Mexican culture if they attended U.S. schools. Not only did the parents raise money and supplies for their Mexican schools, they fought to have the SEP assign teachers that were more qualified, move the school to a location outside of tolerance zones aimed at U.S. tourists, and end sex education, the latter a central tenet of socialist pedagogy. Perhaps the most surprising thing about the adoption of the common language of consent and dissent in relation to Calles' post-revolutionary cultural modernizing project is that so many different groups adopted this common language to pursue widely disparate goals.

The U.S.-Mexican border created a unique milieu within which Mexicans and agents of the government undertook their negotiations. Unlike other parts of Mexico, the border provided citizens and a unique group of mediators with distinctive leverage vis-à-vis the federal government. Most obviously, Pablo used the Papago Reservation in southern Arizona as both a threat and an example for SEP officials. Pablo's 'play-off system' used the border to not so subtly argue that while the Tohono O'odham loved Mexico and were connected to it by custom and tradition, they were quickly becoming assimilated into the fabric of U.S. society. The fact that this was only true for a small percentage of Tohono O'odham, those associated with the Papago Good Government League, was beside the point given that Education Ministry officials were ignorant of these internal tribal divisions. Nevertheless, the use of the Papago Reservation was not just a threat; it was also a suggestion: provide us with resources similar to those that the U.S. government gives us and we will adhere ourselves to your cultural program. This was a message that borderlands residents repeatedly sent to the SEP, especially those Mexicans who were the targets of frontier schools. That non-indigenous residents were more successful in getting the federal government to comply with their requests – for English instruction, more resources, and secondary schools, for example – was probably a reflection of the perceived costs and benefits. Indigenous groups were smaller, geographically isolated, and had much more ground to cover before they would be ready to move from "proto-citizens" to citizens.

The Seri, through Thompson and Davis, used the border as leverage in a different manner. By employing indigenous assimilation approaches common in the United States – the payment of tribal officials, restricting the Seri to Tiburon Island and requiring them to have 'passports' to leave, and proposing an Indian show – the Seri's benefactors tapped into threads of U.S. cultural imperialism that had long predominated in Sonora.[8] More concretely, they also tried to tap into U.S. markets through the sale of Seri crafts as well as the rejected Indian show. Interestingly, Thompson and Davis's modernizing project and the SEP's modernizing project, although accepting of different means, had nearly identical ends.

Perhaps the most interesting mediators between everyday Mexicans and the Education Ministry were Enrique and Simon Fernández. Even as they competed with governor Rodrigo Quevedo's faction for control over the drug and alcohol bootlegging industry in Ciudad Juárez, they worked to shore up their support with the Education Ministry and local residents by donating land, buildings, and supplies for local schools (and their anti-alcohol campaigns). Enrique's sister-in-law went so far as to engage in a PR campaign, writing letters to the editors of borderlands newspapers proclaiming the morally upstanding character of her husband's brother and his unjustified harassment at the hands of federal authorities.[9] Given the publicity of the campaign against the Fernández brothers, it is highly unlikely that J. Reyes Pimentel, the education inspector assigned to the area, was not aware of the Fernández brothers' activities. Without further information, we are left to wonder if Pimentel's support of the Fernández brothers was a reflection of popular sentiments in the area, a cynical response to local conditions, or a sign that Pimentel did not support the federal government's anti-alcohol campaign. In any case, the SEP's collusion with the Fernández brothers demonstrates the fractured and contradictory nature of the post-revolutionary nation-building project.

Not all of the roles that mediators played were unique to the borderlands. The case that most closely resembles the mediating role that permitted indigenous people "to challenge the terms of their own domination" that Dawson found in indigenous communities scattered across Mexico was that of Ignacio León and the Tarahumara. When the Education Ministry named León's as head of boarding school at Tónachich at the suggestion of Odorico García in 1933, the SEP was implementing a strategy that they had long embraced rhetorically, that of taking indigenous graduates from the Casa in Mexico City and placing them back in their communities to direct the "redemption" of their own people. By 1940, León and his wife had trained numerous indigenous students at the boarding school who would go on to play pivotal roles in promoting Tarahumara governance and local democracy. Nonetheless, the SEP avoided implementing (or trying to implement) García's suggestion that the federal government intervene in local politics to appoint at least one Tarahumara to serve in each municipal government in the Sierra Tarahumara. Although there is no evidence that the Education Ministry ever did put García's suggestion into place, it is clear that the Cárdenas administration more fully empowered León than preceding administrations did. This was probably the result of both the ephemeral nature of the federal government's presence in the Sierra Tarahumara prior to 1934 and the lack of Callista dedication to the issue. Puig and Sáenz were disheartened with the failure of their program to change drastically the way that campesinos and indigenous people lived.[10] It would take Cárdenas to reinvigorate the modernizing cultural project.

An analysis of Calles' attempt to put his modernizing, anti-religious liberal stamp on northern Mexico through a vastly expanded federal education system clearly demonstrates the difficulties and limitations that his nation-building program encountered.[11] The first obstacles to the implementation of his program arose within the government's own bureaucracy. Some teachers and inspectors offered only a token effort at implementing the government's programs. Local power holders rebuffed others in their ardent attempts to do their jobs. Still others sided with local campesinos in their protestations against the government. Meanwhile, the mass mobilization of Mexican society in the wake of the Mexican Revolution led to pressure from below which caused the "ray of liberal enlightenment" to pass "through the looking glass of peasant perspectives."[12] This pressure from below was especially apparent along the U.S.-Mexican border. It was also evident in the government's dealings with Northern Mexico's various indigenous groups. Indigenous people forced the government to adjust to their desires or face the complete loss of influence over them.

Despite the many failures of Calles' educational program between 1924 and 1935, it nonetheless played an important part in the institutional birth of Mexico's later corporate governmental structure.[13] In many places, SEP officials made the first contacts between the nascent federal government and local power brokers. Later, under Cárdenas, the government co-opted many of these power brokers into the system. Still, the federal government's inability to attack the structural problems that were the actual roots of rural poverty – such as caciquismo and the uneven distribution of land – left its schools in a precarious position. In the end, federal rural schools seldom had enough power or leverage against local power holders to overcome the systemic poverty and inequality that they were mandated to fight against.[14] In fact, the many connections that the PNR made with local power holders in order to keep itself in office and later to construct its corporate machine often served to undermine its educational and economic goals.[15] This contradiction was evident in federal government's willingness to accept the support of gambling and contraband interests in Ciudad Juárez at the same time that it was sponsoring anti-alcohol leagues through the education department. The need for the nascent federal government to make its peace and strengthen its ties with both members of the pre-revolutionary elites and those who rose to prominence during and after the revolution is not surprising given the weakness of the post-revolutionary Mexican state.[16] Nevertheless, the government's primary education program was not completely ineffectual. While neither Calles nor rural recipients of Mexico's post-revolutionary liberal educational program received exactly what they might have wished for, Calles' program did provide the necessary educational infrastructure to catapult his country on to its unprecedented post–World War II economic growth.[17]

Notes

INTRODUCTION: THE ROLE OF THE STATE AND EDUCATIONAL REFORM IN MEXICAN NATION BUILDING

1   Mary Kay Vaughan, "Cambio Ideológico en la Política Educativa de la SEP: Programas y Libros de Texto, 1921–1940," in *Escuela y sociedad en el periodo cardenista*, ed. Susana Quintanilla y Mary Kay Vaughan (México: Fondo de Cultura Económica, 1997), 76–108; Alberto Arnaut, *La federalización educativa en México: Historia del debate sobre la centralización y la descentralización educative, 1889–1994* (México: El Colegio de México and Centro de Investigación y Docencia Económicas, 1998), 147–99.

2   Although Porfirio Díaz instituted a positivist pedagogy meant to counteract the influence of the Catholic Church, the Mexican government focused on creating an "illustrious elite" and mostly ignored education for the masses, especially for rural dwellers. See Jorge Alonso, "La educación en la emergencia de la sociedad civil," in *Un Siglo de Educación en México*, vol. 1, ed. Pablo Latapí Sarre (México: Biblioteca Mexicana, 1998), 150–74.

3   Alan Knight, *The Mexican Revolution: Counter-revolution and Reconstruction*, vol. 2 (Lincoln: University of Nebraska Press, 1986); Gilbert M. Joseph, *Revolution from Without: Yucatán, Mexico, and the United States, 1880–1924* (Durham, NC: Duke University Press, 1988); Linda B. Hall, *Oil, Banks, and Politics: The United States and Postrevolutionary Mexico, 1917–1924* (Austin: University of Texas Press, 1995); Linda B. Hall, *Alvaro Obregon: Power and Revolution in Mexico, 1911–1920* (College Station: Texas A & M Press, 1981); Linda B. Hall, "Alvaro Obregón and the Politics of Land Reform, 1920–1924," *Hispanic American Historical Review* 60, no. 2 (May 1980): 213–38; Lorenzo Meyer, *Mexico and the United States in the Oil Controversy, 1917–1942*, trans. Muriel Vasconcelos (Austin: University of Texas Press, 1977); Randall Hansis, "The Political Strategy of Military Reform: Álvaro Obregón and Revolutionary Mexico, 1920–1924," *The Americas* 36, no. 2 (October 1979): 199–233; Edgar Llinas Alvarez, *Revolucion, educación y mexicanidad: La busqueda de la identidad nacional en el pensamiento educativo* (México: UNAM, 1979); Ana Maria Alonso, "Conforming Disconformity: 'Mestizaje,' Hybridity, and the Aesthetics of Mexican Nationalism," *Cultural Anthropology* 19, no. 4 (November 2004): 459–90; Louise Schoenhals, "Mexico Experiments in Rural and Primary Education, 1921–1930," *Hispanic American Historical Review* 44, no. 1 (February 1964): 22–43; John A. Britton, "Indian Education, Nationalism, and Federalism in Mexico, 1910–1921," *The Americas* 32, no. 3 (January 1976): 445–58.

4   Susana Quintanilla and Mary Kay Vaughan, eds., *Escuela y sociedad en el periodo cardenista* (México: Fondo de Cultura Económica, 1997); Ben Fallaw, *Cárdenas Compromised: The Failure of Reform in Postrevolutionary Yucatán* (Durham, NC: Duke University Press, 2001); Adrian A. Bantjes, *As If Jesus Walked on Earth: Cardenismo, Sonora, and the Mexican Revolution* (Wilmington, DE: Scholarly Resources, 1998); Mary Kay Vaughan, *Cultural Politics in Revolution: Teachers, Peasants, and Schools in Mexico, 1930–1940* (Tucson: University of Arizona Press, 1997); Marjorie Becker, *Setting the Virgin on Fire: Lázaro Cárdenas, Michoacán Peasants, and the Redemption of the Mexican Revolution* (Berkeley: University of California Press, 1995); Nora Hamilton, *The Limits of State Autonomy: Post-Revolutionary Mexico* (Princeton: Princeton University Press, 1982); Marjorie Becker, "Black and White and Color: Cardenismo and the Search for a Campesino Ideology," *Comparative Studies in Society and History* 29, no. 3 (July 1987): 453–65; Ben Fallaw, "The Life and Death of Felipa Poot: Women, Fiction, and Cardenismo in Postrevolutionary Mexico," *Hispanic American Historical Review* 82, no. 4 (November 2002): 645–83.

5   Kevin J. Middlebrook, *The Paradox of Revolution: Labor, the State, and Authoritarianism in Mexico* (Baltimore: Johns Hopkins University Press, 1995); Enrique Krauze, Jean Meyer, and Cayetano Reyes, *Historia*

de la Revolución Mexicana, 1924–1928: La reconstrucción económica, vol. 10 (México: El Colegio de México, 1977); Jean Meyer, Enrique Krauze, and Cayetano Reyes, Historia de la Revolución Mexicana, 1924–1928: Estado y sociedad con Calles, vol. 11 (México: El Colegio de México, 1977); Lorenzo Meyer, Rafael Segovia and Alejandro Lajous, Historia de la Revolución Mexicana, 1928–1934: Los inicios de la institucionalización, vol. 12 (México: El Colegio de México, 1977); Lorenzo Meyer, Historia de la Revolución Mexicana, 1928–1934: El conflicto social y los gobiernos del maximato, vol. 13 (México: El Colegio de México).

6   Engracia Loyo, "El largo camino hacia la centralización educativa," in Federalización e innovación educativa en México, ed. Maria del Carmen Pardo (México: El Colegio de México, 1999), 49–58; Mark Wasserman, "Chihuahua: Politics in an Era of Transition," in Provinces of the Revolution: Essays on Regional Mexican History, 1910–1929, ed. Thomas Benjamin and Mark Wasserman (Albuquerque: University of New Mexico Press, 1990), 218–35; Gerardo Rénique, "Anti-Chinese Racism, Nationalism, and State Formation in Post-Revolutionary Mexico," in Political Power and Social Theory, vol. 14 (2001): 91–140; Middlebrook, The Paradox of Revolution.

7   John W.F. Dulles, Yesterday in Mexico: A Chronicle of the Revolution, 1919–1936 (Austin: University of Texas Press, 1961), 118; James W. Wilkie, The Mexican Revolution: Federal Expenditure and Social Change Since 1910 (Berkeley and Los Angeles: University of California Press, 1967), 58–59; Frank Brandenburg, The Making of Modern Mexico (New York: Prentice Hall, 1964), 70; and Mary Kay Vaughan, The State, Education, and Social Class in Mexico, 1880–1928 (DeKalb: Northern Illinois University Press, 1982), 215–38.

8   Héctor Aguilar Camín and Lorenzo Meyer, In the Shadow of the Revolution: Contemporary Mexican History, 1910–1989, trans. Luis Alberto Fierro (Austin, University of Texas Press, 1993), 123. To see the impact of peasant mobilization on rural education,

see Elsie Rockwell, "Schools of the Revolution: Enacting and Contesting State Forms (Tlaxcala 1910–1930)," in Everyday Forms of State Formation: Revolution and the Negotiation of Rule in Modern Mexico, ed. Gilbert Joseph and Daniel Nugent (Durham, NC: Duke University Press, 1994), 170-208.

9   Harold H. Punke, "Extent and Support of Popular Education in Mexico," Peabody Journal of Education 11, no. 3 (November 1933): 122–37. The lack of numerical data has made it difficult for researchers to pinpoint with any accuracy the PRI's level of support in any one sector of Mexican society. See Barry Ames, "Bases of Support for Mexico's Dominant Party," The American Political Science Review 64, no. 1 (March 1970): 153–67. Nonetheless, many peasants were not eager to adopt the most radical, and especially the anticlerical, tenets of either Callismo or Cardenismo. See Stuart F. Voss, "Nationalizing the Revolution: Culmination and Circumstance," in Provinces of the Revolution: Essays on Regional Mexican History, 1910–1929, ed. Thomas Benjamin and Mark Wasserman (Albuquerque: University of New Mexico Press, 1990), 298–306; Fallaw, Cárdenas Compromised; Bantjes, As If Jesus Walked on Earth; Becker, Setting the Virgin on Fire; Benjamin Thomas Smith, "Anticlericalism and Resistance: The Diocese of Huajuapam de León, 1930–1940," Journal of Latin American Studies 37, no. 3 (August 2005): 469–505; and Stanley E. Hilton, "The Church-State Dispute over Education in Mexico from Carranza to Cardenas," The Americas 21, no. 2 (October 1964): 163–83. For an example of the limitations on regime support in the 1940s, see Daniel Newcomer, Reconciling Modernity: Urban State Formation in 1940s León, Mexico (Lincoln: University of Nebraska Press, 2004), and Thomas Rath, "'Que el cielo un soldado en cada hijo te dio ...' Conscription, Recalcitrance and Resistance in Mexico in the 1940s," Journal of Latin American Studies 37, no. 3 (August 2005): 507–31.

10   Middlebrook, The Paradox of Revolution, 10–14; Guillermo O'Donnell, "Corporatism and the Question of the State," in

Authoritarianism and Corporatism in Latin America, ed. James M. Malloy (Pittsburgh: University of Pittsburgh Press, 1977); 47–87; and Meyer, *El conflicto social*, 173–87.

11   Dale Story, *The Mexican Ruling Party: Stability and Authority* (New York: Praeger, 1986); Roderic A. Camp, "Mexican Political Elites 1935–1973: A Comparative Study," *The Americas* 31, no. 4 (April 1975): 452–69; Dulce Maria Sauri Riancho, "Mexico visto por el Partido Revolucionario Institucional," *Mexico Studies/Estudios Mexicanos* 17, no. 2 (Summer 2001): 261–71; Mary Kay Vaughan, *The State, Education, and Social Class*; Pablo Latapí Sarre, "Un siglo de educación nacional: una sistematización," in *Un Siglo de Eduación en México*, Volume 1, ed. Pablo Latapí Sarre (México: Biblioteca Mexicana, 1998), 21–42: and Loyo, *Gobiernos Revolucionarios y educación popular en México, 1911–1928* (Mexico: Centro de Estudios Históricos, 1998).

12   Jürgen Buchenau, *Plutarco Elías Calles and the Mexican Revolution* (Lanham, MD: Rowman & Littlefield, 2007), 6–8; Ana María Alonso, *Thread of Blood: Colonialism, Revolution, and Gender on Mexico's Northern Frontier* (Tucson: University of Arizona Press, 1995), 51–71; Héctor Aguilar Camín, *Saldos de la revolucion: cultura y política de México, 1910–1980* (México: Editorial Nuevo Imagen, 1982), 34–38.

13   Buchenau, *Plutarco Elías Calles*, 20.

14   Ricardo Aragón Pérez, ed., *Historia de la Educación en Sonora*, Tomo 2 (Hermosillo: Gobierno del Estado de Sonora, 2003); Ana Mai Giese, "The Sonoran Triumvirate: Preview in Sonora, 1910–1920," Ph.D. dissertation, University of Florida, 1975, 546–58.

15   Aguilar Camín, *Saldos de la revolucion*, 17–18 and 23–28.

16   Deborah J. Baldwin, *Protestants and the Mexican Revolution: Missionaries, Ministers, and Social Change* (Urbana and Chicago: University of Illinois Press, 1990), 137; Alexander Dawson, *Indian and Nation in Revolutionary Mexico* (Tucson: University of Arizona Press, 2004), xix; and Schoenhals,

"Mexico Experiments in Rural and Primary Education," 30–32.

17   Friedrich Katz, *The Life and Times of Pancho Villa* (Stanford: Stanford University Press, 1998), 417–19.

18   Miguel Tinker Salas, *In the Shadow of the Eagles: Sonora and the Transformation of the Border during the Porfiriato* (Berkeley: University of California Press, 1997), 9; Thomas E. Sheridan, *Where the Dove Calls: The Political Ecology of a Peasant Corporate Community in Northwestern Mexico* (Tucson: University of Arizona Press, 1988), 1–25; Jonathan Coatsworth, *Growth Against Development: The Economic Impact of Railroads in Porfirian Mexico* (DeKalb: Northern Illinois University Press, 1981); William K. Meyers, *Forge of Progress, Crucible of Revolt: The Origins of the Mexican Revolution in La Comarca, Lagunera, 1880–1911* (Albuquerque: University of New Mexico Press, 1994), 9–35; *Historia General de Sonora*, Tomo IV (Hermosillo: Gobierno del Estado de Sonora, 1997); Mark Wasserman, *Capitalists, Caciques, and Revolution: The Native Elite and Foreign Enterprise in Chihuahua, Mexico, 1854–1911* (Chapel Hill: University of North Carolina Press, 1984); Stuart F. Voss, *On the Periphery of Nineteenth-Century Mexico: Sonora and Sinaloa, 1810–1877* (Tucson: University of Arizona Press, 1982); Alan Knight, "Land and Society in Revolutionary Mexico: The Destruction of the Great Haciendas," *Mexican Studies/Estudios Mexicanos* 7, no. 1 (Winter 1991): 73–104.

19   Mary Kay Vaughan, "Primary Education and Literacy in Nineteenth-Century Mexico: Research Trends, 1968–1988," *Latin American Research Review* 25, no. 1 (1990): 43.

20   Stephen E. Lewis, *Ambivalent Revolution: Forging State and Nation in Chiapas, 1910–1945* (Albuquerque: University of New Mexico Press, 2005), 10–11.

21   William K. Meyers, *Forge of Progress*, 4–6.

22   Mark Wasserman, *Persistent Oligarchs: Elites and Politics in Chihuahua, Mexico, 1910–1940* (Durham, NC: Duke University Press, 1993), 2–7.

23 Tinker Salas, *In the Shadow of the Eagles*, 6–12.

24 The federalization of education at the time meant that the education system went from being under the jurisdiction of the state to that of the federal government.

25 Vaughan, *State, Education, and Social Class*,134.

26 Ibid., 138–39.

27 Both Rafael Ramirez and José Manuel Puig Casauranc viewed solving the indigenous question as a major, if not the most important, obstacle to Mexico's overall economic advancement. See Rafael Ramirez, *La Escuela Rural Mexicana* (México: Secretaría de Educación Pública, 1976), and José Manuel Puig Casauranc, *La Cosecha y la Siembra* (México: Secretaría de Educación Pública, 1929).

28 The United States' increasing vigilance along the Mexican border during and after the revolution would become an ever-increasing source of confrontation. See Alexandra Minna Stern, "Buildings, Boundaries, and Blood: Medicalization and Nation-Building on the U.S.-Mexican Border, 1910–1930," *Hispanic American Historical Review* 79, no. 1 (February 1999): 41–81.

29 Knight, "Land and Society in Revolutionary Mexico," 73–104; John Mason Hart, *Revolutionary Mexico: The Coming and Process of the Mexican Revolution* (Berkeley: University of California Press, 1987), 1–18.

30 Alan Knight, "Popular Culture and the Revolutionary State in Mexico, 1910–1940," *Hispanic American Historical Review* 74, no. 3 (August 1994): 393–444; Alberto Arnaut, *La federalización educativa* (México: Reflexiones sobre el Cambio, A.C., 1999), 12.

31 Alan Knight notes that the post-revolutionary nationalist regime, of which Calles was a major player, had several close calls, especially in 1923–24. Knight, "Popular Culture and the Revolutionary State," 394.

32 Luz Elena Galván de Terraza, *Los maestros y la educación pública en México: un estudio histórico* (Hidalgo y Matamoros, Tlalpan:

Centro de Investigaciones y Estudios Superiores en Antropología Social, 1985), 27.

33 Fernando Solana et. al., *Historia de la educación pública en México*, vol. 1 (Mexico City: Fondo de Cultura Económica, 1982), vi; Isidro Castillo, *México: sus revoluciones sociales y la educación*, vol. 2 (Mexico City: Gobierno del Estado de Michoacán, 1976), 325.

34 Galván de Terrazas, *Los maestros*, 29.

35 Castillo, *México: sus revoluciones*, 341.

36 Ibid., 341–47.

37 John Kenneth Turner, *Barbarous Mexico* (Austin: University of Texas Press, 1984), 269; Vaughan, "Primary Education and Literacy," 42–43.

38 Turner, *Barbarous Mexico*, 285.

39 Vaughan, *The State, Education, and Social Class*, 26.

40 Castillo, *México: sus revoluciones*, 314.

41 Ibid., 304.

42 Galván de Terrazas, *Los maestros*, 28; Vaughan, *The State, Education, and Social Class*, 38; Guillermo de la Peña, "Educación y cultura en el México del siglo XX," in *Un siglo de educación en México*, vol. 1, ed. Pablo Latapi Sarre (Mexico: Fondo de Cultura Económica, 1998). 50.

43 Vaughan, *The State, Education, and Social Class*, 84; James Cockcroft, *Intellectual Precursors of the Mexican Revolution, 1900–1910* (Austin: University of Texas Press, 1968), 193.

44 Ricardo and Jesús Flores Magón, *Batalla a la Dictadura* (Mexico City: Empresas Editoriales, 1948), 127.

45 Galván de Terrazas, *Los maestros*, 35.

46 Arnaldo Córdova, *La ideología de la revolución mexicana: la formación del nuevo régimen* (Mexico City: Editorial Era, 1973), 112.

47 Galván de Terrazas, *Los maestros*, 36; Castillo, *México: sus revoluciones*, 44–45.

48 Michael C. Meyer and William L. Sherman, *The Course of Mexican History*, 5th ed. (New York: Oxford University Press, 1995), 514.

49 Loyo, *Gobiernos Revolucionarios*, 22–23.

50 Galván de Terrazas, *Los maestros*, 37.

51 Castillo, *México: sus revoluciones*, 124; Vaughan, *The State, Education, and Social Class*, 99.

52 Castillo, *México: sus revoluciones*, 125–30.

53 Galván de Terrazas, *Los maestros*, 42–43, Loyo, *Gobiernos Revolucionarios*, 42–43.

54 Galván de Terrazas, *Los maestros*, 45.

55 De la Peña, "Educación y cultura," 54.

56 Galván de Terrazas, *Los Maestros*, 72–73.

57 Castillo, *México: sus revoluciones*, 130.

58 Dulles, *Yesterday in Mexico*, 118.

59 Wilkie, *Federal Expenditure and Social Change*, 58–59.

60 Brandenburg, *The Making of Modern Mexico*, 70.

61 Vaughan, *The State, Education, and Social Class*, 215–38.

62 De la Peña, "Educación y cultura," 51.

63 Vaughan, *The State, Education, and Social Class*, 136–37; José Vasconcelos, *el desastre*, in *Obras Completas*, vol. 2 (Mexico City: Libreros Mexicanos Unidos, 1958), 1251.

64 Galván de Terrazas, *Los maestros*, 77.

65 Vaughan, *The State, Education, and Social Class*, 171.

66 Lewis, *Ambivalent Revolution*, 218.

67 Dawson, *Indian and Nation*, xv.

CHAPTER 1: THE CALLISTA PROGRAM

1 Carlos Macías Richard, *Vida y Temperamento: Plutarco Elías Calles, 1877–1920* (Hermosillo: Instituto Sonorense de Cultura, 1995), 157–63.

2 Camín, *Saldos de la revolucion*, 23–28.

3 Arce Gurza, "En Busca de una educación revolucionaria: 1924–1934," in *Ensayos sobre historia de la eduación en México*, ed. Josefina Zoraida Vázquez (Mexico: El Colegio de

Mexico, 1981), 173; Middlebrook, *The Paradox of Revolution*, 23–24.

4 Middlebrook, *The Paradox of Revolution*, 23–24.

5 Krauze, *Mexico: Biography of Power: A History of Modern Mexico, 1810–1996*, trans. Hank Heirtz (New York: Harper Collins, 1997), 416–17.

6 Joel S. Migdal has argued that "with only isolated exceptions, political leaders have sought to head a transformative state. They have seen it as an organization that can (or, at least, should) dominate in every corner of society.… Indeed, transformative states go beyond trying to establish people's identities; they aim to shape people's entire moral orders." Cited in Migdal, "The State in Society: An Approach to Struggles for Domination," in *State Power and Social Forces: Domination and Transformation in the Third World*. ed. Joel S. Migdal, Atul Kohli, and Vivienne Shue (Cambridge: Cambridge University Press, 1994), 13–14.

7 Jean Meyer, "Revolution and Reconstruction in the 1920s," in *Mexico Since Independence*, ed. Leslie Bethell (Cambridge: Cambridge University Press, 1991), 237–38; Middlebrook, *Paradox of Revolution*, 25.

8 James C. Scott has argued that these "soft" policy options are seen by elites as the optimum reform programs as they seldom undermine the stability of the state or the economy. Cited in Scott, *Weapons of the Weak: Everyday Forms of Peasant Resistance* (New Haven, CT: Yale University Press, 1985), 54; Elsie Rockwell also notes that "when postrevolutionary agrarian policy became increasingly conservative, the expansion of rural schooling may have been politically motivated by an attempt to offset the demand for land." Cited in Rockwell, "Schools of the Revolution: Enacting and Contesting State Forms in Tlaxcala, 1910–1930," in *Everyday Forms of State Formation: Revolution and the Negotiation of Rule in Modern Mexico*, ed. Gilbert M. Joseph and Daniel Nugent (Durham, NC: Duke University Press, 1994), 190.

9   Enrique Krauze, Jean Meyer, and Cayetano Reyes, *Historia de la Revolución Mexicana,1924–1928: La reconstrucción económica*, ed. Luis González (México: El Colegio de México, 1977), 18.

10 Eric Zolov, *Refried Elvis: The Rise of the Mexican Counterculture* (Berkeley: University of California Press, 1999), 1–11; Alan Knight, "Mexico, c. 1930–1946," in *Cambridge History of Latin America*, vol. 7, ed. Leslie Bethell (New York: Cambridge University Press, 1990), 3–82.

11 Vaughan, *The State, Education, and Social Class*, 130.

12 Macías Richard, *Vida y Temperamento*, 240.

13 Carlos Macías Richard, *Plutarco Elías Calles: Pensamiento politico y social, antología (1913–1936)* (Mexico: Fondo de Cultura Económica, 1988), 121.

14 Krauze, *Biography of Power*, 405; Macías Richard, *Vida y Temperamento*,55–60.

15 Macías Richard, *Vida y Temperamento* 57; Buchenau, *Plutarco Elías Calles*, 15.

16 Buchenau, *Plutarco Elías Calles*, 15–16; Mary Kay Vaughan, *The State, Education, and Social Class*, 17–20.

17 Alan Knight, "The United States and the Mexican Peasantry, circa 1880–1940," in *Rural Revolt in Mexico: U.S. Intervention and the Domain of Subaltern Politics*, ed. Daniel Nugent (Durham, NC: Duke University Press, 1998), 62.

18 Buchenau, *Plutarco Elías Calles*, 16–18.

19 Cited in Tinker Salas, *In the Shadow of the Eagles*, 252.

20 Macías Richard, *Pensamiento político*, 32–39.

21 Ibid., 35.

22 For an example of the active role that Calles took with the school, see the series of letters between himself and school and local officials, *Archivo General de la Nacion / Obregón-Calles* (hereafter AGN/OC), 121-E-E-50.

23 See *Patronato de la Historia de Sonora* (hereafter PHS), Roll 1, Decree #8.

24 See PHS, Roll 1, Decree #1.

25 See PHS, Roll 1, Decree #4; Macías Richard, *Vida y Temperamento*, 193–94

26 Krauze, *Biography of Power*, 410.

27 See PHS, Roll 1, Decree #14.

28 Vaughan, *Cultural Politics in Revolution*, 57.

29 Macías Richard, *Vida y Temperamento*, 197–201; citation on page 199.

30 See PHS, Roll 1, Law #69.

31 "Calles Presidente, sostendrá los mismos principios que Calles candidato," by Braulio Rodríguez, AGN/OC 241-E-E-94.

32 Macías Richard, *Pensamiento político*, 70–71.

33 Ibid., 116.

34 Buchenau, *Plutarco Elías Calles*, 16; Macías Richard, *Pensamiento político*, 124.

35 Macías Richard, *Pensamiento politico*, 145–46.

36 Ibid., 156–57.

37 Ibid., 161.

38 Krauze, *Biography of Power*, 415.

39 *Boletín de la Secretaría de Educación Pública* (hereafter BSEP) 4, no. 7 (October 1925): 183.

40 *La educación pública en México a traves de los mensajes presidenciales desde la consumación de la independencia hasta nuestros dias*, 1926, Table Number 1.

41 Ibid., 261–62.

42 BSEP 4, nos. 9–10 (December 1925): 7.

43 BSEP 5, no. 9 (1926): 5; BSEP 5, no. 4 (1926): 5–12.

44 Arnaut, *La federalización educativa*, 13.

45 *Mensajes presidenciales*, 268; BSEP 5, no. 1 (1926): 5–8.

46 Presidential Resolution, AGN / OC 121-E-E-71.

47 Krauze, *Biography of Power*, 415.

48 *Mensajes presidenciales*, 176.

49 Krauze, Meyer, and Reyes, *La reconstrución económica*, 18–23; Pamphlet, "Plutarco Elías Calles: Primer Presidente de la Etapa Institucional de la Revolución Mexicana,"

Fideicomiso Archivos Plutarco Elías Calles y Fernando Torreblanca (hereafter FAPE-CFT), Exp. 40: "Homenajes 1984," Fojas 22–23, Inv. 7988.

50   Krauze, Meyer, and Reyes, *La reconstrución económica*, 20.

51   Arce Gurza, "En Busca," 180.

52   Krauze, Meyer, and Reyes, *La reconstrución económica*, 317–18.

53   *El esfuerzo educativo*, 21.

54   *Mensajes presidenciales*, 262.

55   Tannenbaum, *Peace by Revolution: Mexico After 1910* (New York: Columbia University Press, 1933), 276.

56   BSEP 4, no. 7 (1925): 237.

57   BSEP 4, no. 7 (1925): 240; *El esfuerzo educativo*, 12

58   *Mensajes presidenciales*, 305.

59   BSEP 4, no. 6 (1925): 246–48.

60   *Mensajes presidenciales*, 261.

61   BSEP 5, no. 4 (1926): 29–31; Tannenbaum, *Peace by Revolution*, 288–89.

62   BSEP 4, no. 6 (1925): 248.

63   BSEP 5, no. 3 (1926): 33.

64   BSEP 4, no. 7 (1925): 74.

65   BSEP 5, no. 2 (1926): 21–28; BSEP 6, no. 11 (1927): 26; Vaughan, *The State, Education, and Social Class*, 173–74.

66   BSEP 5, no. 10 (1926): 86–93; Krauze, Meyer, and Reyes, *La reconstrución económica*, 318.

67   BSEP 5, no. 1 (1926): 5–8.

68   *El esfuerzo educativo*, 27.

69   Ibid., 21.

70   Lewis, *Ambivalent Revolution*, 100; Vaughan, "Modernizing Patriarchy: State Policies, Rural Households, and Women in Mexico, 1930-1940," in *Hidden Histories of Gender and the State in Latin America*, ed. Elizabeth Dore and Maxine Molyneux, (Durham, NC: Duke University Press, 2000), 199–202.

71   BSEP 5, no. 3 (1926): 28–29.

72   Spicer, *Cycles of Conquest: The Impact of Spain, Mexico, and the United States on the Indians of the Southwest, 1533–1960* (Tucson: University of Arizona Press, 1962), 539–40; Proyecto del Plan Sexenal, en lo que Corresponde a la Secretaría de Agricultura y Fomento, FAPECFT, Exp. 1: Plan Sexenal, Leg. ½, foja 26, nv. 4526.

73   Galván de Terrazas, *Los maestros*, 91; Macías Richard, *Pensamiento político*, 116.

74   Camín, *Saldos de la revolución*, 22–23.

75   *Memoria que indica el estado que guarda el ramo de educación pública* (hereafter *Memoria*) (1932): 26.

76   Joel Spring, *Deculturalization and the Struggle for Equality: A Brief History of the Education of Dominated Cultures in the United States*, 4th ed. (Boston: McGraw-Hill Higher Education, 2004), 27–31.

77   Alexander S. Dawson, "From Models for the Nation to Model Citizens: Indigenismo and the 'Revindication' of the Mexican Indian, 1920–1940," *Journal of Latin American Studies* 30, no. 2 (May 1998): 279–308; Rick A. López, "The India Bonita Contest of 1921and the Ethnicization of the Mexican National Culture," *Hispanic American Historical Review* 82, no. 2 (May 2002): 291–328.

78   BSEP, 5, no. 6 (1926): 13; Galván de Terrazas, *Los maestros*, 91–92.

79   *Mensajes presidenciales*,176.

80   BSEP 5, no. 6 (1926): 13

81   Ibid., 5–7.

82   Ibid., 7–8.

83   Ibid., 8.

84   Ibid., 15.

85   Ibid., 13–14.

86   Ibid., 17.

87   Galvan de Terrazas, Los maestros, 92–93.

88   Engracia Loyo, "La empresa redentora: La Casa del Estudiante Indígena," *Historia Mexicana 46, no. 1* (1996): 111.

89   Ibid., 114–16.

90   *El esfuerzo educativo*, 20.

91 Krauze, Meyer, and Reyes, *La reconstrucción económica*, 231–68, de la Peña, "Educación y cultura," 66.

92 BSEP 7, no. 1 (1928): 5–8.

93 BSEP 7, no. 4 (1928): 106.

94 BSEP 7, no. 5 (1928): 233–34.

95 Ibid., 218.

96 BSEP 7, no. 4 (1928): 25.

97 *El esfuerzo educativo*, xix and 36.

98 Ibid., xii.

99 Ibid., 23.

100 Ibid., 29.

101 BSEP 7, no. 1 (1928): 9–12.

102 BSEP 7, no. 4 (1928): 184.

103 *El esfuerzo educativo*, xiii–xiv.

104 Concepción Jiménez Alarcón, ed., *Rafael Ramírez y la escuela rural mexicana* (Mexico City: Secretaria de Educación Pública, 1998), 14.

105 BSEP 7, no. 5 (1928): 16–19.

106 Vaughan, *Cultural Politics in Revolution*, 28–29.

107 BSEP 7, no. 1 (1928): 168–69.

108 Gilberto M. Lopez to Rafael Ramírez, Chihuahua, 8 April 1929, *Archivo Historico de la Secretaría de la Educación Pública – Escuelas Rurales* (hereafter AHSEP-ER), Box 1653, Exp. IV/000 (II-5)(721.5).

109 BSEP 8, no. 1 (1929): v–vi.

110 BSEP 8, no. 4 (1929): 41.

111 Lewis, *Ambivalent Revolution*, 81.

112 BSEP 8, no. 5 (1929): 27–28.

113 *Memoria*, 22, no. 4 (1929): 401–2.

114 BSEP 9, no. 6 (1930): 26–29.

115 Tannenbaum, *Peace by Revolution*, 291.

116 BSEP 9, nos. 1–3 (1930): 23–24.

117 BSEP 9, nos. 9–10 (1930): 30.

118 Ibid., 33.

119 Ibid., 34.

120 Ibid., 35

121 Ibid., 36.

122 Ibid.

123 *Memoria* (1931): 8.

124 *Memoria* (1932): xxvii.

125 Rafael Ramírez to Director of Federal Education, Chihuahua, 18 October 1934, AHSEP-ER, Box 1079, Exp. IV/202; Celso Flores Zamora to Chief of Juridical Department, Chihuahua, 9 November 1935, AHSEP-ER, Box 1360, Exp. IV/161.1 (721.4); Ralph B. Keeler to SEP, Chihuahua, 1 October 1935, AHSEP-ER, Box 1360, Exp. 221/1/21.

126 Kristina A. Boylan, "Gendering the Faith and Altering the Nation: Mexican Catholic Women's Activism, 1917–1940," in *Sex in Revolution: Gender, Politics, and Power in Modern Mexico*, ed. Jocelyn Olcott, Mary Kay Vaughan, and Gabriela Cano (Durham, NC: Duke University Press, 2007), 211.

127 *Memoria* (1933): 22.

128 Ibid., 9–10.

129 BSEP 10, no. 5 (1931): 20–22.

130 *Memoria* (1932): xxv–xxvii.

131 BSEP 10, no. 6 (1931): 27–28.

132 *Memoria* (1931): 25.

133 *Memoria* (1931): 11–14.

134 *El Maestro Rural* 3, no. 2 (15 June 1933), 1; FAPECFT, Exp. 1: Plan Sexenal, Leg. 1 and 2, Inv. 4526.

135 FAPECFT, Exp. 1: Plan Sexenal, Leg. 1 of 2, Fojas 26 and 37, Inv. 4526.

136 Cited in Vaughan, *Cultural Politics in Revolution*, 34.

137 *Memoria* (1933): 26; Vaughan, *Cultural Politics in Revolution*, 32.

138 *Memoria* (1933): 41.

139 Ibid., xiv.

140 *Memoria* (1933): 107.

141 Elena Torres, "Económia domestica: descanso del ama de casa y acción civica del hogar," *El Maestro Rural* 3, no. 3 (1 July 1933), n.p.; Borderland gender norms were

such that the ideal Mexican woman embraced *marianismo*, a paradoxical virgin/mother mix based on the patterning of one's life on the Virgin Mary. She was feminine and lived a life of *abnegación*: selflessness, self-sacrifice, and the willingness to give up her public existence for the benefit of others. Her place was the home. She needed to be chaperoned by close male relatives while in public and was "incapable of wielding [public] power." Mainstream society saw women who overstepped these bounds as *marimachos*, the equivalent of butches or dykes. Yet, women had "a measure of moral authority" and a taming influence over men. It was this moral authority and taming influence that Education Ministry officials both wanted to harness and feared (especially in the religious sphere). See Jocelyn Olcott, *Revolutionary Women in Postrevolutionary Mexico* (Durham, NC: Duke University Press, 2005), 15–17, and Alonso, *Thread of Blood*, 87.

142 *Memoria* (1933): 4.

143 Ibid., 6.

144 *Memoria* (1934): xiv.

145 *Memoria* (1933): 12–13.

146 Ibid., xiii–xv.

147 Cited in Solano, *Historia de la educación*, 270.

148 Cited in Vaughan, *Cultural Politics in Revolution*, 34–35.

CHAPTER 2: FEDERALIZATION OF EDUCATION IN CHIHUAHUA

1 Mary Kay Vaughan has argued that the expansion of federal schooling was seen by government officials as a means to "restrain and co-opt" the popular forces that arose during and after the Mexican Revolution. Mary Kay Vaughan, "Education and Class in the Mexican Revolution," *Latin American Perspectives* 2, no. 2 (Summer 1975): 17. For additional perspectives on clientelism and the co-optation of popular forces see: Vivian

Brachet-Marquez, "Explaining Sociopolitical Change in Latin America: The Case of Mexico," *Latin American Research Review* 27, no. 3 (1992): 91–122; Frederick Pike, *Spanish America, 1900–1970: Tradition and Social Innovation* (New York: Norton, 1973), Chapter 4; and John A. Britton, "Teacher Unionization and the Corporate State in Mexico, 1931–1945," *Hispanic American Historical Review* 59, no. 4 (November 1979): 674–90.

2 Mary Kay Vaughan, "Primary Schooling in the City of Puebla, 1821–60," *Hispanic American Historical Review* 67, no. 1 (February 1987): 39; Schoenhals, "Mexico Experiments in Rural and Primary Education, 22–23; Carlos Newland, "The *Estado Docente* and its Expansion: Spanish American Elementary Education, 1900–1950," *Journal of Latin American Studies* 26, no. 2 (May 1994): 450; and David E. Cronon, "American Catholics and Mexican Anticlericalism," *Mississippi Valley Historical Review* 45, no. 2 (September 1958): 201–31.

3 Pablo Sarre Latapí and Manuel Ulloa Herrero, *El financiamiento de la eduación básica en el marco del federalismo* (México: Fondo de Cultura de Económica, 2000), 17.

4 Cecilia Greaves Lainé, "El debate sobre una antigua polémica: La integración indígena," *Historia de la eduación y enseñanza de la historia* (México: El Colegio de México, 1998), 138; and Alan Knight, *The Mexican Revolution: Porfirians, Liberals and Peasants*, Volume 1 (Lincoln, NE: University of Nebraska Press, 1986), 2–3.

5 On support for rural education, see Britton, "Teacher Unionization," 675–76.

6 Vaughan, *The State, Education and Social Class*, 134; Arnaut, *La federalización*, 163–69; and Latapí and Ulloa, *El financiamiento*, 18–19.

7 Loyo, "Los mecanismos de la 'federalización' educativa, 1921–1940," in *Historia de la educación y enseñanza de la historia* (Mexico: Colegio de México, 1998), 118; Knight, *Porfirians, Liberals, and Peasants*, 142.

8 Vasconcelos, *El Ulises criollo*, 3rd ed. (Mexico: Jus, 1968), 9.

9   Loyo, *Gobiernos revolucionarios*, 138.

10   Loyo, "Los mecanismos," 116.

11   BSEP 1, no. 3 (1923): 187.

12   *El esfuerzo educativo*, 13.

13   Loyo, "Los mecanismos," 119.

14   Thomas Benjamin, "Laboratories of the New State, 1920–1929," in *Provinces of the Revolution: Essays on Regional Mexican History, 1910–1929*, ed. Thomas Benjamin and Mark Wasserman (Albuquerque: University of New Mexico Press, 1990), 72.

15   Moises Sáenz, *Memoria* (México: Secretaría de la Educación Pública, 1928), 13.

16   Neither Obregón nor any of his successors would manage to remove unofficial local politicking from the policy-making equation; for example, see Rockwell, "Schools of the Revolution," 170–208.

17   Katz, Pancho Villa, 17. See also Alonso, Thread of Blood, and Nugent, Spent Cartridges of Revolution: An Anthropological History of Namiquipa, Chihuahua (Chicago: University of Chicago Press, 1993).

18   Cited in Knight, *Porfirians, Liberals, and Peasants*, 120–22.

19   Knight, *Porfirians, Liberals, and Peasants*, 180–81; Katz, *Pancho Villa*, 17.

20   Luis Aboites, *Breve historia de Chihuahua* (México: El Colegio de México, 1994), 143–44.

21   Wasserman, *Persistent Oligarchs*, 32.

22   Katz, *Pancho Villa*, 731; Aboites, *Breve historia*, 143–44.

23   Contrato Celebrado entre la Secretaría de la Educación Pública y el Gobierno Constitucional del Estado de Chihuahua, 1 September 1922, AHSEP-ER, Box 5600, Exp. 28.

24   Katz, *Pancho Villa*, 731–32; Aboites, *Breve historia*, 143–44.

25   Knight, "The United States and the Mexican Peasantry, 34.

26   BSEP 3, no. 10 (March 1925): Table 1.

27   BSEP 4, no. 7 (October 1925): 183.

28   BSEP 5, no. 9 (1926): 5; and BSEP 5, no. 4 (1926): 5–12.

29   This policy was still in effect at the beginning of the 1930s. See, for example, José M. Padilla, Inspection Report, Chihuahua, 28 June 1930, AHSEP-ER, Box 26, Exp. 2595; and Salvador Varela to the Rafael Ramírez, Chihuahua, 9 September 1931, AHSEP-ER, Box 26, Exp. 2595.

30   Loyo, "Los mecanismos," 119.

31   Arnaut, *Historia del debate*, 171.

32   *Memoria* (1928): 13.

33   *Mensajes presidenciales*, 261–62; Loyo, "Los mecanismos," 121.

34   BSEP 5, no. 1 (1926): 6–8.

35   José Valdés Acosta to SEP, Chihuahua, 23 December 1927, AHSEP-ER, Box 23, Exp. IV/161 (IV-14)/2569; Juan R. Salazar to Ignacio Ramírez, Chihuahua, 20 August 1928, AHSEP-ER, Box 19, Exp. IV/161 (IV-14)/2637; and Rockwell, "Schools of the Revolution," 188.

36   Ramón Espinosa Villanueva, Inspection Report, Chihuahua, AHSEP-ER, Box 19, Exp. IV/161 (IV-14)/2541.

37   *Memoria* (1928): 13–14.

38   BSEP 6, no. 3 (1927): 17–18.

39   BSEP 6, no. 4 (1927): 11–12.

40   BSEP 5, no. 3 (1926): 28–29; BSEP 5, no. 1 (1926): 119–20.

41   Salvador Varela to Abelardo de la Rosa, Chihuahua, 1 April 1930, AHSEP-ER, Box 1731, Exp. IV/166 (IV-4) 721.4.

42   Buchenau, *Plutarco Elías Calles*, 147.

43   Aboites, *Breve historia*, 146.

44   Wasserman, *Persistent Oligarchs*, 37–41 and 201.

45   Aboites, *Breve historia*, 146–47.

46   Wasserman, *Persistent Oligarchs*, 40.

47   *El esfuerzo educativo*, 12.

48   *Noticia estadística*, 1930, 762–65.

49   BSEP 5. no. 7 (1926): 5–7.

50   BSEP 5, no. 1 (1926): 25.

51 BSEP 9, nos. 1–3 (1930): 9.

52 Loyo, "Los mecanismos," 123.

53 Salvador Varela to Rafael Ramírez, Chihuahua, 9 September 1931, AHSEP-ER, Box 26, Exp. IV/161 (IV-14)/2595.

54 BSEP 8, no. 1 (1929): vi.

55 *Memoria* (1932): 587. Expenditures on rural schools rose from 12.19 per cent of the budge in 1927 to 25.61 per cent by 1930.

56 Wasserman, *Persistent Oligarchs*, 52–60; Aboites, *Breve historia*, 151–52.

57 The early unionization of teachers occurred at the grassroots level. Bassol's attempts and failure to centralize federal government control over these unions played a significant role in his stepping down from his post as Minister of Education. See Britton, "Teacher Unionization," 677–87; and Vaughan, *Cultural Politics in Revolution*, 33.

58 Engracia Loyo, "Escuelas Rurales 'Artículo 123', (1917–1940)." *Historia Mexicana* 40, no. 2 (1991): 321–24; and Hall, "Alvaro Obregón and the Politics of Mexican Land Reform," 213–38.

59 Loyo, "Los mecanismos," 126.

60 Rafael Ramírez to Salvador Varela, Chihuahua, 25 July 1934, AHSEP-ER, Box 46, Exp. IV/161 (IV-15)/2897; M. Ramos and H.G. Mendoza to Gobernador de Chihuahua, 8 November 1934, AHSEP-ER, Box 46, Exp. IV/161 (IV-15)/2897; Salvador Varela to Manager of Compañía Maderera de Chihuahua, S.A., Chihuahua, 29 April 1935, AHSEP-ER, Box 46, Exp. IV/161 (IV-15)/2897; Director of Federal Education to Rafael Ramírez, Chihuahua, 29 May 1934, AHSEP-ER, Box 44, Exp. IV/161 (IV-15)/602; Salvador Varela to Manager of Compañía Industrial 'El Potosi,' S.A., Chihuahua, 2 November 1934, AHSEP-ER, Box 44, Exp. IV/161 (IV-15)/3745; Compañía Industrial 'El Potosi,' S.A. to SEP, 13 October 1934, AHSEP-ER, Box 44, Exp. IV/161 (IV-15)/3745; Salvador Varela to SEP, 15 November 1934, AHSEP-ER, Box 44, Exp. IV/161 (IV-15)/3745; Salvador Varela to Secretary General of Sindicato no. 12 of Mine, Industrial and Metallurgical Workers of the Republic, 4 April 1936, AHSEP-ER, Box 44, Exp. IV/161 (IV-15)/3745; and Loyo, "Articulo 123," 321–24.

61 Vaughan, *Cultural Politics in Revolution*, 31.

62 *El Maestro Rural* 3, no. 2 (1933): 1.

63 Aboites, *Breve historia*, 152–53.

64 Jesús Coello, Bimonthly Report, Chihuahua, 28 February 1934, AHSEP-ER, Box 860, Exp. IV/100 (04)(IV-4)(721.4), and President of the Revolutionary Union of Parents to the Minister of SEP, Chihuahua, 19 September 1933, AHSEP-ER, Box 936, Exp. IV/200; Aboites, *Breve historia*, 153.

65 Salvador Varela to Rafael Ramírez, Chihuahua, 3 October 1933, AHSEP-ER, Box 936, Exp. IV/200.

66 Vaughan, *Cultural Politics in Revolution*, 34–35.

67 Wasserman, *Persistent Oligarchs*, 52.

68 Robert Fierro (Substitute Governor) to the SEP, Chihuahua, 18 June 1932, AHSEP-ER, Box 867, Exp. IV/161 (IV-15)(721.4).

69 Rafael Ramírez to Secretario del Ramo, Chihuahua, 6 December 1932, AHSEP-ER, Box 867, Exp. IV/161 (IV-15)(721.4).

70 Rodrigo M. Quevedo to Diputación Permanente de la Legislatura del Estado, Chihuahua, 24 July 1933, AHSEP-ER, Box 936, Exp. IV/200.

71 J. Borunda E. to Gobernado Constitucional del Estado del Estado, Chihuahua, 26 July 1933, AHSEP-ER, Box 936, Exp. IV/200.

72 *Memoria* 2 (1933): 27–32.

73 Rafael Ramírez to Salvador Varela, Chihuahua, 11 August 1933, AHSEP-ER, Box 936, IV/200.

74 Rafael Ramírez to Director of Federal Education, Chihuahua, 17 August 1933, AHSEP-ER, Box 936, Exp. IV/200.

75 Relación de Datos Generales en la Organización de Personal de las Escuelas del Estado por José A. Espejo, Chihuahua, 9 August 1933, AHSEP-ER, Box 936, Exp. IV/200.

76   Rafael Ramírez to Director of Federal Education, Chihuahua, 17 August 1933, AHSEP-ER, Box 936, Exp. IV/200.

77   Salvador Varela to Rafael Ramírez, 10 November 1933, AHSEP-ER, Box 936, Exp. IV/200.

78   Inés Estrada to Rafael Ramírez, 21 August 1933, AHSEP-ER, Box 958, Exp. IV/100 (721.4).

79   Guillermo Castillo, Inspection Report, Chihuahua, 14 November 1932, AHSEP-ER, Box 15, Exp. IV/161 (IV-14)/2451; Ramón Espinosa Villanueva, Inspection Report, Chihuahua, 18 March 1933, AHSEP-ER, Box 15, Exp. IV/161 (IV-14)/2451; Jesús Coello, to the SEP, Chihuahua, 30 September 1933, AHSEP-ER, Box 23, Exp. IV/161 (IV-14)/2704; Jesús Coello, Monthly Report, Chihuahua, 30 September 1933, AHSEP-ER, Box 958, Exp. IV/100 (721.4); Jesús Coello, Bimonthly Report, Chihuahua, 5 December 1933, AHSEP-ER, Box 958, Exp. IV/100 (721.4); Miguel Ceballos Durán to Rafael Ramírez, Chihuahua, 3 October 1933, AHSEP-ER, Box 958, Exp. IV/100 (721.4); Miguel Ceballos Durán to Salvador Varela, Chihuahua, 13 October 1933, AHSEP-ER, Exp. IV/100 (721.4); Miguel Ceballos Durán, Monthly Report, 2 October 1933, AHSEP-ER, Box 958, Exp. IV/100 (721.4); Guillermo Castillo, Monthly Report, Chihuahua, 4 November 1933, AHSEP-ER, Box 958, Exp. IV/100 (721.4); and Manuel Castellanos, Bimonthly Report, Chihuahua, 7 May 1934, AHSEP-ER, Box 860, Exp. IV/100 (04)(IV-4)(721.4).

80   Miguel Ceballos Durán to Eduardo Zarza, Chihuahua, 29 April 1934, AHSEP-ER, Box 1057, Exp. IV/166 (04)(721.4).

81   "Hace una reclamación el Gobernador de Chihuahua," in El Heraldo, Prof. Manuel López Dávila, Chihuahua, 6 August 1935, AHSEP-ER, Box 1360, Exp. 221/1/21.

82   The SEP argued that the agreement that it signed gave Quevedo no right to make public declarations against the SEP, which, it was afraid, might turn public sentiment against it. See Director of Federal Education to the General Secretary of Government, Chihuahua, 6 August 1935, AHSEP-ER, Box 1360, 221/1/21.

83   "Cumplimiento del Convenio de Educación," El Heraldo, Prof. Manuel López Dávila, Chihuahua, 7 August 1935, AHSEP-ER, Box 1360, Exp. 221/1/21.

84   Jacinto Maldonado to the SEP, Chihuahua, 20 August 1935, AHSEP-ER, Box 1359, Exp. 220/1/19.

85   Celso Flores Zamora to Subsecretario de Educación, Chihuahua, 22 August 1935, AHSEP-ER, Box 1360, Exp. IV/202 (04)(721.4).

86   Jacinto Maldonado to the SEP, Chihuahua, 26 August 1935, AHSEP-ER, Box 1360, Exp. 221/1/21.

87   Rodrigo M. Quevedo to SEP, Chihuahua, 10 September 1935, AHSEP-ER, Box 1360, Exp. 221/1/21.

88   Rodrigo M. Quevedo to SEP, Chihuahua, 24 September 1935, AHSEP-ER, Box 1360, Exp. 221/1/21.

89   Loyo, "Los mecanismos," 125.

90   Ibid., 126.

91   Plan Sexenal, FAPECFT, Exp. 1: Plan Sexenal, legajo ½, Inv. 4526.

92   Loyo, "Los mecanismos," 128.

93   Ibid.

94   Ibid.

95   Ibid., 129–30.

96   Ibid., 130–31.

97   Arnaut, Historia del debate, 203–11.

98   The creation of the SNTE marked the end of a "decentralized and flexible" collection of teachers' unions. See Latapí and Ulloa, El financimiento, 19, and Britton, "Teacher Unionization," 687.

CHAPTER 3: THE TARAHU-
MARA

1   Lewis, *Ambivalent Revolution*, 45.

2   Héctor Aguilar Camín notes that haci-
     enda owners regularly protected loyal Yaqui
     workers from that state war of extermina-
     tion against barbaric Yaqui. See Aguilar
     Camín, *Saldos de la revolución*, 18–23.

3   Oscar Chamosa has argued that attempts by
     intellectuals to collect data on indigenous
     people coincided closely with their attempts
     to eradicate that culture. See Chamosa,
     "Indigenous or Criollo: The Myth of White
     Argentina in Tucumán's Calchaquí Valley,"
     Hispanic American Historical Review 88, no.
     1 (February, 2008): 91.

4   Dawson, *Indian and Nation*, xix–xx; Clau-
     dio Lomnitz, *Deep Mexico, Silent Mexico: An
     Anthropology of Nationalism* (Minneapolis:
     University of Minnesota Press, 2001),
     73–78.

5   Luis Aboites, *La Irrigación Revolucionaria.
     México. Historia del Sistema Nacional de
     Riego del Rio Conchos Chihuahua. 1927–1938*
     (México: CIESAS, 1988), 11.

6   Vaughan, *Cultural Politics in Revolution*,
     28.

7   Guillermo Palacios, *La Pluma y El Arado:
     Los intelectuales pedagogos y la construcción
     socio-cultural del 'problema campesino' en
     México, 1930–1934* (México: El Colegio
     de México and Centro de Investigación y
     Docencia Económicas, 1999), 198–99.

8   Lewis, *Ambivalent Revolution*, 46.

9   BSEP 5, no. 6 (1926): 5–8.

10   Ibid., 5–7.

11   Dawson, *Indian and Nation*, 21.

12   Alexander Dawson, "'Wild Indians,' 'Mexi-
     can Gentlemen,' and the Lessons Learned
     in the Casa del Estudiante Indígena,
     1926–1932," *The Americas* 57, no. 3 (January
     2001): 330; Knight, *Porfirians, Liberals and
     Peasants*, 3–10. In Sonora, the Seri Indians,
     for example, had previously withstood de-
     portation and extermination campaigns at

the hands of the Mexican government and
private forces. See Thomas Bowen, "Seri,"
Handbook of the North American Indians, vol.
10: Southwest, ed. Alfonso Ortiz (Washington: Smithsonian Institution, 1983),
232–34; Spicer, *Cycles of Conquest*,107–8;
Tinker Salas, *In the Shadow of the Eagles*,
60–61; On similar campaigns against the
Yaqui Indians see Turner, *Barbarous Mexico*
and Vaughan, *Cultural Politics in Revolution*,140–43.

13   Plutarco Elías Calles, for example, argued
     that given a proper education, indigenous
     people could overcome their years of exploi-
     tation at the hands of whites and *mestizos*
     and elevate and incorporate themselves into
     the Mexican nation; see Macias Richard,
     Pensamiento político y social, 124.

14   Dawson, "From Models for the Nation to
     Model Citizens," 279–308. Although the
     Maya were seen as noble, worthy of dignity,
     and redeemable, the Mexican government,
     especially under Cárdenas, was unable to
     use *indigenismo* to advance their political
     project in the Yucatán peninsula. See Ben
     W. Fallaw, "Cárdenas and the Caste War
     that Wasn't: State Power and Indigenismo in
     Post-Revolutionary Yucatán," *The Americas*
     53, no. 4 (April 1997): 563–76, and Fallaw,
     Cárdenas Compromised; Ben Fallaw, "The
     Life and Death of Felipa Poot: Women,
     Fiction, and Cardenismo in Postrevolution-
     ary Mexico," *HAHR* 82, no. 4 (November
     2002): 645–83.

15   Rick A. López, "The India Bonita Contest
     of 1921 and the Ethnicization of Mexican
     National Culture," *HAHR* 82, no. 2 (May
     2002).

16   Dawson, "From Models for the Nation to
     Model Citizens," 282–84, and Dawson,
     "'Wild Indians', 'Mexican Gentlemen,'"
     331.

17   The reaction to the federal government's
     education program in relation to the two
     other major indigenous groups in Sonora,
     the Mayo and the Yaqui, has already been
     extensively researched, the latest works be-
     ing Vaughan, *Cultural Politics in Revolution*,
     and Bantjes, *As if Jesus Walked on Earth*.

18 Dawson, *Indian and Nation*, xxiii.

19 Ibid., 158.

20 Ibid., 161.

21 José Macillas Padilla, Bimonthly Report, September and October 1927, Chihuahua, AHSEP-ER, Box 1057, Exp. IV/162 (721.4). On previous failed attempts to force the Tarahumara into Spanish-style settlements, see D. Carleton Gajdusek, "The Sierra Tarahumara," *Geographical Review* 43:1 (January 1953): 16, and Olivia Arrieta, "Religion and Ritual among the Tarahumara Indians of Northern Mexico: Maintenance of Cultural Autonomy Through Resistance and Transformation of Colonizing Symbols," *Wicazo Sa Review* 8, no. 2 (Autumn 1992): 12–13.

22 Roberto de la Cerdasilva, "Los Tarahumaras," *Revista Mexicana de Sociología* 5, no. 3 (3rd Quarter, 1943): 403–5; Herbert Passin, "A Note on the Present Indigenous Population of Chihuahua," *American Anthropologist*, New Series, 46, no. 1, Part 1 (January–March 1944): 145–47; and John G. Kennedy, "Tesguino Complex: The Role of Beer in Tarahumara Culture," *American Anthropologist*, New Series, 65, no. 3, Part 1 (June 1963): 622. Famed anthropologist Robert M. Zingg argued that the Tarahumara population was probably closer to 40,000. Robert M. Zingg, "The Genuine and Spurious Values in Tarahumara Culture," *American Anthropologist*, New Series, 44, no. 1 (January–March 1942): 78–79.

23 Jacob Fried, "An Interpretation of Tarahumara Interpersonal Relations," *Anthropological Quarterly* 34, no. 2 (April 1962): 112.

24 Kennedy, "Tesguino Complex," 621.

25 Fried, "An Interpretation of Tarahumara Interpersonal Relations," 111.

26 Kennedy, "Tesguino Complex," 620–21.

27 José Anchieta de Gracia, Representate de la Capitanía General de la Alta y Baja Tarahumara to Plutarco Elías Calles, 6 November 1923, Exp. 27, Inv. 289, Indios Tarahumaras, FAPECFT.

28 Wasserman, *Persistent Oligarchs*.

29 BSEP 4, no. 7 (1925): 236.

30 Valentina Torres Septién, *La educación privada en México, 1903–1976* (México: El Colegio de México and Universidad Iberoamericana, 2004), 18.

31 Delfino Bazán, Extract from the Annual Report of the Director of Federal Education in Chihuahua, Corresponding to 1927, Chihuahua, AHSEP-ER, Box 1653, Exp. IV/100 (II-5)(721.4).

32 Tannenbaum, *Peace by Revolution*, 272.

33 After closing down the state-run boarding schools, the governor of Chihuahua, Jesús Antonio Almeida, asked the federal government to fund one in its place. See Almeida to Calles, 26 April 1926, OC 731-I-7, AGN; Almeida to Calles, 21 December 1925, OC 816-Ch-20, AGN; SEP to Delfino Bazán, 20 September 1926, Chihuahua, AHSEP-ER, Box 1465, Exp. IV/221 (II-3)(06).

34 José Macias Padilla to Juan Salazar, 22 February 1928, Chihuahua, AHSEP-ER, Box 19, Exp. IV/161 (IV-14)/2213; Gregorio Lozano to Juan Salazar, 2 July 1928, Chihuahua, AHSEP-ER, Box 19, Exp. IV/161 (IV-14)/2588.

35 Frances M. Slaney, "Double Baptism: Personhood and Ethnicity in the Sierra Tarahumara of Mexico," *American Ethnologist* 24, no. 2 (May, 1997): 279–80.

36 Arrieta, "Religion and Ritual among the Tarahumara," 12–17.

37 Cecilio Bustillos, Report, 17 September 1926, Chihuahua, AHSEP-ER, Box 1465, Exp. IV/243 (4)(06).

38 Indalecio Sandoval to Carlos Basauri, 20 November 1925, Chihuahua, AHSEP-ER, Box 1465, Exp. IV/221 (II-3)(06).

39 Emilio Carrasco to SEP, 14 April 1926, Chihuahua, AHSEP-ER, Box 1465, Exp. IV/221 (II-3)(06).

40 Nicolás Pérez to José Manuel Puig Casauranc, 23 October 1926, Chihuahua, AHSEP-ER, Box 1653, Exp. IV/161 (ii-5)(721.4).

41 Delegados de la Alta y Baja Tarahumara to Calles, 19 November 1925, OC 816-Ch-20, AGN.

42 Lisa Emmerich, "'To Respect and Love and Seek the Ways of White Women,' Field Matrons, the Office of Indian Affairs, and Civilization Policy, 1890–1938," Dissertation, University of Maryland, 1987, and Robert Trennert, "Educating Indian Girls at Nonreservation Boarding Schools, 1878–1920," *Western Historical Quarterly* 13, no. 3 (July 1982): 271–90.

43 Gustavo Jarquín to Ignacio Ramírez, 14 January 1926, Chihuahua, AHSEP-ER, Box 1057, Exp. IV/100 (721.4).

44 Carlos Basauri to SEP, 28 December 1925, Chihuahua, AHSEP-ER, Box 1465, Exp. IV/221 (II-3)(06).

45 Delfino Bazán to SEP, 23 December 1926, Chihuahua, AHSEP-ER, Box 1465, Exp. IV/221 (II-3)(06).

46 Salvador Varela to Delfino Bazán, 12 November 1926, Chihuahua, AHSEP-ER, Box 17, Exp. IV/161 (IV-14)/2222.

47 Delfino Bazán to SEP, 10 October 1926, Chihuahua, AHSEP-ER, Box 1637, Exp. IV/161 (721.4).

48 Delfino Bazán to SEP, 17 January 1927, Chihuahua, AHSEP-ER, Box 1637, Exp. IV/161 (721.4).

49 Ignacio Ramírez to Delfino Bazán, 8 February 1927, Chihuahua, AHSEP-ER, Box 1637, Exp. IV/161 (721.4).

50 This suggestion is similar to the practice of "outing" Native American girls adopted by the Bureau of Indian Affairs in the United States. See Eric V. Meeks, "The Tohono O'odham, Wage Labor, and Resistant Adaptation, 1900–1930," *Western Historical Quarterly* 34 (Winter 2003): 473–77; Reports of the Field Matrons, 1910–1932; Sells Indian Agency (Papago); Records of the Bureau of Indian Affairs, Record Group 75; National Archives and Records Administration – Pacific Region (Laguna Niguel) (hereafter SIA-RG75-NARA/PR/LN).

51 Delfino Bazán to Ignacio Ramírez, 7 February 1927, Chihuahua, AHSEP-ER, Box 1637, Exp. IV/161 (721.4); Salvador Varela to Ignacio Ramírez, 3 October 1927, Chihuahua, AHSEP-ER, Box 1057, Exp. IV/100 (721.4); Salvador Varela to Delfino Bazán, 19 November 1927, Chihuahua, AHSEP-ER, Box 1057, Exp. IV/162 (721.4); Loyo, "Los centros de educación indígena y su papel en el medio rural (1930–1940)," in *Educación rural e indígena en Iberoamérica*, ed. Pilar Gonzalbo Aizpuru (Mexico City: El Colegio de México, 1996).

52 H. Aizpuru to Ignacio Ramírez, 23 January, Chihuahua, AHSEP-ER, Box 26, Exp. IV/161 (IV-14)/2227; Delfino Bazán to Ignacio Ramírez, 29 March 1927, Chihuahua, AHSEP-ER, Box 26, IV/161 (IV-14)/2227.

53 Delfino Bazán, Extract from the Annual Report of the Director of Federal Education in Chihuahua, Corresponding to 1927, Chihuahua, AHSEP-ER, Box 1653, Exp. IV/100 (II-5)(721.4).

54 Salvador Varela to Delfino Bazán, 1 June 1927, Chihuahua, AHSEP-ER, Box 24, Exp. IV/161 (IV-14)/2217.

55 Cited in Allen G. Pastron, "Collective Defenses of Repression and Denial: Their Relationship to Violence among the Tarahumara Indians of Northern Mexico," *Ethos* 2, no. 4 (Winter 1974): 390; see also Jerome M. Levi, "Hidden Transcripts among the Rarámuri: Culture, Resistance, and Interethnic Relations in Northern Mexico," *American Ethnologist* 26, no. 1 (February 1999): 91.

56 Arrieta, "Religion and Ritual among the Tarahumara Indians," 11–23.

57 José Macillas, Bimonthly Report, September and October 1927, Chihuahua, AHSEP-ER, Box 1057, Exp. IV/162 (721.4).

58 Robert Zingg, *Behind the Mexican Mountains*, ed. Howard Campbell, John Peterson, and David Carmichael (Austin: University of Texas Press, 2001), 239–60; and Zingg, "The Genuine and Spurious Values in Tarahumara Culture," 78–92.

59 Efrén Ramírez, Report, 5 December 1927, Chihuahua, AHSEP-ER, Box 1057, Exp. IV/000 (IV-4)(721,4).

60 SEP officials noted problems with teachers in Naráchic, Batopilas, and Estación Creel. Some were the result of lack of training while others occurred because the areas were so remote that SEP officials could not find any teachers who wanted to live there: see Efrén Ramírez, Inspection Report, 19 September 1927, Chihuahua, AHSEP-ER, Box 24, Exp. IV/161 (IV-14)/2072; Alfredo E. Uruchurto to Juan Salazar, 24 November 1927, Chihuahua, AHSEP-ER, Box 26, Exp. IV/161 (IV-14)/2227; Juan Salazar to Alfredo E. Uruchurto, 29 November 1927, Chihuahua, AHSEP-ER, IV/161 (IV-14)/2227; El Gobernador Constl. Subst. to SEP, 11 January 1928, Chihuahua, AHSEP-ER, Box 26, IV/161 (IV-14)/2227; José Valdés Acosta to SEP, 23 December 1927, Chihuahua, AHSEP-ER, Box 23, Exp. IV/161 (IV-14)/2569.

61 SEP to Juan Salazar, 24 February 1928, Chihuahua, AHSEP-ER, Box 1653, Exp. IV/160 (II-5)(721.4).

62 Salvador Varela to Rafael Ramírez, 18 November 1929, Chihuahua, AHSEP-ER, Box 24, Exp. IV/161 (IV-14)/2218; Salvador Varela to Villagers of Agua Escondida, 22 November 1929, Chihuahua, AHSEP-ER, Box 19, Exp. IV/161 (IV-14)/2645.

63 Ramón E. Villanueva to Jesús E. Fuentes, 17 September 1929, Chihuahua, AHSEP-ER, Box 1213, Exp. IV/100.

64 Ramón E. Villanueva to Jesús E. Fuentes, 20 September 1929, Chihuahua, AHSEP-ER, Box 1213, Exp. IV/166 (721.4); Ramón E. Villanueva to Rafael Ramírez, 21 September 1929, Chihuahua, AHSEP-ER, Box 1213, Exp. IV/166 (721.4).

65 Ramón E. Villanueva to Jesús E. Fuentes, 20 September 1929, Chihuahua, AHSEP-ER, Box 1213, Exp. IV/100 (04)(IV-4)(721.4).

66 Salvador Varela to Rafael Ramírez, 22 October 1929, Chihuahua, AHSEP-ER, Box 1213, Exp. IV/100 (IV-4)(721.4).

67 Kennedy, "Tesguino Complex," 623–28.

68 Salvador Varela to Rafael Ramírez, 3 January 1930, Chihuahua, AHSEP-ER, Box 1731, Exp. IV/100 (II-5)(721.4).

69 The worldwide Depression first began to affect the Mexican economy in 1929. It resulted in a substantial drop in the value of primary products and the return of many Mexican workers who had been expelled from the United States. Although the Mexican government struggled to fund many of its programs, the Depression was not as severe in Mexico as it was in the United States. See, for example, Leslie Bethell, ed., *Mexico Since Independence* (Cambridge: Cambridge University Press, 1991), 204–5, 221, 233, 324.

70 Inspectors and community members remarked about the poor quality of teachers in the region, their complaints ranging from a teacher's "indolence … and a lack of spirit" to teachers' unwillingness even to be associated with the Tarahumara. See Abelardo de la Rosa, Monthly Report, 31 October 1931, Chihuahua, AHSEP-ER, Box 1731, Exp. IV/100 (IV-4)(721.4); Ramón Espinosa Villanueva, Inspection Report, 24 March 1930, Chihuahua, AHSEP-ER, Box 24, Exp. IV?161 (IV-14)/2217; Abelardo de la Rosa, Inspection Report, 15 March 1930, Chihuahua, AHSEP-ER, Box 26, Exp. IV/161 (IV-14)/2226; Salvador Varela to Abelardo de la Rosa, 1 April 1930, Chihuahua, AHSEP-ER, Box 1731, Exp. IV/166 (IV-4)(721.4).

71 Holguín had placed another of his nieces, Victoriana Yañez, into another nearby circuit school in La Soledad. Victoriana was less than 18 years old, had only a third-grade education, and had kicked a third of the children out of school to lighten her load after using their initial attendance to justify the school's existence to the SEP. Salvador Varela cautioned against firing Victoriana, however, because he did not think he could find anyone more qualified to take the position. See Abelardo de la Rosa to Salvador Varela, 27 March 1930, Chihuahua, AHSEP-ER, Box 19, Exp. IV/161 (IV-14)/2201; Salvador Varela to Abelardo de la Rosa, 2 April 1930, Chihuahua, AHSEP-ER, Box 19, Exp. IV/161 (IV-14)/2201.

72 Abelardo de la Rosa, Inspection Report, January 1931, Chihuahua, AHSEP-ER,

Box 13, Exp. IV/161 (IV-14)/2319; Jesús Coello, Inspection Report, 6 May 1932, Chihuahua, AHSEP-ER, Box 13, Exp. IV/161 (IV-14)/2319.

73 Ramón Espinosa Villanueva, "Supersticiones, prejuicios y tradiciones dominantes en la zona suroeste del estado de Chihuahua," 18 August 1930, Chihuahua, AHSEP-ER, Box 1731, Exp. IV/100 (IV-4)(721.4).

74 BSEP 8, no. 4 (1929): 141–49; Vidal G. Chávez to Ramón E. Villanueva, 20 May 1930, Chihuahua, AHSEP-ER, Box 24, Exp. IV/161 (IV-14)/2219.

75 Abelardo de la Rosa, Inspection Report, 10 March 1930, Chihuahua, AHSEP-ER, Box 26, Exp. IV/161 (IV-14)/2630.

76 For example, in Tenoriva an inspector discovered that the head of the police and the municipal president were working together to ferment and sell tesgüino to the Tarahumara. See Ramón Espinosa Villanueva, Monthly Report, 5 May 1930, Chihuahua, AHSEP-ER, Box 1731, Exp. IV/100 (IV-4)(721.4).

77 Ramón Espinosa Villanueva, Monthly Report, 10 March 1930, Chihuahua, AHSEP-ER, Box 1731, Exp. IV/100 (IV-4)(721.4).

78 Ramón Espinosa Villanueva, Inspection Report, 28 April 1930, Chihuahua, AHSEP-ER, Box 22, Exp. IV/161 (IV-14)/2599.

79 De la Cerdasilva, "Los Tarahumaras," 403.

80 Abelardo de la Rosa, Monthly Report, 30 June 1930, Chihuahua, AHSEP-ER, Box 1731, Exp. IV/100 (IV-4)(721.4).

81 One teacher, José Fierro Ventura, however, had a different and novel idea. He sent his second-, third-, and fourth-grade students out to visit the surrounding Tarahumara settlements on weekends in hopes of convincing children there to attend his school. See Salvador Varela to Rafael Ramírez, n.d., Chihuahua, AHSEP-ER, Box 19, Exp. IV/161 (IV-14)/2323.

82 Ramón Espinosa Villanueva, Inspection Report, 10 March 1932, Chihuahua, AHSEP-ER, Box 12, Exp. IV/161 (IV-14)/19816.

83 Ramón Espinosa Villnueva to Salvador Varela, 30 June 1930, Chihuahua, AHSEP-ER, Box 1731, Exp. IV/166 (IV-4)(721.4).

84 Ramón Espinosa Villanueva to Salvador Varela, 31 March 1930, Chihuahua, AHSEP-ER, Box 12, Exp. IV/161 (IV-14)/19816.

85 There is no evidence that the school closed, but it was never officially recognized as a boarding school. See Ramón Espinosa Villanueva, Inspection Report, 17 June 1930, Chihuahua, AHSEP-ER, Box 12, Exp. IV/161 (IV-14)/19816.

86 Abelardo de la Rosa, Monthly Report, 13 March 1930, Chihuahua, AHSEP-ER, Box 1731, Exp. IV/100 (IV-4)(721.4).

87 Salvador Varela, Visita, 31 May 1930, Chihuahua, AHSEP-ER, Box 1805, Exp. IV/100 (II-5)(721.6); Salvador Varela, General Report, 27 September 1930, Chihuahua, AHSEP-ER, Box 1805, Exp. IV/100 (II-5)(721.6).

88 For example, one inspector asked local mestizos in Bajisóchic to provide food for Tarahumara children so that they could continue attending school. Another asked the mestizos in Ciénega Prieta to give local Tarahumara families work so that they would, through exposure to mestizo culture, change their habits. See Jesús Coello, Inspection Report, 24 May 1931, Chihuahua, AHSEP-ER, Box 18, Exp. IV/161 (IV-14)/2280; Jesús Coello, Monthly Report, 1 February 1932, Chihuahua, AHSEP-ER, Box 977, Exp. IV/100.

89 J. Miguel Ceballos D., Inspection Report, 3 December 1931, Chihuahua, AHSEP-ER, Box 13, Exp. IV/161 (IV-14)/2657.

90 Primitivo Holguín to Salvador Varela, 27 June 1932, Chihuahua, AHSEP-ER, Box 19, Exp. IV/161 (IV-14)/2645; Jesús Coello, Inspection Report, 4 November 1932, Chihuahua, AHSEP-ER, Box 19, Exp. IV/161 (IV-14)/2645.

91 Ramón Espinosa Villanueva to Salvador Varela, November 1932, Chihuahua, AHSEP-ER, Box 1465, Exp. IV/161 (IV-15)(721.4)/1.

92 Lorenzo Basulto, Inspection Report, 6 May 1932, Chihuahua, AHSEP-ER, Box 15, Exp. IV/161 (IV-14)/2479.

93 Odorico García to SEP, 10 October 1932, Chihuahua, AHSEP-ER, Box 867, Exp. IV/161 (IV-2)(721.4); Luis Leony to SEP, 27 October 1932, Chihuahua, AHSEP-ER, Box 867, Exp. IV/128.1 (721.4); Salvador Varela to Luis Leony, 29 October 1932, Chihuahua, AHSEP-ER, Box 867, Exp. IV/128.1 (721.4).

94 Salvador Varela, Monthly Report, 17 February 1932, Chihuahua, AHSEP-ER, Box 867, Exp. IV/100 (04)(IV-5)(721.4).

95 Dawson, *Indian and Nation*, 34–37.

96 Salvador Varela, Annual Report, 3 September 1932, Chihuahua, AHSEP-ER, Box 867, Exp. IV/100 (04)(IV-5)(721.4).

97 José Vázquez Luna, Trimonthly Report, 1 January 1932, Chihuahua, AHSEP-ER, Box 977, Exp. IV/100 (04)(IV-5)(721.3).

98 Dawson, *Indian and Nation*, 55 and 123–24.

99 Odorico García to SEP, 10 October 1932, Chihuahua, AHSEP-ER, Box 867, Exp. IV/161 (IV-2)(721.4).

100 Salvador Varela to Rafael Ramírez, 26 January 1933, Chihuahua, AHSEP-ER, Box 1360, Exp. IV/161 (IV-2)(721.4).

101 J. Humberto Paniagua, Bimonthly Report, 4 March 1933, Chihuahua, AHSEP-ER, Box 958, Exp. IV/100 (721.4).

102 Salvador Varela, Annual Report, 3 September 1932, Chihuahua, AHSEP-ER, Box 958, Exp. IV/100 (04)(IV-5)(721.4).

103 Wilbert H. Ahern, "An Experiment Aborted: Returned Indian Students in the Indian School Service, 1881–1908," *Ethnohistory* 44, no. 2 (Spring 1997): 273 and 292.

104 J. Humberto Paniagua, Bimonthly Report, 4 March 1933, Chihuahua, AHSEP-ER, Box 958, Exp. IV/100 (721.4).

105 J. Humberto Paniagua, Monthly Report, 31 March 1933, Chihuahua, AHSEP-ER, Box 958, Exp. IV/100 (721.4).

106 J. Humberto Paniagua, Monthly Report, 30 April 1933, Chihuahua, AHSEP-ER, Box 958, Exp. IV/100 (721.4).

107 Loyo, "Los centros de educación indígena," 139.

108 J. Humberto Paniagua, Bimonthly Report, 8 January 1934, Chihuahua, AHSEP-ER, Box 958, Exp. IV/100 (721.4).

109 Jacinto Maldonado, Report on February to August, 3 October 1935, Chihuahua, AHSEP-ER, Box 1359, Exp. 220/1/19.

110 Dawson, *Indian and Nation*, 55 and 123–24.

111 Spicer, *Cycles of Conquest*, 43.

CHAPTER 4: THE SERI

1 Fernando F. Dworak to Chief of Rural Schools, 10 November 1926, Sonora, AHSEP-ER, Box 8415, Exp. 68.

2 On the "Indian problem," see Judith Friedlander, "The National Indigenist Institute of Mexico Reinvents the Indian: The Pame Example," *American Ethnologist* 13, no. 2 (May 1986): 363–67. On the construction of post-revolutionary hegemony, see Vaughan, *Cultural Politics in Revolution*, 20.

3 Population numbers range from 175 to 350. See Jack D. Forbes, "Historical Survey of the Indians of Sonora, 1821–1910," *Ethnohistory* 4, no. 4 (Autumn 1957): 350; W.J. McGee, "Expedition to Papagueria and Seriland: A Preliminary Note," *American Anthropologist* 9:3 (March 1896): 98; and Luis Arturo Gonzalez Bonilla, "Los Seris," *Revista Mexicana de Sociología* 3:2 (2nd Quarter, 1941): 94–95.

4 Robert Thompson to Governor, 31 August 1923, *Archivo Historico General del Estado de Sonora* (hereafter AHGES), Tribus/Seris, Tomo 3611.

5 Delegación de la Secretaría de Educación Pública Federal, 1923, AHGES, Tribus/Seris, Tomo 3577.

6 W.J. McGee, "The Beginning of Marriage," *American Anthropologist* 9, no. 11 (November

1896): 375. Stephen Lewis notes a similar preoccupation (that we also saw with the Tarahumara) with indigenous endogamy. SEP officials feared that refusal to interbreed meant that "civilization" through mestizaje was impossible. Nonetheless, Gonzalez Bonilla claims that Seri men often prostituted their wives to white fishermen. See Lewis, *Ambivalent Revolution*, 49, and Gonzalez Bonilla, "Los Seris," 99.

7   McGee, "Expedition to Papagueria," 95; Robert Ascher, "Ethnography for Archeology: A Case from the Seri Indians," *Ethnology* 1, no. 3 (July 1962): 361–62; and Gonzalez Bonilla, "Los Seris," 94.

8   Spicer, Cycles of Conquest, 107–8; Cynthia Radding, *Wandering People: Colonialism, Ethnic Spaces, and Ecological Frontiers in Northwestern Mexico, 1700–1850* (Durham, NC: Duke University Press, 1997), 155–56.

9   Cited in Tinker Salas, *In the Shadow of the Eagles*, 60–61.

10   Bowen, "Seri," 232–34.

11   Edward H. Davis and E. Yale Dawson, "The Savage Seris of Sonora – II," *Scientific Monthly* 60, no. 4 (1945): 263, and Gonzalez Bonilla, "Los Seris," 94.

12   Thompson's name varies in the primary documents between Roberto and Robert and between Thompson and Thomson. I have decided to adopt the most common usage, Robert Thompson.

13   Spicer, *Cycles of Conquest*, 114.

14   It is possible that Thompson had settled in Sonora as early as 1897 when a smallpox epidemic struck the Seri. See Gonzalez Bonilla, "Los Seris," 104.

15   Robert Thompson to Fernando F. Dworak, n.d., Sonora, AHSEP-ER, Box 8415, Exp. 68.

16   He called himself "el comisionado del gobierno ante la tribu seri." See Robert Thompson to Governor, 31 August 1923, AHGES, Tribus/Seris, Tomo 3611.

17   "Los Indios Seris," Robert Thompson, 26 July 1927, Sonora, AHSEP-ER, Box 8415,

Exp. 68; Aragón Pérez, *Eduación en Sonora*, 82.

18   Robert Thompson to Fernando F. Dworak, Sonora, AHSEP-ER, Box 8415, Exp. 68.

19   AHGES, Tribus/Seris, Tomo 3611 (1923).

20   Edward H. Davis and E. Yale Dawson claim that the elder Encinas put up with the Seri just like "the rodents of the rancheria." See Davis and Dawson, "The Savage Seris of Sonora – II," 262. On Pablo, see McGee, "Expedition to Papagueria," 93–94.

21   Gail Bederman, *Manliness and Civilization: A Cultural History of Gender and Race in the United States, 1880–1917* (Chicago: University of Chicago Press, 1995), 31–41; Paul Redden, *Wild West Shows* (Urbana and Chicago: University of Illinois Press, 1999); Louis S. Warren, *Buffalo Bill's America: William Cody and the Wild West Show* (New York: Vintage Books, 2005), 190–210; Michael Gonzales, "Imagining Mexico in 1910: Visions of the Patria in the Centennial Celebration in Mexico City," *Journal of Latin American Studies* 39:3 (August 2007): 512–14; López, "The India Bonita Contest," 291–328; and Rick A. López, "The Noche Mexicana and the Exhibition of Popular Arts: Two Ways of Exalting Indianness," in *The Eagle and the Virgin: Nation and Cultural Revolution in Mexico, 1920–1940*, ed. Mary Kay Vaughan and Stephen E. Lewis (Durham, NC: Duke University Press, 2006), 23–42.

22   Museo de los Seris, Ave. Mar de Cortés, Bahía de Kino, Sonora.

23   Davis and Dawson, "The Savage Seris of Sonora – II," 263–64.

24   Museo de los Seris, Ave. Mar de Cortés, Bahía de Kino, Sonora; Secretary of State to Juan Tomás, 10 February 1922, AHGES, Tribus/Seris, Tomo 3546; Secretary of State to Municipal President of Guaymas, 30 November 1922, AHGES, Tribus/Seris, Tomo 3546; Francisco Molina to Francisco Elías, 1 January 1922, AHGES, Tribus/Seris, Tomo 3546; Governor to State Treasurer, 11 December 1923, AHGES, Tribus/Seris, Tomo 3611.

25 Although the Mexican government tried to hire graduates of the Casa as teachers in their home communities, the Seri declined to send anyone to the Casa for training. On BIA practices, see Ahern, "An Experiment Aborted," 263–304, and Anne Ruggles Gere, "Indian Heart/White Man's Head: Native-American Teachers in Indian Schools, 1880–1930," *History of Education Quarterly* 45, no. 1 (Spring 2005): 38–65.

26 SEP archives have no records prior to 1926 of their involvement with the Seri. Robert Thompson to Governor, December 1923, AHGES, Tribus/Seris, Tomo 3611.

27 Governor to Robert Thompson, December 1923, AHGES, Tribus/Seris, Tomo 3611. Bay was far more interested in running his anti-Chinese campaign. See Evelyn Hu-DeHart, "Racism and the Anti-Chinese Persecution in Sonora, Mexico, 1876–1932," *Amerasia* 9, no. 2 (Fall/Winter 1982); Gerardo Renique, "Race, Region and Nation: Sonora's Anti-Chinese Racism and Mexico's Post-Revolutionary Nationalism, 1920s-1930s," in *Race and Nation in Modern Latin America*, ed. Nancy P. Appelbaum, Anne S. MacPherson, and Karin Alejandra Rosemblatt (Chapel Hill: University of North Carolina Press, 2003), 211-36.

28 Unlike many other states, Sonora was spending just as much as the federal government on education. See Puig to Director of Federal Education in Sonora, 18 December 1925, AHGES, Expediente General, Tomo 3764, and Governor to SEP, 26 November 1925, AHGES, Expediente General, Tomo 3764.

29 Puig to Governor, 15 December 1925, AHGES, Expediente General, Tomo 3764.

30 Governor to Francisco Molina, 17 September 1924, AHGES, Tribus/Seris, Tomo 3713.

31 Luis Thompson, Luis Felix, and Robert Thompson to Secretary of Government, 26 February 1925, AHGES, Tribus/Seris, Tomo 3814; Governor to General Treasurer, 27 February 1925, AHGES, Tribus/Seris, Tomo 3814.

32 Thompson's title had now morphed into "Comisionado Especial del Gobierno para Vigilar el Rancho del Carrizal y toda la Costa Frente a la Isla del Tiburón." Governor to Robert Thompson, 12 February 1925, AHGES, Tribus/Seris, Tomo 3814.

33 Robert Thompson to Governor, 21 February 1925, AHGES, Tribus/Seris, Tomo 3814.

34 Robert Thompson to Governor, 25 February 1925, AHGES, Tribus/Seris, Tomo 3814.

35 Pascual Blanco to Alejo Bay, n.d., AHGES, Tribus/Seris, Tomo 3814.

36 W.J. McGee, "Expedition to Papagueria," 96.

37 Secretary of Government to Thompson, 28 February 1925, AHGES, Tribus/Seris, Tomo 3814.

38 Robert Thompson to Secretary of Government, 2 March 1925, AHGES, Tribus/Seris, Tomo 3814.

39 Given Thompson's proclamation that he was a long-time friend of the Seri, why he would need a guide to meet up with them is unclear.

40 Robert Thompson to Secretary of Government, 2 March 1925, AHGES, Tribus/Seris, Tomo 3814; Secretary of Government to Robert Thompson, 7 March 1925, AHGES, Tribus/Seris, Tomo 3814; Thompson to Secretary of Government, 24 March 1925, AHGES, Tribus/Seris, Tomo 3814; Secretary of Government to Chief of Customs in Guaymas, 7 March 1925, AHGES, Tribus/Seris, Tomo 3814; Secretary of Government to Chief of Customs in Puerto de Guaymas, 7 March 1925, AHGES, Tribus/Seris, Tomo 3814; Secretary of Government to Chief of Customs in Altar, 7 March 1925, AHGES, Tribus/Seris, Tomo 3814; Secretary of Government to Chief of Customs in Pitiquito, 7 March 1925, AHGES, Tribus/Seris, Tomo 3814; Secretary of Government to Chief of Customs in Caborca, 7 March 1925, AHGES, Tribus/Seris, Tomo 3814.

41 Governor to Police Chief, 17 April 1925, AHGES, Tribus/Seris, Tomo 3814; Governor to Treasurer, 17 April 1925, AHGES, Tribus/Seris, Tomo 3814.

42 Luis Felix to Governor, 13 May 1925, AH-GES, Tribus/Seris, Tomo 3814.

43 William T. Hagan, "Kiowas, Comanches, and Cattlemen, 1867–1906: A Case Study of the Failure of U.S. Reservation Policy," *Pacific Historical Review* 40, no. 3 (August 1971): 333.

44 Chief of Purchasing Department to Secretary of State, 9 May 1925, AHGES, Tribus/Seris, Tomo 3814.

45 Purchasing Department to Secretary of State, 15 July 1925, AHGES, Tribus/Seris, Tomo 3814.

46 Convenio Celebrado entre el Gobierno del Estado y el Gobernador de los Seris, 4 August 1925, AHGES, Tribus/Seris, Tomo 3814.

47 Secretary of Government to Manuel Davila, 4 August 1925, AHGES, Tribus/Seris, Tomo 3814.

48 Imre Sutton, "Sovereign States and the Changing Definition of the Indian Reservation," *Geographical Review* 66, no. 3 (July 1976): 281, and Evelyn C. Adams, *American Indian Education: Government Schools and Economic Progress* (Morningside Heights, NY: King's Crown Press, 1946), 47–48.

49 By the end of 1927, the Seri's population had dropped to about 170. See Cynthia Radding, ed., *Historia General de Sonora, Tomo IV* (Hermosillo: Gobierno del Estado de Sonora, 1997), 360.

50 For example, the state government paid "Indio Herrera" 15 pesos to be tribal police officer. The federal government, as will be shown below, also began paying tribal members. See Governor to Indio Herrera, 10 November 1927, AHGES, Tribus/Seris, Tomo 82.

51 Fernando F. Dworak to SEP, 10 November 1926, Sonora, AHSEP-ER, Box 8415, Exp. 68.

52 Fernando F. Dworak to SEP, 10 November 1926, Sonora, AHSEP-ER, Box 8415, Exp. 68; SEP to Fernando F. Dworak, 24 November 1926, Sonora, AHSEP-ER, Box 8415, Exp. 68.

53 SEP to Fernando F. Dworak, 6 December 1926, Sonora, AHSEP-ER, Box 8415, Exp. 68.

54 Plutarco Elías Calles founded 'Cruz Galvez' to help educate Sonora's orphans. See Engracia Loyo, "Las Escuelas J. Cruz Gálvez: Fundación y Primeros Años (1915–1928)," *Boletín* 40 (México: Fideicomiso Archivos Plutarco Elías Calles y Fernando Torreblanca and Secreetaría de Educación Pública, 2002). School officials wrote Governor Bay asking him if what the Seri said was true and wondering if they were really in need of clothing. See 'Cruz Galvez' School for Girls to Alejo Bay, 13 December 1926, AHGES, Tribus/Seris, Tomo 88.

55 Fernando F. Dworak to SEP, 10 November 1926, Sonora, AHSEP-ER, Box 8415, Exp. 68.

56 Ibid.

57 Contract, 13 December 1926, Sonora, AHSEP-ER, Box 8415, Exp. 68.

58 Fernando F. Dworak to SEP, 22 December 1926, Sonora, AHSEP-ER, Box 8415, Exp. 68.

59 Robert Thompson to Dworak, 12 December 1926, Sonora, AHSEP-ER, Box 8415, Exp. 68.

60 The demand to simplify the curriculum also suggests that both the curriculum and Thompson's pedagogical approach, of which there are no surviving records, were inappropriate for the Seri.

61 BSEP 6, no. 3 (1927): 5–19.

62 Fernando F. Dworak to SEP, 17 February 1927, Sonora, AHSEP-ER, Box 8415, Exp. 68.

63 Fernando F. Dworak to SEP, 14 February 1927, Sonora, AHSEP-ER, Box 8446, Exp. IV/100 (04)(II-5)(721.5).

64 Ibid.

65 Ibid.

66 Ibid.

67 See, for example, Lewis, *Ambivalent Revolution*, 99–116; Dawson, *Indian and Nation*,

88–89 and 145–46; and Fallaw, *Cárdenas Compromised*, 92–5.

68   Fernando F. Dworak to SEP, 24 February 1927, Sonora, AHSEP-ER, Box 8446, Exp. IV/100 (04)(II-5)(721.5).

69   Fernando F. Dworak to SEP, 18 March 1927, Sonora, AHSEP-ER, Box 8415, Exp. 68.

70   SEP to Fernando F. Dworak, 30 March 1927, Sonora, AHSEP-ER, Box 8415, Exp. 68.

71   Alexandra Minna Stern, "Buildings, Boundaries, and Blood: Medicalization and Nation-Building on the U.S.-Mexico Border, 1910–1930, *HAHR* 79, no. 1 (February 1999); Katherine Bliss, "The Science of Redemption: Syphilis, Sexual Promiscuity, and Reformism in Revolutionary Mexico City," *HAHR* 79, no. 1 (February 1999).

72   Patience A. Schell, *Church and State Education in Revolutionary Mexico City* (Tucson: University of Arizona Press, 2003), 27.

73   Fernando F. Dworak to Thompson, 22 March 1927, Sonora, AHSEP-ER, Box 8446, Exp. IV/100 (04)(II-5)(721.5).

74   'Los Indios Seris,' Robert Thompson, 26 July 1927, Sonora, AHSEP-ER, Box 8415, Exp. 68.

75   Robert Thompson to Primitivo Alvarez, 4 August 1927, AHSEP-ER, Box 8415, Exp. 68.

76   'Los Indios Seris,' Robert Thompson, 26 July 1927, Sonora, AHSEP-ER, Box 8415, Exp. 68.

77   Tinker Salas, *In the Shadow of the Eagles*, 6 and 202–3.

78   Robert Thompson to Fernando F. Dworak, Sonora, AHSEP-ER, Box 8446, 13 August 1927, Exp. IV/000 (04)(721.5)

79   Neither Dworak nor Thompson reported an epidemic until 1928. See Fernando F. Dworak, Monthly Report (May), 15 June 1928, Sonora, AHSEP-ER, Box 8420, Exp. 1.

80   Fernando F. Dworak to SEP, 13 August 1927, Sonora, AHSEP-ER, Box 8446, Exp. IV/000 (04)(721.5).

81   Fernando F. Dworak to SEP, 28 September 1927, Sonora, AHSEP-ER, Box 8446, Exp. IV/077.1 (04)(721.5).

82   Fernando F. Dworak to SEP, 19 May 1928, Sonora, AHSEP-ER, Box 8415, Exp. 68.

83   'Los Indios Seris,' Robert Thompson, 26 July 1927, Sonora, AHSEP-ER, Box 8415, Exp. 68.

84   Mitchell Hudgins, "The White Chief: The Story of Edward H. Davis," M.A. Thesis, University of San Diego, 1987.

85   Edward H. Davis and E. Yale Dawson, "The Savage Seris of Sonora – I," *Scientific Monthly* 60, no. 3 (1945): 193.

86   Davis and Dawson, "The Savage Seris of Sonora – II," 201.

87   Cited in Fernando F. Dworak to SEP, 15 May 1928, Sonora, AHSEP-ER, Box 8415, Exp. 68. For BIA policy see E.B. Meritt, Assistant Commissioner, Bureau of Indian Affairs, to August F. Duclos, Superintendent, Colorado Indian School, William E. Thachery, Superintendent, Fort Mojave School, John J. Terrell, Inspector in Charge, San Carlos School, Wilbur F. Haygood, Superintendent, Pima School, T.F. McCormick, Superintendent, San Xavier School, November 21, 1918; Commissioner of Indian Affairs, Office of, July–December 1918; Subject Files of the Superintendent, Thomas F. McCormick; SIA-RG75-NARA/PR/LN; and Ira Jacknis, "A New Thing? The NMAI in Historical and Institutional Perspective," *American Indian Quarterly* 30, nos. 3–4 (Summer and Fall 2006): 511–42.

88   Fernando F. Dworak to SEP, 15 May 1928, Sonora, AHSEP-ER, Box 8415, Exp. 68.

89   Warren, *Buffalo Bill's America*, 190; Philip J. Deloria, *Indians in Unexpected Places* (Lawrence: University Press of Kansas, 2004), 52–108; L.G. Moses, *Wild West Shows and the Images of American Indians, 1883–1933* (Albuquerque: University of New Mexico Press, 1996); Burton Benedict, *The Anthropology of World's Fairs* (Berkeley: Scolar Press, 1983); and Erik Larson, *The Devil in the White City: Murder, Magic, and Madness*

at the Fair that Changed America (New York: Crown, 2002).

90 Hudgins, "The White Chief."

91 Warren, *Buffalo Bill's America*, 190–210.

92 Davis to Robert Thompson, n.d., Sonora, AHSEP-ER, Box 8415, Exp. 68; SEP to Dworak, 2 June 1928, Sonora, AHSEP-ER, Box 8415, Exp. 68.

93 Fernando F. Dworak to SEP, 21 July 1928, Sonora, AHSEP-ER, Box 8415, Exp. 68.

94 Ibid.

95 Fernando F. Dworak to SEP, 6 September 1928, Sonora, AHSEP-ER, Box 8415, Exp. 68.

96 Luis Arturo Romo to Fernando F. Dworak, 17 September 1928, Sonora, AHSEP-ER, Box 8415, Exp. 68.

97 Fernando F. Dworak to SEP, 9 January 1929, Sonora, AHSEP-ER, Box 8415, Exp. 68.

98 Fernando F. Dworak to SEP, 16 January 1929, Sonora, AHSEP-ER, Box 8415, Exp. 68.

99 Ramón G. Bonfil, Report, 1 November 1929, Sonora, AHSEP-ER, Box 8415, Exp. 68; Ramón G. Bonfil to SEP, Sonora, AHSEP-ER, 5 November 1929, Box 8415, Exp. 68.

100 Dawson, *Indian and Nation*, 135 and 140.

101 Spicer, *Cycles of Conquest*, 116, and Davis and Dawson, "The Savage Seris of Sonora – II," 267–68.

102 Robert Thompson to Secretary of Government, 7 August 1929, AHGES, Tribus/Seris, Tomo 82; Governor to Chico Romero, 8 July 1929, AHGES, Tribus/Seris, Tomo 82; Francisco S. Elías to State Treasurer, 9 July 1929, AHGES, Tribus/Seris, Tomo 82.

CHAPTER 5: THE TOHONO O'ODHAM

1 Winston P. Erickson, *Sharing the Desert: The Tohono O'odham in History* (Tucson: University of Arizona Press, 1994), 104–6; Bernard L. Fontana, "History of the Papago," in *Handbook of North American Indians*, vol. 10, *Southwest*, ed. Alfonzo Ortiz (Washington, D.C.: Smithsonian Institute Press, 1983): 143–45; David Rich Lewis, *Neither Wolf Nor Dog: American Indians, Environment, & Agrarian Change* (New York: Oxford University Press, 1994), 143; Bernard L. Fontana, *Of Earth and Little Rain* (Tucson: University of Arizona Press, 1989), 120.

2 Fernando F. Dworak to SEP, 25 May 1928, Sonora, AHSEP-ER, Box 8420, Exp. 6. Pablo made a far different argument when the Arizona Legislature threatened to reclaim 3.1 million acres of the Papago Reservation in 1917: "[T]he Papagos in asking for the preservation of the reservation to bounds as set aside are only asking for what they feel is due them in simple justice. They are asking for nothing except to be let alone to pursue their own way in peace without aid from the Government or anyone. In this they are more modest than the Tucson citizens who are clamoring for assistance from the Government for public buildings, land offices, etc." See Minutes of Council with Papago, 1916; Subject Files of the Superintendent, Jewell D. Martin; SIA-RG75-NARA/PR/LN.

3 Fernando F. Dworak to SEP, 25 May 1928, Sonora, AHSEP-ER, Box 8420, Exp. 6.

4 José X. Pablo to Jules Martin, 26 August 1916; Pablo, José X., Stockman; Reports of the Agency Farmers and Stockmen, 1910–1934; SIA-RG75-NARA/PR/LN.

5 For a historical parallel on the adoption of a 'play-off system' by the Choctaws, see Richard White, *The Roots of Dependency: Subsistence, Environment, and Social Change among the Choctaws, Pawnees, and Navajos* (Lincoln: University of Nebraska Press, 1983), 34–68.

6   Margaret Connell Szasz, *Education and the American Indian: The Road to Self-Determination since 1928* (Albuquerque: University of New Mexico Press, 1999), 8–15; Macías Richard, *Pensamiento político y social*, 156–57.

7   Meeks, "Wage Labor, and Resistant Adaptation," 469–89.

8   Gary Paul Nabhan, *The Desert Smells Like Rain: A Naturalist in Papago Country* (New York: North Point Press, 1982), 68–69.

9   Superintendent to Commissioner of Indian Affairs, 5 June 1920; Commissioner of Indian Affairs, Office of, January–June 1920; Subject Files of the Superintendent, Thomas F. McCormick; and Reverend Nicholas Pershl to T.F. McCormick, 12 October 1917; Commissioner of Indian Affairs, Office of, 1917; Subject Files of the Superintendent, Thomas F. McCormick; SIA-RG75-NARA/PR/LN.

10 Antonio Bustamante to Governor of Sonora, 12 December 1921, AHGES, Tribus/Papagos, Tomo 3472.

11 On one occasion, BIA officials caught Pablo and fellow member of the Papago Good Government League, Joshua Cachora, attempting to convince tribal officials to reimburse them for the costs of their official trip to BIA headquarters in Washington, D.C., when, in fact, the federal government had already paid them for the trip and for their expenses. On another occasion, Pablo asked to be reimbursed for cattle lost in Mexico. When confronted with the fact that he had lost no cattle in Mexico, he noted that he was trying to be reimbursed on behalf of others who were not literate. See Cato Sells to Jewell D. Martin, 30 March 1917; Jewell D. Martin to Cato Sells, 8 April 1917; and Jewell D. Martin to Cato Sells, 12 April 1917; Commissioner of Indian Affairs, January–June 1917; Subject Files of the Superintendent, Jewell D. Martin; and Superintendent to Commissioner of Indian Affairs, 5 December 1916; Mexican Conflict with Papagos, 1916–1917; Subject Files of the Superintendent, Jewell D. Martin; SIA-RG75-NARA/PR/LN.

12 The Catholic and Presbyterian churches competed directly with each other in their attempts to assimilate the Tohono O'odham. In 1874, Catholic nuns began instructing Tohono O'odham children at the San Xavier Mission. The Presbyterians began arriving in the late 1880s and set up a boarding school in Tucson primarily for the Tohono O'odham. In 1912 Franciscan friar Father Bonaventure Oblasser opened the first Tohono O'odham day school in Little Tucson and a regular school in Topawa. The Tohono O'odham, for their part, agreed to dig wells, donate or construct school buildings, and provide the teachers, two fourth-grade-educated tribal women. By 1916, the U.S. government had finished construction of three schools and had three more under construction; the Catholic Church had provided eight additional schools for indigenous children and the Tohono O'odham donated reservation land to the Board of Home Missions of the Presbyterian Church of the United States to construct another school. See Erickson, *Sharing the Desert*, 102; Fontana, "History of the Papago," 142–44; and E.B. Meritt, Assistant Commissioner, to the Secretary of the Interior (Through the Commissioner of the General Land Office), 20 September 1916; Land-Site for Presbyterian Mission, 1916–1917; Subject Files of the Superintendent, Jewell D. Martin; SIA-RG75-NARA/PR/LN.

13 Carl Lumholtz, *New Trails in Mexico: An Account of One Year's Exploration in North-Western Sonora, Mexico, and South-Western Arizona, 1909–1910* (Tucson: University of Arizona Press, 1990), 30.

14 Meeks, "Wage Labor, and Resistant Adaptation," 470; Lewis, *Neither Wolf Nor Dog*, 143; Fontana, *Of Earth and Little Rain*, 120; Jewell D. Martin to Commissioner of Indian Affairs, 24 July 1917; Commissioner of Indian Affairs, June–September 1917; Subject Files of the Superintendent, Jewell D. Martin; SIA-RG75-NARA/PR/LN.

15 Executive Order, February 1917; Land, 1916–1917; Subject Files of the Superintendent, Jewell D. Martin; SIA-RG75-NARA/PR/LN.

16   Thomas E. Sheridan, *Landscapes of Fraud: Mission Tumacácori, the Baca Float, and the Betrayal of the O'odham* (Tucson: University of Arizona Press, 2006), 34–38.

17   Lewis, *Neither Wolf Nor Dog*, 128–29; A.M. Philipson, Individual Weekly Report for Extension Workers, February 1934; Farmer, A.M. Philipson, 1933–1934; Reports of the Agency Farmers and Stockmen, 1910–1934; SIA-RG75-NARA/PR/LN.

18   Lewis, *Neither Wolf Nor Dog*, 123–24.

19   Meeks, "Wage Labor and Resistant Adaptation," 473–77; see also Reports of the Field Matrons, 1910–1932; SIA-RG75-NARA/PR/LN.

20   Cato Sells, Commissioner of Indian Affairs, to José X. Pablo, 29 January 1917; Pablo, José X., Stockman; Reports of the Agency Farmers and Stockmen, 1910–1934; SIA-RG75-NARA/PR/LN.

21   Cato Sells, Commissioner of Indian Affairs, to Thomas F. McCormick, Superintendent, 18 October 1919; Commissioner of Indian Affairs, Office of, July–December 1919; Subject Files of the Superintendent, Thomas F. McCormick; SIA-RG75-NARA/PR/LN; Meeks, "Wage Labor and Resistant Adaptation," 473; Erickson, *Sharing the Desert*, 93–95 and 102–3.

22   Radding, Entre el desierto y la sierra: las naciones O'odham y Teguima de Sonora, 1530–1840 (Mexico: INI and SEP, 1995), 138; Radding, Wandering Peoples, 253–54; and Sheridan, Landscapes of Fraud, 25–28.

23   Meeks, "Wage Labor and Resistant Adaptation," 473.

24   Spicer, *Cycles of Conquest*, 138.

25   Fontana, "History of the Papago," 141. The Tohono O'odham removed from their land were often forced into the army and then used against the Yaqui Indians. See Lumholtz, *New Trails in Mexico*, 75.

26   Cited in James Honey, "Policy and Politics in the Papaguería: A Twentieth-Century, Cross-Border History of the Tohono O'odham," History Honors Thesis, Stanford University, 1997, 18.

27   Mexican Conflict with Papagos, 1916–17; Subject Files of the Superintendent, Jewell D. Martin; SIA-RG75-NARA/PR/LN.

28   Erickson, *Sharing the Desert*, 111–12, and E.B. Meritt, Assistant Commissioner, to Jewell D. Martin, 5 December 1916; Commissioner of Indian Affairs, 1916; Subject Files of the Superintendent, Jewell D. Martin; SIA-RG75-NARA/PR/LN.

29   Authority, Department of the Interior, Office of Indian Affairs, Fiscal Year 1919; Land, International Boundary Between Papagos and Mexico; Subject Files of the Superintendent, Thomas F. McCormick; SIA-RG75-NARA/PR/LN.

30   José León to State Government, 27 August 1920, AHGES, Aguas/Papagos, Tomo 3411; Governor to José León, 28 August 1920.

31   José León to Governor, 21 March 1921, AHGES, Aguas/Papagos, Tomo 3411.

32   Reyes O. Carrasco to Secretary of State, Sonora, 18 April 1921, AHGES, Aguas/Papagos, Tomo 3411.

33   Antonio L. Bustamante to Governor of Sonora, 25 June 1921, and Governor to Consulate of Mexico, San Fernando, Arizona, 4 July 1921, AHGES, Aguas/Papagos, Tomo 3411;

34   Buchenau, *Plutarco Elías Calles*, 20.

35   Jesus M. Zepeda to Governor of Sonora, 3 October 1921; Mose Drachman to Governor of Sonora, 3 October 1921; Governor to Jesus M. Zepeda, 7 October 1921; Mose Drachman to Governor of Sonora, 17 October 1921; Governor to Municipal President of Altar, 24 October 1921; Municipal President of Altar to Governor, 1 November 1921; AHGES, Tribus/Papagos, Tomo 3472.

36   Antonio L. Bustamante, 12 December 1921, AHGES, Tribus/Papagos, Tomo 3472.

37   Governor to Antonio L. Bustamante, 31 December 1921, and Governor of Sonora to Comisión Nacional Agraria, 31 December 1921, AHGES, Tribus/Papagos, Tomo 3472.

38 Secretary General of Sonora to Governor of Sonora, 23 January 1922, AHGES, Tribus/Papagos, Tomo 3472.

39 José Angel Baviche, Luis Lopéz, and Antonio L. Bustamante to Governor of Sonora, 13 February 1923; Governor to José Angel Baviche, 7 April 1923; El Oficial Primero E. del D. to Lucas Segundo, Lucas Campillo, and José Ventura, 20 July 1923; Local Agrarian Commission to Governor of Sonora, 25 July 1923; José Angel Baviche and Rafael Ortiz to Governor of Sonora, 20 June 1923; AHGES, Tribus/Papagos, Tomo 3472.

40 Municipal President of Sari to Secretary of Government, 14 July 1922, and Secretary of Government to Antonio L. Bustamante, 2 March 1922; AHGES, Tribus/Papagos, Tomo 3546.

41 Raúl Hernández León, Police Commander, to don Alejo Bay, Governor, 22 April 1925, and Jesus Siqueros to Governor, 8 May 1925; AHGES, Tribus/Papagos, Tomo 3814.

42 Fontana, "History of the Papago," 141.

43 Fontana, "History of the Papago," 141; Bantjes, As if Jesus Walked on Earth, 130.

44 Lumholtz, New Trails in Mexico.

45 One of the Tohono O'odham children played a central role in the opening ceremonies of the Casa. See Lewis, Ambivalent Revolution, 61.

46 Fernando F. Dworak to SEP, 25 May 1928; Sonora, AHSEP-ER, Box 8420, Exp. 6.

47 Ibid.

48 Meeks, "Wage Labor and Resistant Adaptation," 473; Lewis, Neither Wolf Nor Dog, 126. BIA officials lauded Tohono O'odham dry-farming capabilities. See T.F. McCormick to Commissioner of Indian Affairs, October 24, 1918; Commissioner of Indian Affairs, Office of, July–December 1918; Subject Files of the Superintendent Thomas F. McCormick; SIA-RG75-NARA/PR/LN.

49 David Torres Orozco to Fernando F. Dworak, 2 June 1928, Sonora, AHSEP-ER, Box 8433, Exp. 2.

50 Bantjes, As if Jesus Walked on Earth, 13. Some BIA officials thought that the Tohono O'odham were being held back from 'civilization' by their Catholicism, but most officials believed that both the Catholic and Presbyterian missions had helped them. See Annual Reports, Narrative and Statistical, 1925; Subject Files of the Superintendent, Thomas F. McCormick; SIA-RG75-NARA/PR/LN.

51 Lewis, Neither Wolf Nor Dog, 135; Superintendent to Commissioner of Indian Affairs, 24 July 1917; Commissioner of Indian Affairs, June–September 1917; Subject Files of the Superintendent, Jewell D. Martin; and Father Bonaventure Oblasser to Jewell D. Martin, 1 August 1916; Education: Catholic Mission Day Schools; Subject Files of the Superintendent, Jewell D. Martin; SIA-RG75-NARA/PR/LN.

52 David Torres Orozco to Fernando F. Dworak, 15 June 1928, Sonora, AHSEP-ER, Box 8433, Exp. 2.

53 T.F. McCormick to Malcolm McDowell, Secretary, 12 April 1922; Board of Indian Commissioners; Subject Files of the Superintendent, Thomas F. McCormick; SIA-RG75-NARA/PR/LN.

54 U.S. officials, however, had a different view. In spite of the drilling of 29 wells and the grant of 3.1 million acres of land (of which some 17,500 acres were arable), by the end of the 1920s only 850 of the 5,000 Tohono O'odham were engaged in agriculture.

55 David Torres Orozco to Fernando F. Dworak, 15 June 1928, Sonora, AHSEP-ER, Box 8433, Exp. 2.

56 Fernando F. Dworak to SEP, 5 June 1928, Sonora, AHSEP-ER, Box 8420, Exp. 6.

57 Gustavo A. Serrano to Ezequiel Padilla, 18 July 1929, Sonora, AHSEP-ER, Box 8420, Exp. 6.

58 Meeks, "Wage Labor and Resistant Adaptation," 473.

59 Gustavo A. Serrano to Ezequiel Padilla, Sonora, 18 July 1929, AHSEP-ER, Box 8420, Exp. 6.

60 Ramón G. Bonfil to SEP, Sonora, 5 November 1929, AHSEP-ER, Box 8420, Exp. 6.

61 Ramón Reyes, Annual Report, August 1932, Sonora, AHSEP-ER, Box 8433, Exp. 4.

62 Dip. Fernando P. Serrano, Com. Vicente Ochoa, Com. Anselmo Figueroa, Insp. de Caza y Pesca Ygnacio Mendoza, Prof. Insp. Ramón R. Reyes, Report, 2 February 1932, Sonora, AHSEP-ER, Box 8433, Exp. 4.

63 Proposal – Pozo Verde, Municipio Saric, Pápago, 31 August 1932, Sonora, AHSEP-ER, Box 8415, Exp. IV/161 (IV-14)/19194.

64 Ramón R. Reyes, Special Report, 12 December 1932, Sonora, AHSEP-ER, Box 8415, Exp. IV/161 (IV-14)/19194.

65 Rafael Ramírez to Ramón R. Reyes, 4 October 1932, Sonora, AHSEP-ER, Box 8433, Exp. IV/100 (04)(IV-4)(721.5).

66 Elpidio López to SEP, 9 January 1933, Sonora, AHSEP-ER, Box 8415, Exp. IV/161 (IV-14)/19141.

67 Ramón R. Reyes, Inspection Report, 25 February 1933, Sonora, AHSEP-ER, Box 8415, Exp. IV/161 (IV-14)/19141.

68 Ramón R. Reyes, 23 February 1933, Sonora, AHSEP-ER, Box 8433, Exp. 4.

69 Cited in Vaughan, *Cultural Politics in Revolution*, 57.

70 Elpidio López, Monthly Report, 25 March 1933, Sonora, AHSEP-ER, Box 8446, Exp. 21.

71 Ahern, "An Experiment Aborted," and Ruggles Gere, "Indian Heart/White Man's Head."

72 According to BIA officials, the average Tohono O'odham could earn up to $90 per year collecting wood and selling it in Tucson. See Annual Report, Statistical, 1917; Subject Files of the Superintendent, Jewell D. Martin; SIA-RG75-NARA/PR/LN.

73 Erickson, *Sharing the Desert*, 123–25.

74 Janette Woodruff, Outing Matron, to E.S. Stewart, Superintendent, June 30, 1928; Field Matron's Weekly Reports, Janette Woodruff, 1927–1929; Reports of the Field Matrons, 1910–1932; SIA-RG75-NARA/PR/LN.

75 Elpidio López, Monthly Report, 25 March 1933, Sonora, AHSEP-ER, Box 8446, Exp. 21.

76 Carlos Soto V., Municipal President, Magdalena, to Rodolfo Elías Calles, Governor, 19 February 1932, AHGES, Fondo Ejecutivo / Cultos y Templos, 1932–1938, Caja 1, Tomo 1, Expediente 4.

77 Spicer, *Cycles of Conquest*, 139; Bantjes, *As if Jesus Walked on Earth*, 13.

78 Rodolfo Elías Calles to Plutarco Elías Calles, FPEC, Exp. 4: Elías Calles Chacon, Rodolfo, leg. 19/24, fojas 957–58, "Inv. 1733; Vaughan, *Cultural Politics in Revolution*, 57; and Rodolfo Elías Calles to Carlos Soto V., 12 September 1932, AHGES, Fondo Ejecutivo/Cultos y Templos, 1932–1938, Caja 1, Tomo 1, Expediente 4.

79 Rodolfo Elías Calles Chacon, FPEC, Exp. 4, Leg. 19/24, Fojas 956 and 972, Inv. 1733. Also see Rodríguez, Abelardo L. (Gral.), FPEC, Exp. 189, Leg. 11/11, Fojas 540–41, Inv. 5010.

80 Bantjes, *As if Jesus Walked on Earth*, 6–15; Vaughan, *Cultural Politics in Revolution*, 62.

81 Thomas E. Sheridan, "The O'odham (Pimas and Papagos): The World Would Burn Without Rain," *Paths of Life: American Indians of the Southwest and Northern Mexico*, ed. Thomas E. Sheridan and Nancy J. Parezo (Tucson: University of Arizona Press, 1996), 118–20.

82 Ernesto Camou Healy, *Historia General de Sonora: Historia Contemporánea de Sonora, 1929–1984* (Hermosillo: Colegio de Sonora, 1988), 138–40.

83 Sheridan, *Landscapes of Fraud*, 237; Superintendent to Thomas Childs, 24 March 1917; Law and Order, 1916–1917; Subject Files of the Superintendent, Jewell D. Martin; A.M. Philipson to T.F. McCormick, 26 June 1924; A.M. Philipson to T.F. McCormick, 3 September 1924; Farmer, A.M. Philipson, 1924–1926; Reports of the Agency Farmers

and Stockmen, 1910–1934; "No Violation of Indian Rights is Asked, but only Fair Play," El Paso Herald, Editorial Page, 18 January 1917; Subject ·Files of the Superintendent, Jewell D. Martin; E.B. Meritt, Assistant Commissioner, to Thomas F. McCormick, 19 January 1918; Commissioner of Indian Affairs, Office of, January–July 1918; Subject Files of the Superintendent, Thomas F. McCormick; Land, Bowie Report, Volume I and Volume II; Irrigation, Superintendent, A.L. Wathen, Subject Files of the Superintendent, Thomas F. McCormick; SIA-RG75-NARA/PR/LN.

84 Miguel Espinosa R., Monthly Report, 10 November 1934, Sonora, AHSEP-ER, Box 8433, Exp. 20.

85 A.M. Philipson, Weekly Report of Farm Agent, 14 October 1933; Farmer, A.M. Philipson 1933–1934; Reports of the Agency Farmers and Stockmen, 1910–1934; SIA-RG75-NARA/PR/LN.

86 Spicer, Cycles of Conquest, 144.

87 Juan Antony Kachica to Commissioner of Sonoyta, 30 June 1939, AHGES, Tribus/Papagos, Tomo 214.4.

CHAPTER 6: FRONTIER SCHOOLS

1 Although 500,000 people of Mexican descent, both U.S. citizens and non-U.S. citizens, would eventually be forced across the border into Mexico, most of the early refugees to return to Mexico did so because they lost their jobs. After the initial wave of returnees slowed to a trickle, a "decentralized but vigorous campaign" forced the rest across the boarder (almost none were legally deported). Changes in U.S. visa policy meant that almost none of them would be able to return legally to the United States after the end of the Great Depression. See Josiah McConnell Heyman, Life and Labor on the Border: Working People of Northeastern Sonora, Mexico, 1886–1986 (Tucson: University of Arizona Press, 1991), 33–35.

2 Josefina Zoraida Vázquez, Nacionalismo y educación en México (México: El Colegio de México, 2005), 151–224; Mary Kay Vaughan and Stephen E. Lewis, eds., The Eagle and the Virgin: Nation and Cultural Revolution in Mexico, 1920–1940 (Durham, NC: Duke University Press, 2006); William H. Beezely, Cheryl English Martin, and William E. French, eds., Rituals of Rule, Rituals of Resistance: Public Celebrations and Popular Culture in Mexico (Lanham, MD: Rowman & Littlefield, 1994); Vaughan, Cultural Politics in Revolution; Lewis, Ambivalent Revolution; and Bantjes, As if Jesus Walked on Earth.

3 Engracia Loyo, "Las escuelas fronterizas en México, (1930–1940): un esfuerzo a favor de la unidad nacional," XII Congress of Mexican, United States, and Canadian Historians, Vancouver, British Columbia, October 2006.

4 Relación general de palabras incorrectas más usadas en la frontera, Profesora Elisa Dosamantes, n.d., Chihuahua, AHSEP-ER, Box 1360, Exp. Iv/180 (IV-16)(721.4).

5 When discussing frontier I mean that which "describes both a zone and a process, an interaction between two or more different cultures." See Sarah Deutsch, No Separate Refuge: Culture, Class, and Gender on an Anglo-Hispanic Frontier in the American Southwest, 1880–1940 (New York: Oxford University Press, 1987), 10.

6 For example, William Walker and a number of filibusters invaded Baja California in 1853 and declared it an independent country before being overwhelmed by Mexican forces and surrendering. In 1857, Henry Crabb and 100 men attacked Sonora in hopes that the state would later be annexed by U.S. officials as Texas was. Other less well-known, and less successful, filibusters continued throughout the Porfiriato (1876–1911). See Oscar J. Martínez, Troublesome Border (Tucson: University of Arizona Press, 1988), 38–47.

7 Knight, Counter-revolution and Reconstruction, 139. See also Andrés Reséndez, Changing National Identities at the Frontier: Texas

and *New Mexico, 1800–1850* (Cambridge: Cambridge University Press, 2005); Joseph E. Chance, *José María de Jesús Carvajal: The Life and Times of a Mexican Revolutionary* (San Antonio: Trinity University Press, 2006).

8   For an in-depth account of both U.S. and Mexican responses to the invasion see Knight, *Counter-revolution and Reconstruction*, 155–62.

9   U.S. Senate, *Investigation of Mexican Affairs*, 3 (Washington, D.C.: U.S. Government Printing Office, 1920), 3327–3381.

10 Tinker Salas, *In the Shadow of the Eagles*, 173.

11 Knight, "The United States and the Mexican Peasantry," 40.

12 Cited in Loyo, *Gobiernos revolucionarios*, 217.

13 BSEP 8, no. 8 (1929): 63.

14 BSEP 8, nos. 9–11 (1929): 49–50.

15 BSEP 9, no. 6 (1930): 9. For details on the SEP's educational works on Mexico's southern border during this time period, see Lewis, *Ambivalent Revolution*, 65–116.

16 BSEP 9, nos. 1–3 (1930): 21–22.

17 BSEP 9, nos. 9–10 (1930): 37–38.

18 Ramón Méndez, Jefe del Departamento, to Rafael Ramírez, 7 January 1930, Coahuila, AHSEP-ER, Box 32, Exp. IV/161 (IV-12)/132.

19 Ramón Méndez, Jefe del Departmento, to Rafael Ramírez, 13 January 1930, Coahuila, AHSEP-ER, Box 32, Exp. IV/161 (IV-12)/132.

20 Ramón Méndez, Jefe del Departmento, to Rafael Ramirez, 10 February 1930, Coahuila, AHSEP-ER, Box 32, Exp. IV/161 (IV-12)/132.

21 Rafael Castro, Monthly Reports, 28 February 1930 and 2 June 1930, Coahuila, AHSEP-ER, Box 20, Exp. IV/161 (IV-12)/134.

22 When Nazario S. Ortiz finished his term in office as governor in 1934, he went into business selling foodstuffs to the federal government. Nazario S. Ortiz Garza, FAPECFT, Exp. 32, Leg. 3/3, Inv. 4220.

23 Rafael Ramírez to Jefe del Departmento, 21 February 1930, Coahuila, AHSEP-ER, Box 32, Exp. IV/161 (IV-12)/132.

24 Schell, *Church and State Education*, 132.

25 Rafael Castro, Monthly Report, 2 June 1930, Coahuila, AHSEP-ER, Box 20, Exp. IV/161 (IV-12)/134.

26 Ramón Méndez, Monthly Report, 31 May 1930, Coahuila, AHSEP-ER, Box 6037, Exp. IV/100.

27 Inocente M. Hernández, Monthly Report, 30 June 1930, Coahuila, AHSEP-ER, Box 6037, Exp. IV/100.

28 Rafael Castro, Inspection Report, 24 May 1930, Coahuila, AHSEP-ER, Box 20, Exp. IV/161 (IV-12)/134.

29 Rafael Castro, Inspection Report, 5 December 1930, Coahuila, AHSEP-ER, Box 52, Exp. IV/161 (IV-14)/714.

30 Rafael Castro, Inspection Report, 24 March 1931, Coahuila, AHSEP-ER, Box 31, Exp. IV/161 (IV-14)/511.

31 According to education officials, colonists were those settlers who already had the necessary capital to settle without the support of the government, while ejidatarios were those settlers who lacked the necessary resources. See Rafael Castro, Monthly Report, 2 January 1934, Coahuila, AHSEP-ER, Box 6039, Exp. IV/100. For further information on the reneging on provisional land grants in the interests of greater economic output in post-revolutionary Mexico, see Hall, "Alvaro Obregón and the Politics of Mexican Land Reform," 213–38.

32 Rafael Castro, Inspection Report, 21 May 1931, Coahuila, AHSEP-ER, Box 31, Exp. IV/161 (IV-14)/602; Rafael Castro, Inspection Report, 8 January 1931, Coahuila, AHSEP-ER, Box 51, Exp. IV/161 (IV-14)/606.

33 Jefe del Departamento, Report, 4 November 1932, Coahuila, AHSEP-ER, Box 31, Exp. IV/161 (IV-14)/563.

34 Jefe del Departamento, Reports, 13 November 1931 and 25 November 1932, Coahuila, AHSEP-ER, Box 55, Exp. IV/161 (IV-14)/632.

35 Rafael Castro, Monthly Report, 4 November 1933, Coahuila, AHSEP-ER, Box 6039, Exp. IV-100.

36 Rafael Castro, Inspection Report, 20 June 1933, Coahuila, AHSEP-ER, Box 51, Exp. IV/161 (IV-14)/697.

37 J. Alcázar Robledo, Inspection Report, 26 September 1931, Coahuila, AHSEP-ER, Box 51, Exp. IV/161 (IV-14)/606.

38 Rafael Castro, Monthly Report, 31 January 1932, Coahuila, AHSEP-ER, Box 24, Exp. IV/161 (IV-14)/762.

39 Nazario S. Ortiz Garza, FAPECFT, Exp. 32, Leg. 2/3, Fojas 93–94 and 100–101, Inv. 4220.

40 G. Elías to Secretario de Gobernación, 16 July 1929; Marcos de León, El Administrador (in Villa Acuña) to Director de Aduanas, 29 July 1929; Felipe Canales, Departamento de Gobernacion, to Gobernador del Estado de Coahuila, 13 August 1929; Municipal President of Villa Acuña to Gobernacion, 12 August 1929; G. Elías (Aduana in Villa Acuña) to Secretario de Gobernación, 1 November 1929; El Comandante J. del Resguardo, Alejandro Bernal to Administrador de la Aduana, 2 October 1929; Manuel Collado, Dept. de Gobernación, to Gobernador del Estado, 12 November 1929; G. Elías to Administrador de la Aduana de Villa Acuña, 21 November 1929; 2.015.3(3)2 Casas Asignaciones, AGN – Dirreción General de Gobierno – Ramo Gobernación.

41 Rafael Castro, Monthly Report, 30 April 1932, Coahuila, AHSEP-ER, Box 24, Exp. IV/161 (IV-14)/762.

42 Rafael Castro, Monthly Report, 3 February 1934, Coahuila, AHSEP-ER, Box 6039, Exp. IV/100.

43 Abraham Arellano, Monthly Report, 31 December 1932, Coahuila, AHSEP-ER, Box 6039, Exp. IV/100.

44 Rafael Castro, Inspection Report, 25 November 1932, Coahuila, AHSEP-ER, Box 52, Exp. IV/161 (IV-14)/701.

45 Maurilio P. Nañez, Director of Federal Education, to SEP, 16 February 1933, Coahuila, AHSEP-ER, Box 32, Exp. IV/161 (IV-12)/132.

46 Eliseo Ruiz Vadillo to the President of XETN, 6 March 1933, Coahuila, AHSEP-ER, Box 32, Exp. IV/161 (IV-12)/132.

47 Maurilio P. Nañez to Rafael Castro, 17 April 1933, Coahuila, AHSEP-ER, Box 32, Exp. IV/161 (IV-12)/132.

48 Fabian García R. to Maurilio P. Nañez, 20 April 1933, Coahuila, AHSEP-ER, Box 32, Exp. IV/161 (IV-12)/132.

49 Fabian García, Monthly Report, 30 April 1933, Coahuila, AHSEP-ER, Box 32, Exp. IV/161 (IV-12)/132.

50 Gobernador Constitucional del Estado to Narciso Bassols, 29 January 1933, Coahuila, AHSEP-ER, Box 37, Exp. IV/161 (IV-12)/140. SEP officials had considered but been unable to open a frontier school in Villa Acuña in 1930. See Rafael Castro, Monthly Report, 2 June 1930, Coahuila, AHSEP-ER, Box 20, Exp. IV/161 (IV-12)/134.

51 Maurilio P. Nanez to SEP, 1 February 1933, Coahuila, AHSEP-ER, Box 37, Exp. IV/161 (IV-12)/140.

52 Rafael Castro, Monthly Report, 1 June 1933, Coahuila, AHSEP-ER, Box 52, Exp. IV/161 (IV-14)/727.

53 Rafael Castro, Monthly Report, 31 January 1933, Coahuila, AHSEP-ER, Box 6039, Exp. IV/100.

54 Micaela Zuñiga R., Bimonthly Report, 24 December 1934, Coahuila, AHSEP-ER, Box 37, Exp. IV/161 (IV-12)/140.

55 Micaela Zuñiga R. Annual Report 1934–1935, 30 June 1935, Coahuila, AHSEP-ER, Box 37, Exp. IV/161 (IV-12)/140.

56 Rafael Castro, Monthly Report, 1 March 1933, Coahuila, AHSEP-ER, Box 52, Exp. IV/161 (IV-14)/727.

57 Rafael Castro, Monthly Report, 3 April 1933, Coahuila, AHSEP-ER, Box 52, Exp. IV/161 (IV-14)/727.

58 Rafael Castro, Monthly Report, 4 May 1933, Coahuila, AHSEP-ER, Box 52, Exp. IV/161 (IV-14)/727.

59 Rafael Castro, Monthly Report, 3 February 1934, Coahuila, AHSEP-ER, Box 6039, Exp. IV/100.

60 Rafael Castro, Bimonthly Report, 5 March 1935, Coahuila, AHSEP-ER, Box 6039, Exp. IV/100.

61 Rafael Castro to Maurilio P. Nañez, 24 June 1935, Coahuila, AHSEP-ER, Box 6034, Exp. 1.

62 Ibid.

63 Lawrence D. Taylor, "The Battle of Ciudad Juárez: Death Knell of the Porfirian Regime in Mexico," *New Mexico Historical Review* 74, no. 2 (April 1999): 181.

64 "Protestan los Padres de Familia de C. Juárez," *El Mexicano del Norte*, p. 4, Chihuahua, AHSEP-ER, Box 936, Exp. IV [082].

65 Linda B. Hall and Don M. Coerver, *Revolution on the Border: The United States and Mexico, 1910–1920* (Albuquerque: University of New Mexico Press, 1988), 8.

66 James R. Sheffield, U.S. Ambassador, to Aáron Saenz, Secretario de Relaciones Exteriores, 7 February 1927, 2.015.4.(1-4)-1, Caja 3, Bebidas Embriagantes (Cantinas), AGN – Dirrección General de Gobierno – Ramo Gobernación.

67 Salvador Varela to Rafael Ramírez, 26 November 1929, Chihuahua, AHSEP-ER, Box 57, Exp. IV/161 (IV-12)/221; Wasserman, *Persistent Oligarchs*, 57.

68 Alfredo G. Basurto, Informe General del Instituto Extraordinario de Ciudad Juárez, 4 August 1934, Chihuahua, AHSEP-ER, Box 1079, Exp. IV/203.7.

69 Wasserman, *Persistent Oligarchs*, 56–60.

70 Buchenau, *Plutarco Elías Calles*, 31–32; Loyo, "Las Escuelas J. Cruz Gálvez," 6–7.

71 Salvador Varela, Report, 29 November 1929, Chihuahua, AHSEP-ER, Box 1653, Exp. IV/000 (II-5)(721.5); Ramón Espinosa Villanueva, Monthly Report, 10 April 1933, Chihuahua, AHSEP-ER, Box 860, Exp. IV/100 (04)(IV-4)(721.4).

72 Blasa S. de Fernandez to President of Mexico, 30 August 1928; F. Orozco, Substitute Governor of Chihuahua, to Secretario de Gobernación, 25 September 1928; Lic. E. Padilla, Procurador General, to Secretario de Gobernación, 24 October 1928; and Ignacio Dosamantes to Emilio Portes Gil, 10 November 1928; 2.015.4(6)3 Bebidas Embriagantes (Cantinas), AGN – Dirreción General de Gobierno – Ramo Gobernación.

73 J.Reyes Pimentel, Reports, 4 April 1930, 26 February 1930, 15 March 1930, 23 July 1930, Chihuahua, AHSEP-ER, Box 19, Exp. IV/161 (IV-14)/2576.

74 BSEP 8, no. 4 (1929): 141–49.

75 J. Reyes Pimentel, Reports, 4 April 1930, 26 February 1930, 15 March 1930, 23 July 1930, Chihuahua, AHSEP-ER, Box 19, Exp. IV/161 (IV-14)/2576.

76 Ramón Espinosa Villanueva, Inspection Reports, 19 May 1931 and 30 April 1932, Chihuahua, AHSEP-ER, Box 19, Exp. IV/161 (IV-14)/2576.

77 Wasserman, *Persistent Oligarchs*, 58.

78 J. Reyes Pimentel, Monthly Report, 24 December 1929, Chihuahua, AHSEP-ER, Box 1213, Exp. IV/100 (IV-4)(721.4).

79 Salvador Varela to Rafael Ramírez, 26 November 1929, Chihuahua, AHSEP-ER, Box 57, Exp. IV/161 (IV-12)/221.

80 Salvador Varela, Report, 22 November 1929, Chihuahua, AHSEP-ER, Box 1653, Exp. IV/000 (II-5)(721.5).

81 Various Parents to Rafael Ramírez, 24 January 1930, Chihuahua, AHSEP-ER, Box 57, Exp. IV/161 (IV-12)/215.

82 Rafael Ramírez to Jefe del Departmento de Administrativo Edificio, 19 January 1932, Chihuahua, AHSEP-ER, Box 57, Exp. IV/161 (IV-12)/215.

83 Ramón Espinosa Villanueva to the SEP, 22 August 1933, Chihuahua, AHSEP-ER, Box 57, Exp. IV/161 (IV-12)/215.

84 Ramón Espinosa Villanueva, Inspection Reports, 26 January 1932, 14 November 1932, 16 January 1933, 20 June 1933, and 17 April 1934, Chihuahua, AHSEP-ER, Box 57, Exp. IV/161 (IV-12)/215. The radio proved to be less than useful for educational purposes as the SEP's radio signal was drown out by the more powerful U.S. signals from across the border. See Eduardo Zarza to Rafael Ramírez, 17 April 1934, Chihuahua, AHSEP-ER, Box 1079, Exp. IV/354.2.

85 Daniel M. Perea, President of the Confederation of Parents and Teachers, to SEP, 28 June 1933, Chihuahua, AHSEP-ER, Box 936, Exp. IV/082/1561/7.

86 M. Campos, E.E. Sada and others to Governor Rodrigo M. Quevedo, n.d. (but received on 15 March 1933), 2.015.4(6)1 Bebidas Embriagantes (Cantinas), AGN – Dirreción General de Gobierno – Ramo Gobernación; Wasserman, *Persistent Oligarchs*, 56–58.

87 Parents of Ciudad Juárez to Rafael Ramírez, 24 August 1933, Chihuahua, AHSEP-ER, Box 936, Exp. IV/082/561/7.

88 Boylan, "Gendering the Faith and Altering the Nation," 211.

89 Ramón Espinosa Villanueva to D. Eduardo Azarza, 8 February 1934, Chihuahua, AHSEP-ER, Box 1057, Exp. IV/100.

90 D. Pedro Moreno, Bimonthly Report, November and December 1934, Chihuahua, AHSEP-ER, Box 1057, Exp. IV/100; Alfredo G. Basurto, Informe General del Instituto Extraordinario de Ciudad Juárez, 4 August 1934, Chihuahua, AHSEP-ER, Box 1079, Exp. IV/203.7.

91 Bantjes, *As If Jesus Walked on Earth*, 19.

92 Ramón Espinosa Villanueva to SEP, 9 January 1935, Chihuahua, AHSEP-ER, Box 5736, Exp. 328/11.

93 Alfredo G. Basurto, Informe de la Visita Practicada a la "AOY School" de El Paso, Texas, 5 June 1934, Box 1079, Exp. IV/203.7.

94 Celso Flores Zamora to the Director de Educación Federal, 16 May 1935, Chihuahua, AHSEP-ER, Box 1360, Exp. IV/161 (IV-2)(721.4).

95 Ramón Espinosa Villanueva to the Director de Educación Federal, 27 July 1935, Chihuahua, AHSEP-ER, Box 1360, Exp. IV/161 (IV-2)(721.4).

96 Jesús Coello to the Departmento de Escuelas Rurales, 31 October 1935, Chihuahua, AHSEP-ER, Box 1333, Exp. IV/100 (04)(IV-4)(721.4).

97 Sindical de Obreros Industriales de C. Juárez to SEP, 14 February 1935, Chihuahua, AHSEP-ER, Box 5736, Exp. 328/11; Gran Liga Textil Socialista to SEP, 19 February 1935, Chihuahua, AHSEP-ER, Box 5736, Exp. 328/11; Bloque de Estudiantes Socialistre, Escuela de Agricultura, C. Juárez to Licenciado Ignacio García Tellez, 12 April 1935, Chihuahua, AHSEP-ER, Box 867, Exp. IV/161 (IV-4)(721.4); Ramón Espinosa Villanueva, Bimonthly Report, 9 January 1936, Chihuahua, AHSEP-ER, Box 867, Exp. IV/100 (04)(IV-4)(721.4).

98 Sintesis de Carta de Inspector Alfonso G. Alanis, 11 September 1935, Chihuahua, AHSEP-ER, Box 6041, Exp. IV/166 (IV-6)(721.3).

99 Ramón Espinosa Villanueva, Bimonthly Report, 30 April 1935, Chihuahua, AHSEP-ER, Box 867, Exp. IV/100 (04)(IV-4)(721.4).

100 Ramón Espinosa Villanueva to Jacinto Maldonado, 20 July 1935, Chihuahua, AHSEP-ER, Box 867, Exp. IV/100 (04)(IV-4)(721.4).

101 Tinker Salas, *In the Shadow of the Eagles*, 152.

102 Quote from Hall and Coerver, *Revolution on the Border*, 31–32; Tinker Salas, *In the Shadow of the Eagles*, 6.

103 Tinker Salas, *In the Shadow of the Eagles*, 6 and 202–3.

104 F.F. Dworak to the Jefe del Departamento de Escuelas Rurales, n.d., Sonora, AHSEP-ER, Box 8420, Exp. 12.

105 Rosalío E. Moreno, Monthly Report, September 1928, Sonora, AHSEP-ER, Box 8420, Exp. 12.

106 Rosalío E. Moreno, Monthly Report, October 1928, Sonora, AHSEP-ER, Box 8420, Exp. 12.

107 Rosalío E. Moreno, Monthly Report, January 1929, Sonora, AHSEP-ER, Box 8420, Exp. 12.

108 Rosalío E. Moreno, Monthly Report, February 1929, Sonora, AHSEP-ER, Box 8420, Exp. 12.

109 Fernando F. Dworak, Monthly Report, March 1929, Sonora, AHSEP-ER, Box 8420, Exp. 1.

110 Rosalío E. Moreno, Monthly Report, March 1929, Sonora, AHSEP-ER, Box 8420, Exp. 12.

111 Alfonso Acosta V., Monthly Report, May 1930, Sonora, AHSEP-ER, Box 8420, Exp. 12.

112 Agapito Constantino, Monthly Report, October 1930, Sonora, AHSEP-ER, Box 8420, Exp. 12.

113 Ramón G. Bonfil, Memorandum, Sonora, AHSEP-ER, Box 8446, Exp. 20.

114 Elpidio López, Annual Report, Sonora, AHSEP-ER, Box 8446, Exp. 20.

115 Elpidio López, Monthly Report, Sonora, AHSEP-ER, Box 8446, Exp. 21; Elpidio López, Annual Report 1933–1934, Sonora, AHSEP-ER, Box 8420, Exp. 12.

116 Rodolfo Elías Calles Chacon, FAPECFT, Exp. 4, Leg. 13/24, Fojas 663–706, Inv. 1733; Juventino Espinosa, General, FAPECFT, Exp. 67, Leg. 1, Fojas 4–7, Inv. 1898.

117 See, Fondo Ejecutivo, Cultos y Templos, 1932–1938, AHGES, Box 1; Bantjes, *As if Jesus Walked on Earth*, 10–15.

CONCLUSION

1 Palacios, *La Pluma y el Arado*, 178–86; Alan Knight, "Peasants into Patriots: Thoughts on the Making of the Mexican Nation," *Mexican Studies/Estudios Mexicanos*, 10, no. 1 (1994): 135; Vaughan, *Cultural Politics in Revolution*, 4 and 40–44; Bantjes, *As If Jesus Walked on Earth*, 6–10; Loyo, *Gobiernos Revolucionarios*, 225.

2 Loyo, "Los mecanismos," 116.

3 *Memoria* (1928): 13; *Mensajes presidenciales*, 261–62; Loyo, "Los mecanismos," 121.

4 Dawson, *Indian Nation*, 155.

5 Elsie Rockwell, "Reforma constitucional y controversias locales: la eduación socialista en Tlaxcala, 1935–1936," in *Escuela y sociedad en el periodo cardenista*, ed. Susana Quintanilla and Mary Kay Vaughan (México: Fondo de Cultura Económica, 1997), 196–228; Vaughan, *Cultural Politics in Revolution*, 163–88 and 65; Lewis, *Ambivalent Revolution*, 194–201.

6 Lewis, *Ambivalent Revolution*, 194–200.

7 Vaughan, *Cultural Politics in Revolution*, 20.

8 Shelley Bowen Hatfield, *Chasing Shadows: Apaches and Yaquis Along the United States–Mexico Border, 1876–1911* (Albuquerque: University of New Mexico Press, 1998), 7 and 12.

9 Blasa S. de Fernandez to President of Mexico, 30 August 1928; 2.015.4(6)3 Bebidas Embriagantes (Cantinas), AGN – Dirreción General de Gobierno – Ramo Gobernación.

10 Sáenz would give up on the simple assimilation of indigenous people with the failure of his experiments with the Tarascan Indians in 1932. See Dawson, *Indian and Nation*, 30–33.

11 Palacios, *La Pluma y el Arado*, 86–92; Vaughan, *Cultural Politics in Revolution*, 34–35; Bantjes, *As If Jesus Walked on Earth*, 6–15; Becker, *Setting the Virgin on Fire*; Lewis, *Ambivalent Revolution*, 67–85.

12   Matthew Butler, "The 'Liberal' Cristero: Ladislao Molina and the *Cristero* Rebellion in Michoacán, 1927–9," *Journal of Latin American Studies* 31, no. 3 (October 1999): 648.

13   On corporatism and its long term effects in Mexico see, Philippe C. Schmitter, "Still the Century of Corporatism?" *Review of Politics* 36, no. 1 (January 1974): 85–131; Jeffrey W. Rubin, "Decentering the Regime: Culture and Regional Politics in Mexico," *Latin American Research Review* 31, no. 3 (1996): 85–126; Alicia Hernandez Chavez, "Mexican Presidentialism: A Historical and Institutional Overview," *Mexican Studies/ Estudios Mexicanos* 10, no. 1 (Winter 1994): 217–25.

14   Access to education is still based on class, race, and ethnic factors, as most elites pay for private schooling for their children, leaving poorer, darker, and indigenous people to go to underfunded public schools. See Carlos Alberto Torres and Adriana Puiggros, "The State and Public Education in Latin America," *Comparative Education Review* 39, no. 1 (February 1995): 1–27.

15   Arnaut, *Historia de una profesión: los maestros de educación primaria en México, 1887–1994* (Mexico: Centro de Investigación y Docencia Económicas, 1996), 86–92; Dawson, *Indian and Nation*, 162–64; Vaughan, *Cultural Politics in Revolution*, 20–24; Lewis, *Ambivalent Revolution*, 207–10; Fallaw, *Cárdenas Compromised*, 158–67; Bantjes, *As If Jesus Walked on Earth*, 224–26; Charles H. Weston, Jr., "The Political Legacy of Lazaro Cardenas," *The Americas* 39, no. 3 (January 1983): 383–405.

16   Wasserman, *Persistent Oligarchs*, 56–60.

17   Aguilar Camín and Meyer, *In the Shadow of the Mexican Revolution*, 159–250.

Bibliography

ARCHIVES

Archivo Géneral de la Nación, Ramo Presidentes, Obregón – Calles. Mexico City.

Archivo Historico del Agua. Mexico City.

Archivo Historico del Estado de Sonora. Hermosillo, Sonora.

Archivo Historico de la Secretaria de Educación Pública. Mexico City.

Biblioteca Nacional. Mexico City.

Edward H. Davis Papers, Huntington Free Library, Cornell University, New York.

Fideicomiso Archivos Plutarco Elías Calles y Fernando Torreblanca. Mexico City.

Fototeca Nacional. Pachuca, Hidalgo.

Hemeroteca Nacional de Antropología e Historia. Mexico City.

Museo Nacional de Culturas Populares. Mexico City.

Patronato de la Historia de Sonora. Museo Nacional de Antropología e Historia. Mexico City.

Programa de Historia Oral, Archivo de la Palabra, Mecanuscriptos, Instituto Dr. José María Luis Mora. Mexico City.

The Silvestre Terrazas Collection, Museo Nacional de Antropología e Historia. Mexico City.

Unidad de Información de Pueblos Indigenas. Hermosillo, Sonora.

UNITED STATES GOVERNMENT SOURCES

Senate Subcommittee on Mexican Affairs (the "Fall Committee"). *Investigation of Mexican Affairs*. 4 vols. Washington, D.C., 1920.

NEWSPAPERS, MAGAZINES, AND BULLETINS

Boletin de la Secretaria de Educación Pública.

Correo de Chihuahua.

La educación pública a través de los mensajes presidenciales desde la consumación de la independencia hasta nuestro días.

El esfuerzo educativo en México. La obra del gobierno federal en el ramo. de educación pública durante la administración del presidente Plutarco Elías Calles.

El Maestro Rural.

Memoria que indica el estado que guarda el ramo de educación pública.

Noticia estadistica sobre la educación pública en México.

SECONDARY MATERIALS

Aboites, Luis. *Breve historia de Chihuahua*. México: El Colegio de México, 1994.

———. *La Irrigación Revolucionaria. México. Historia del Sistema Nacional de Riego del Rio Conchos Chihuahua. 1927–1938*. México: CIESAS, 1988.

Adams, Evelyn C. *American Indian Education: Government Schools and Economic Progress*. Morningside Heights, NY: King's Crown Press, 1946.

Ahern, Wilbert H. "An Experiment Aborted: Returned Indian Students in the Indian School Service, 1881–1908," *Ethnohistory* 44, no. 2 (Spring 1997): 263–304.

Alonso, Ana Maria. "Conforming Disconformity: 'Mestizaje,' Hybridity, and the Aesthetics of Mexican Nationalism," *Cultural Anthropology* 19, no. 4 (November 2004): 459–90.

———. *Thread of Blood: Colonialism, Revolution, and Gender on Mexico's Northern Frontier*. Tucson: University of Arizona Press, 1995.

Alonso, Jorge. "La educación en la emergencia de la sociedad civil." In *Un Siglo de Educación en México*, vol. 1, edited by Pablo Latapí Sarre. México: Biblioteca Mexicana, 1998, 150–74.

Ames, Barry. "Bases of Support for Mexico's Dominant Party," *The American Political Science Review* 64, no. 1 (March 1970): 153–67.

Anderson, Gary L. "Toward Authentic Participation: Deconstructing the Discourses of Participatory Reforms in Education." *American Educational Research Journal* 35, no. 4 (Winter 1998): 571–603.

Anderson, Gary L., and Jaime Grinberg. "Educational Administration as a Disciplinary Practice: Appropriating Foucault's View of Power, Discourse, and Method." *Educational Administration Quarterly* 34, no. 3 (August 1998): 329–53.

Aragón Pérez, Ricardo, ed. *Historia de la educación en Sonora*, Tomo 2. Hermosillo: Gobierno del Estado de Sonora, 2003.

Arce Gurza, Francisco. "En busca de una educación revolucionaria: 1924–1934." In *Ensayos sobre historia de la educación en México*, edited by Josefina Zoraida Vázquez, 171–224. Mexico: El Colegio de Mexico, 1981.

Arnaut, Alberto. *La federalización educativa*. Mexico: Reflexiones sobre el Cambio, A.C., 1999.

———. *La federalización educativa en México: Historia del debate sobre la centralización y la descentralización educativa, 1889–1994*. Mexico: El Colegio de México, Centro de Investigación y Docencia Económicas, 1998.

———. *Historia de una profesión: los maestros de educación primaria en México, 1887–1994*. Mexico: Centro de Investigación y Docencia Económicas, 1996.

Arrieta, Olivia. "Acculturation and the National Integration of the Tarahumara Indians of Northern Mexico." Ph.D. diss., University of Arizona, 1984.

———. "Religion and Ritual among the Tarahumara Indians of Northern Mexico: Maintenance of Cultural Autonomy Through Resistance and Transformation of Colonizing Symbols," *Wicazo Sa Review* 8, no. 2 (Autumn 1992): 11–23.

Ascher, Robert. "Ethnography for Archeology: A Case from the Seri Indians," *Ethnology* 1, no. 3 (July 1962): 360–69.

Bailey, David C. *Viva Cristo Rey! The Cristero Rebellion and the Church-State Conflict in Mexico.* Austin: University of Texas Press, 1974.

Bailey, John J. *Governing Mexico: The Statecraft of Crisis Management.* New York: St. Martin's Press, 1988.

Baldwin, Deborah J. *Protestants and the Mexican Revolution: Missionaries, Ministers, and Social Change.* Urbana: University of Illinois Press, 1990.

Bandala, Eliseo. "Sección pedagogica: ayuda de la mujer en el hogar campesino." *El Maestro Rural* 3, no. 5 (1 August 1933): n.p.

Bantjes, Adrian A. *As if Jesus Walked on Earth: Cardenismo, Sonora, and the Mexican Revolution.* Wilmington: Scholarly Resources, 1998.

Bardach, Eugene. *The Implementation Game: What Happens After a Bill Becomes Law.* Cambridge, MA: M.I.T. Press, 1977.

Becker, Marjorie. *Setting the Virgin on Fire: Lázaro Cárdenas, Michoacán Peasants, and the Redemption of the Mexican Revolution.* Berkeley: University of California Press, 1995.

———. "Black and White and Color: Cardenismo and the Search for a Campesino Ideology," *Comparative Studies in Society and History* 29, no. 3 (July 1987): 453–65.

Bederman, Gail. *Manliness and Civilization: A Cultural History of Gender and Race in the United States, 1880–1917.* Chicago: University of Chicago Press, 1995.

Beezely, William H., Cheryl English Martin, and William E. French, eds. *Rituals of Rule, Rituals of Resistance: Public Celebrations and Popular Culture in Mexico.* Lanham, MD: Rowman & Littlefield, 1994.

Benedict, Burton. *The Anthropology of World's Fairs.* Berkeley: Scolar Press, 1983.

Benjamin, Thomas. "Laboratories of the New State, 1920–1929." In *Provinces of the Revolution: Essays on Regional Mexican History, 1910–1929*, edited by Thomas Benjamin and Mark Wasserman, 71–90. Albuquerque: University of New Mexico Press, 1990.

Bethell, Leslie, ed. *Mexico Since Independence.* Cambridge: Cambridge University Press, 1991.

Bliss, Katherine. "The Science of Redemption: Syphilis, Sexual Promiscuity, and Reformism in Revolutionary Mexico City," *HAHR* 79, no. 1 (February 1999).

Boorstin, Daniel J. *The Americans: The Democratic Experience.* New York: Vintage Books, 1973.

Bowen, Thomas. "Seri." In *Handbook of North American Indians*, vol. 10, Southwest, edited by Alfonso Ortiz, 230-49. Washington: Smithsonian Institution, 1983.

Boylan, Kristina A. "Gendering the Faith and Altering the Nation: Mexican Catholic Women's Activism, 1917–1940," *Sex in Revolution: Gender, Politics, and Power in Modern Mexico*, edited by Jocelyn Olcott, Mary Kay Vaughan, and Gabriela Cano, 199-222. Durham, NC: Duke University Press, 2007.

Brachet-Marquez, Vivian. "Explaining Sociopolitical Change in Latin America: The Case of Mexico," *Latin American Research Review* 27, no. 3 (1992): 91–122.

Brandenburg, Frank. *The Making of Modern Mexico.* New York: Prentice Hall, 1964.

Britton, John A. "Indian Education, Nationalism, and Federalism in Mexico, 1910–1921," *The Americas* 32, no. 3 (January 1976): 445–58.

———. "Teacher Unionization and the Corporate State in Mexico, 1931–1945," *Hispanic American Historical Review* 59, no. 4 (November 1979): 674–90.

Brown, James Chilton. "Consolidation of the Mexican Revolution under Calles, 1924–1928: Politics, Modernization, and the Roots of the Revolutionary National Party." Ph.D. diss., University of New Mexico, 1979.

Buchenau, Jürgen. *Plutarco Elías Calles and the Mexican Revolution.* Lanham, MD: Rowman & Littlefield, 2007.

Bustamante, Jorge. "The Mexico-U.S. Border: A Line of Paradox." In *Identities in North America: A Search for Community*, edited by R.L. Earle and J.D. Wirth, 180-194. Stanford: Stanford University Press, 1995.

Butler, Matthew. "The 'Liberal' *Cristero*: Ladislao Molina and the *Cristero* Rebellion in Michoacán, 1927–9." *Journal of Latin American Studies* 31, no. 3 (October 1999): 645–71.

Camín, Héctor Aguilar. *Saldos de la revolucion: cultura y política de México, 1910–1980.* México: Editorial Nuevo Imagen, 1982.

Camín, Héctor Aguilar, and Lorenzo Meyer. *In the Shadows of the Revolution: Contemporary Mexican History, 1910–1989*, translated by Luis Alberto Fierro. Austin: University of Texas Press, 1993.

Camou Healy, Ernesto. *Historia general de Sonora: historia contemporánea de Sonora, 1929–1984.* Hermosillo, Colegio de Sonora: 1988.

Camp, Roderic A. *Politics in Mexico.* New York: Oxford University Press, 1996.

———. "Mexican Political Elites 1935–1973: A Comparative Study," *The Americas* 31, no. 4 (April 1975): 452–69.

Castillo, Isidro. *México: sus revoluciones sociales y la educación.* 2 vols. Mexico: Gobierno del Estado de Michoacán, 1976.

de la Cerdasilva, Roberto. "Los Tarahumaras," *Revista Mexicana de Sociología* 5, no. 3 (3rd Quarter, 1943): 403–36.

Chamosa, Oscar. "Indigenous or Criollo: The Myth of White Argentina in Tucumán's Calchaquí Valley," *Hispanic American Historical Review* 88, no. 1 (February 2008): 71–106.

Chance, Joseph E. *José María de Jesús Carvajal: The Life and Times of a Mexican Revolutionary.* San Antonio: Trinity University Press, 2006.

Coatsworth, Jonathan. *Growth Against Development: The Economic Impact of Railroads in Porfirian Mexico.* DeKalb: Northern Illinois University Press, 1981.

Cockcroft, James. *Intellectual Precursors of the Mexican Revolution, 1900–1910.* Austin: University of Texas Press, 1968.

Córdova, Arnaldo. *La ideología de la revolución mexicana: la formación del nuevo régimen.* Mexico: Editorial Era, 1973.

Corrigan, Philip, and Derek Sayer. *The Great Arch: English State Formation as Cultural Revolution.* Oxford: Basil Blackwell, 1985.

Cronon, David E. "American Catholics and Mexican Anticlericalism," *Mississippi Valley Historical Review* 45, no. 2 (September 1958): 201–31.

Davis, Edward H., and E. Yale Dawson. "The Savage Seris of Sonora – I," *The Scientific Monthly* 60, no. 3 (1945).

———. "The Savage Seris of Sonora – II," *The Scientific Monthly* 60, no. 4 (1945).

Dawson, Alexander. *Indian and Nation in Revolutionary Mexico*. Tucson: University of Arizona Press, 2004.

———. "From Models for the Nation to Model Citizens: Indigenismo and the 'Revindication' of the Mexican Indian, 1920–1940," *Journal of Latin American Studies* 30, no. 2 (May 1998): 279–308.

———. "'Wild Indians,' 'Mexican Gentlemen,' and the Lessons Learned in the Casa del Estudiante Indígena, 1926–1932," *The Americas* 57, no. 3 (January 2001): 329–61.

Deloria, Philip J. *Indians in Unexpected Places*. Lawrence: University Press of Kansas, 2004.

Deutsch, Sarah. *No Separate Refuge: Culture, Class, and Gender on an Anglo-Hispanic Frontier in the American Southwest, 1880–1940*. Oxford: Oxford University Press, 1987.

Dulles, John W.F. *Yesterday in Mexico: A Chronicle of the Revolution, 1919–1936*. Austin: University of Texas Press, 1961.

Eckstein, Susan. *The Poverty of Revolution: The State and the Urban Poor in Mexico*. Princeton: Princeton University Press, 1977.

Emmerich, Lisa. "'To Respect and Love and Seek the Ways of White Women,' Field Matrons, the Office of Indian Affairs, and Civilization Policy, 1890–1938." Dissertation, University of Maryland, 1987.

Erickson, Winston P. *Sharing the Desert: The Tohono O'odham in History*. Tucson: University of Arizona Press, 1994.

Fallaw, Ben. *Cárdenas Compromised: The Failure of Reform in Postrevolutionary Yucatán*. Durham, NC: Duke University Press, 2001.

———. "The Life and Death of Felipa Poot: Women, Fiction, and Cardenismo in Postrevolutionary Mexico," *Hispanic American Historical Review* 82, no. 4 (November 2002): 645–83.

———. "Cárdenas and the Caste War that Wasn't: State Power and Indigenismo in Post-Revolutionary Yucatán," *The Americas* 53, no. 4 (April 1997): 563–76.

Farmer, Edward. "Un nacionalismo pragmático: El gobierno Callista en Sonroa y el capital extranjero." *Boletín* no. 31 (1999).

Flores Magón, Ricardo and Jesús. *Batalla a la Dictadura*. Mexico: Empresas Editoriales, 1948.

Fontana, Bernard L. "History of the Papago." In *Handbook of the North American Indians*. vol. 10, Southwest, edited by Alfonso Ortiz, 137-48. Washington: Smithsonian Institution, 1983.

———. *Of Earth and Little Rain*. Tucson: University of Arizona Press, 1989.

Forbes, Jack D. "Historical Survey of the Indians of Sonora, 1821–1910," *Ethnohistory* 4, no. 4 (Autumn 1957): 335–68.

French, William E. *A Peaceful Working People: Manners, Morals, and Class Formation in Northern Mexico*. Albuquerque: University of New Mexico Press, 1996.

Fried, Jacob. "An Interpretation of Tarahumara Interpersonal Relations," *Anthropological Quarterly* 34, no. 2 (April 1962): 110–20.

Friedlander, Judith. "The National Indigenist Institute of Mexico Reinvents the Indian: The Pame Example," *American Ethnologist* 13, no. 2 (May 1986): 363–67.

Gajdusek, D. Carleton. "The Sierra Tarahumara," *Geographical Review* 43, no. 1 (January 1953): 15–38.

Galván de Terrazas, Luz Elena. *Los maestros y la educación pública en México: un estudio histórico.* Tlalpan: Centro de Investigaciones y Estudios Superiores en Antropología Social, 1985.

Gibson, A.M. *The Kickapoos: Lords of the Middle Border.* Norman: University of Oklahoma Press, 1963.

Giese, Ana Mai. "The Sonoran Triumvirate: Preview in Sonora, 1910–1920," Ph.D. diss., University of Florida, 1975.

Gonzales, Michael. "Imagining Mexico in 1910: Visions of the Patria in the Centennial Celebration in Mexico City," *Journal of Latin American Studies* 39, no. 3 (August 2007): 495–533.

Gonzalez Bonilla, Luis Arturo. "Los Seris," *Revista Mexicana de Scoiología* 3, no. 2 (2nd Quarter, 1941): 93–107.

Gramsci, Antonio. *Notes from the Prison Notebooks*, edited and translated by Quintin Hoare and Geoffrey Nowell Smith. New York: International Publishers, 1999.

Greaves Lainé, Cecilia. "El debate sobre una antigua polémica: La integración indígena," *Historia de la eduación y enseñanza de la historia.* México: El Colegio de México, 1998.

Hagan, William T. "Kiowas, Comanches, and Cattlemen, 1867–1906: A Case Study of the Failure of U.S. Reservation Policy," *Pacific Historical Review* 40, no. 3 (August 1971): 333–55.

Hall, Linda B. "Alvaro Obregón and the Politics of Mexican Land Reform, 1920–1924," *Hispanic American Historical Review* 60, no. 2 (1980): 213–38.

———. *Alvaro Obregon: Power and Revolution in Mexico, 1911–1920.* College Station: Texas A & M Press, 1981.

———. *Oil, Banks, and Politics: The United States and Postrevolutionary Mexico, 1917–1924.* Austin: University of Texas Press, 1995.

Hall, Linda B. and Don M. Coerver, *Revolution on the Border: The United States and Mexico, 1910–1920.* Albuquerque: University of New Mexico Press, 1988.

Hamilton, Nora. *The Limits of State Autonomy: Post-Revolutionary Mexico.* Princeton: Princeton University Press, 1982.

Hansis, Randall. "The Political Strategy of Military Reform: Álvaro Obregón and Revolutionary Mexico, 1920–1924," *The Americas* 36, no. 2 (October 1979): 199–233.

Hart, John Mason. *Revolutionary Mexico: The Coming and Process of the Mexican Revolution.* Berkeley: University of California Press, 1987.

Hatfield, Shelley Bowen. *Chasing Shadows: Apaches and Yaquis Along the United States-Mexico Border, 1876–1911.* Albuquerque: University of New Mexico Press, 1998.

Hernandez Chavez, Alicia. "Mexican Presidentialism: A Historical and Institutional Overview," *Mexican Studies/Estudios Mexicanos* 10, no. 1 (Winter 1994): 217–25.

Heyman, Josiah McConnell. *Life and Labor on the Border: Working People of Northeastern Sonora, Mexico, 1886–1986.* Tucson: University of Arizona Press, 1991.

Hilton, Stanley E. "The Church-State Dispute over Education in Mexico from Carranza to Cardenas," *The Americas* 21, no. 2 (October 1964): 163–83.

Hirschman, Albert O. *Exit, Voice, and Loyalty: Responses to Decline in Firms, Organizations, and States.* Cambridge: Harvard University Press, 1970.

Honey, James. "Policy and Politics in the Papaguería: A Twentieth Century, Cross-Border History of the Tohono O'odham." History Honors Thesis, Stanford University, 1997.

Hu-DeHart, Evelyn. "Racism and the Anti-Chinese Persecution in Sonora, Mexico, 1876–1932," *Amerasia* 9, no. 2 (Fall/Winter 1982).

Hudgins, Mitchell. "The White Chief: The Story of Edward H. Davis," M.A. Thesis, University of San Diego, 1987.

Jacknis, Ira. "A New Thing? The NMAI in Historical and Institutional Perspective," *American Indian Quarterly* 30, nos. 3–4 (Summer and Fall 2006): 511–42.

Jiménez Alarcón, Concepción, ed. *Rafael Ramírez y la escuela rural mexicana.* Mexico: Secretaria de Educación Pública, 1998.

Joseph, Gilbert M. *Revolution from Without: Yucatán, Mexico, and the United States, 1880–1924.* Durham, NC: Duke University Press, 1988.

Katz, Friedrich. *The Life and Times of Pancho Villa.* Stanford: Stanford University Press, 1998.

Kennedy, John G. "Tesguino Complex: The Role of Beer in Tarahumara Culture," *American Anthropologist*, New Series, 65, no. 3, Part 1 (June 1963): 620–40.

King, Linda. *Roots of Identity: Language and Literacy in Mexico.* Stanford: Stanford University Press, 1994.

Knight, Alan. "Popular Culture and the Revolutionary State in Mexico, 1910–1940." *Hispanic American Historical Review* 74, no. 3 (1994): 393–444.

———. *The Mexican Revolution.* 2 vols. Lincoln: University of Nebraska Press, 1986.

———. "The Rise and Fall of Cardenismo, c. 1930 – c. 1946." In *Mexico since Independence*, edited by Leslie Bethell, 241-320. Cambridge: Cambridge University Press, 1991.

———. "The United States and the Mexican Peasantry, circa 1880–1940." In *Rural Revolt in Mexico: U.S. Intervention and the Domain of Subaltern Politics*, edited by Daniel Nugent, 25–63. Durham, NC: Duke University Press, 1998.

———. "Land and Society in Revolutionary Mexico: The Destruction of the Great Haciendas," *Mexican Studies/Estudios Mexicanos* 7, no. 1 (Winter 1991): 73–104.

———. "Peasants into Patriots: Thoughts on the Making of the Mexican Nation," *Mexican Studies/Estudios Mexicanos*, 10, no. 1 (1994): 135–61.

———. *The Mexican Revolution: Porfirians, Liberals, and Peasants,* Volume 1. Lincoln: University of Nebraska Press, 1986.

Krauze, Enrique. *Mexico: Biography of Power: A History of Modern Mexico, 1810–1996,* translated by Hank Heirtz. New York: Harper Collins, 1997.

Krauze, Enrique, Jean Meyer, and Cayetano Reyes. *Historia de la Revolución Mexicana, 1924–1928: La reconstrucción económica*, edited by Luis González. Mexico: El Colegio de México, 1977.

Labaree, David F. *How to Succeed in School without Really Learning: The Credentials Race in American Education*. New Haven, CT: Yale University Press, 1997.

———. *The Making of an American High School: The Credentials Market and the Central High School of Philadelphia, 1838–1939*. New Haven, CT: Yale University Press, 1988.

Lapatí Sarre, Pablo, ed. "Un siglo de educación nacional: una sistematización." In *Un siglo de educación en México*. Volume 1, edited by Pablo Lapati Sarre, 21–42. Mexico: Fondo de Cultura Económica, 1998.

Lapatí Sarre, Pablo and Manuel Ulloa Herrero. *El financiamiento de la eduación básica en el marco del federalismo*. México: Fondo de Cultura de Económica, 2000.

Larson, Erik. *The Devil in the White City: Murder, Magic, and Madness at the Fair that Changed America*. New York: Crown, 2002.

Latorre, Felipe A., and Dolores L. *The Mexican Kickapoo Indians*. Austin: University of Texas Press, 1976.

Levi, Jerome M. "Hidden Transcripts among the Rarámuri: Culture, Resistance, and Interethnic Relations in Northern Mexico." *American Ethnologist* 26, no. 1 (February 1999): 90–113.

Lewis, David Rich. *Neither Wolf Nor Dog: American Indians, Environment, & Agrarian Change*. New York: Oxford University Press, 1994.

Lewis, Stephen E. *Ambivalent Revolution: Forging State and Nation in Chiapas, 1910–1945*. Albuquerque: University of New Mexico Press, 2005.

Llinas Alvarez, Edgar. *Revolucion, educación y mexicanidad: La busqueda de la identidad nacional en el pensamiento educativo*. México: UNAM, 1979.

Lomnitz, Claudio. *Deep Mexico, Silent Mexico: An Anthropology of Nationalism*. Minneapolis: University of Minnesota Press, 2001.

López, Rick A. "The India Bonita Contest of 1921and the Ethnicization of the Mexican National Culture." *Hispanic American Historical Review* 82, no. 2 (May 2002): 291–328.

———. "The Noche Mexicana and the Exhibition of Popular Arts: Two Ways of Exalting Indianness." In *The Eagle and the Virgin: Nation and Cultural Revolution in Mexico, 1920–1940*, edited by Mary Kay Vaughan and Stephen E. Lewis, 23-42. Durham: Duke University Press, 2006.

Loyo, Engracia. "Escuelas Rurales 'Articulo 123' (1917–1940)." *Historia Mexicana* 40, no. 2 (1991): 299–336.

———. "La empresa redentora: La Casa del Estudiante Indígena." *Historia Mexicana* 46, no. 1 (1996): 99–131.

———. *Gobiernos revolucionarios y educación popular en México, 1911–1928*. Mexico: Centro de Estudios Históricos, 1998.

———. "Los mecanismos de la 'federalización' educativa, 1921–1940." In *Historia de la educación y enseñanza de la historia*, 113–37. Mexico: Colegio de México, 1998.

————. "Los centros de educación indígena y su papel en el medio rural (1930–1940)." In *Educación rural e indígena en Iberoamérica*, edited by Pilar Gonzalbo Aizpuru, 139-59. Mexico: El Colegio de México, 1996.

————. "El largo camino hacia la centralización educativa." In *Federalización e innovación educativa en México*, edited by Maria del Carmen Pardo, 49–58. México: El Colegio de México, 1999.

————. "Las Escuelas J. Cruz Gálvez: Fundación y Primeros Años (1915–1928)," *Boletín* 40. México: Fideicomiso Archivos Plutarco Elías Calles y Fernando Torreblanca and Secreetaría de Educación Pública, 2002.

————. "Las escuelas fronterizas en México, (1930–1940): un esfuerzo a favor de la unidad nacional," XII Congress of Mexican, United States, and Canadian Historians, Vancouver, British Columbia, October 2006.

Lumholtz, Carl. *New Trails in Mexico: An Account of One Year's Exploration in North-Western Sonora, Mexico, and South-Western Arizona, 1909–1910*. Tucson: University of Arizona Press, 1990.

Macías Richard, Carlos, ed. *Plutarco Elías Calles: Pensamiento politico y social, antología (1913–1936)*. Mexico: Fondo de Cultura Económica, 1988.

————. *Plutarco Elías Calles: Correspondencia personal (1919–1945)*. Mexico: Fondo de Cultura Económica, 1991.

————. *Plutarco Elías Calles: Correspondencia pesonal (1919–1945)*. Mexico: Fondo de Cultura Económica, 1993.

————. *Vida y temperamento: Plutarco Elías Calles, 1877–1920*. Hermosillo: Instituto Sonorense de Cultura, 1995.

Mallon, Florencia E. "Reflection on the Ruins: Everyday Forms of State Formation in Nineteenth-Century Mexico." In *Everyday Forms of State Formation: Revolution and the Negotiation of Rule in Modern Mexico*, edited by Gilbert M Joseph and Daniel Nugent, 69–106. Durham, NC: Duke University Press, 1994.

Marcoux, Carl Henry. "Plutarco Elías Calles and the Partido Nacional Revolucionario: Mexican National and Regional Politics in 1928 and 1929." Ph.D. diss., University of California, Riverside, 1994.

Martínez, Oscar J. *Troublesome Border*. Tucson: University of Arizona Press, 1988.

McGee, W.J. "Expedition to Papagueria and Seriland: A Preliminary Note," *American Anthropologist* 9, no. 3 (March 1896): 93–98.

————. "The Beginning of Marriage," *American Anthropologist* 9, no. 11 (November 1896): 371–83.

Meeks, Eric V. "The Tohono O'odham, Wage Labor, and Resistant Adaptation, 1900–1930." In *Western Historical Quarterly* 34 (Winter 2003): 468–89.

Meyer, Jean. "Revolution and Reconstruction in the 1920s." In *Mexico since Independence*, edited by Leslie Bethell, 201–40. Cambridge: Cambridge University Press, 1991.

————. *La cristiada*. 2 vols. Mexico: Siglo Veintiuno Editores, 1973.

Meyer, Lorenzo. *Mexico and the United States in the Oil Controversy, 1917–1942*, translated by Muriel Vasconcelos. Austin: University of Texas Press, 1977.

———. *Historia de la Revolución Mexicana, 1928–1934: El conflicto social y los gobiernos del maximato*. México: El Colegio de México.

Meyer, Lorenzo, Rafael Segovia, and Alejandra Lajous. *Historia de la Revolución Mexicana, 1928–1934: los inicios de la institucionalización*. Mexico: El Colegio de México, 1978.

Meyer, Michael C., and William L. Sherman. *The Course of Mexican History*, 5th ed. New York: Oxford University Press, 1995.

Meyers, William K. *Forge of Progress, Crucible of Revolt: The Origins of the Mexican Revolution in La Comarca, Lagunera, 1880–1911*. Albuquerque: University of New Mexico Press, 1994.

Middlebrook, Kevin J. *The Paradox of Revolution: Labor, the State, and Authoritarianism in Mexico*. Baltimore: John Hopkins University Press, 1995.

Migdal, Joel S. "The State in Society: An Approach to Struggles for Domination." In *State Power and Social Forces: Domination and Transformation in the Third World*. edited by Joel S. Migdal, Atul Kohli, and Vivienne Shue, 7–34. Cambridge: Cambridge University Press, 1994.

———. *Strong Societies and Weak States: State-Society Relations and State Capabilities in the Third World*. Princeton: Princeton University Press, 1988.

Moore, Barrington, Jr. *Injustice: The Social Bases of Obedience and Revolt*. White Plains, NY: M.E. Sharp, 1978.

Morris, Stephen D. "Reforming the Nation: Mexican Nationalism in Context." *Journal of Latin American Studies* 31, no. 2 (May 1999): 363–97.

Moses, L.G. *Wild West Shows and the Images of American Indians, 1883–1933*. Albuquerque: University of New Mexico Press, 1996.

Nabhan, Gary Paul. *The Desert Smells Like Rain: A Naturalist in Papago Country*. New York: North Point Press, 1982.

Newland, Carlos. "The *Estado Docente* and its Expansion: Spanish American Elementary Education, 1900–1950," *Journal of Latin American Studies* 26, no. 2 (May 1994): 449–67.

Newcomer, Daniel. *Reconciling Modernity: Urban State Formation in 1940s León, Mexico*. Lincoln: University of Nebraska Press, 2004.

Nugent, Daniel. *Spent Cartridges of Revolution: An Anthropological History of Namiquipa, Chihuahua*. Chicago: University of Chicago Press, 1993.

Nunley, Mary Christopher. "The Mexican Kickapoo Indians: Avoidance of Acculturation through a Migratory Adaptation." Ph.D. diss., Southern Methodist University, 1986.

O'Donnell, Guillermo. "Corporatism and the Question of the State." In *Authoritarianism and Corporatism in Latin America*, edited by James M. Malloy, 47–87. Pittsburgh: University of Pittsburgh Press, 1977.

Olcott, Jocelyn. *Revolutionary Women in Postrevolutionary Mexico*. Durham, NC: Duke University Press, 2005.

Palacios, Guillermo. *La Pluma y el Arado: Los intelectuales pedagogos y la construcción socio-cultural del 'problema campesino' en México, 1930–1934*. México: El Colegio de México and Centro de Investigación y Docencia Económicas, 1999.

————. "Postrevolutionary Intellectuals, Rural Readings and the Shaping of the 'Peasant Problem' in Mexico: *El Maestro Rural*, 1932–1934." *Journal of Latin American Studies* 30, no. 2 (May 1988): 309–39.

Passin, Herbert. "A Note on the Present Indigenous Population of Chihuahua." *American Anthropologist*, New Series, 46, no. 1, Part 1 (January–March 1944): 145–47.

Pastron, Allen G. "Collective Defenses of Repression and Denial: Their Relationship to Violence among the Tarahumara Indians of Northern Mexico." *Ethos* 2, no. 4 (Winter 1974): 387–404.

de la Peña, Guillermo. "Educación y cultura en el México del siglo XX." In *Un siglo de educación en México*, vol. 1, edited by Pablo Latapi Sarre, 43–83. Mexico: Fondo de Cultura Económica, 1998.

Pennington, Campbell W. "Tarahumara." In *Handbook of North American Indians*. vol. 10, Southwest, edited by Alfonso Ortiz, 276–89. Washington: Smithsonian Institution, 1983.

Pike, Frederick. *Spanish America, 1900–1970: Tradition and Social Innovation*. New York: Norton, 1973.

Portes Gil, Emilio. *Autobiografía de la revolución mexicana*. Mexico: Instituto Mexicano de Culture, 1964.

Puig Casauranc, José Manuel. *El sentido social del proceso historico de méxico*. Mexico: Ediciones Botas, 1936.

————. *La Cosecha y la Siembra*. México: Secretaría de Educación Pública, 1929.

Punke, Harold H. "Extent and Support of Popular Education in Mexico." *Peabody Journal of Education* 11, no. 3 (November 1933): 122–37.

Quintanilla, Susana, ed. *Teoría, campo e historia de la educación*. Mexico: Consejo Mexicano de Investigación Educativa, A.C., 1995.

Quintanilla, Susana, and Mary Kay Vaughan. *Escuela y sociedad en el periodo cardenista*. Mexico: Fondo de Cultura Económica, 1997.

Quirk, Robert E. *Mexico*. Englewood Cliffs, NJ: Prentice Hall, 1971.

Radding, Cynthia. *Wandering People: Colonialism, Ethnic Spaces, and Ecological Frontiers in Northwestern Mexico, 1700–1850*. Durham, NC: Duke University Press, 1997.

————, ed. *Historia General de Sonora, Tomo IV*. Hermosillo: Gobierno del Estado de Sonora, 1997.

————. *Entre el desierto y la sierra: las naciones O'odham y Teguima de Sonora, 1530–1840*. Mexico: INI and SEP, 1995.

Ramirez, Rafael. *La Escuela Rural Mexicana*. México: Secretaría de Educación Pública, 1976.

Rath, Thomas. "'*Que el cielo un soldado en cada hijo te dio ...*' Conscription, Recalcitrance and Resistance in Mexico in the 1940s." *Journal of Latin American Studies* 37, no. 3 (August 2005): 507–31.

Redden, Paul. *Wild West Shows*. Urbana and Chicago: University of Illinois Press, 1999.

Rénique, Gerardo. "Anti-Chinese Racism, Nationalism, and State Formation in Post-Revolutionary Mexico." *Political Power and Social Theory*, vol. 14 (2001): 91–140.

———. "Race, Region and Nation: Sonora's Anti-Chinese Racism and Mexico's Post-Revolutionary Nationalism, 1920s–1930s." In *Race and Nation in Modern Latin America*, edited by Nancy P. Appelbaum, Anne S. MacPherson, and Karin Alejandra Rosenblatt, 211–36. Chapel Hill: University of North Carolina Press, 2003.

Reséndez, Andrés. *Changing National Identities at the Frontier: Texas and New Mexico, 1800–1850.* Cambridge: Cambridge University Press, 2005.

Rockwell, Elsie. "Schools of the Revolution: Enacting and Contesting State Forms in Tlaxcala, 1910–1930." In *Everyday Forms of State Formation: Revolution and the Negotiation of Rule in Modern Mexico*, edited by Gilbert M. Joseph and Daniel Nugent, 170–208. Durham, NC: Duke University Press, 1994.

———. "Reforma constitucional y controversias locales: la eduación socialista en Tlaxcala, 1935–1936." In *Escuela y sociedad en el periodo cardenista*, edited by Susana Quintanilla and Mary Kay Vaughan, 196–228. México: Fondo de Cultura Económica, 1997.

Rubin, Jeffrey W. "Decentering the Regime: Culture and Regional Politics in Mexico." *Latin American Research Review* 31, no. 3 (1996): 85–126.

Ruggles Gere, Anne. "Indian Heart/White Man's Head: Native-American Teachers in Indian Schools, 1880–1930." *History of Education Quarterly* 45, no. 1 (Spring 2005): 38–65.

Sauri Riancho, Dulce Maria. "Mexico visto por el Partido Revolucionario Institucional." *Mexico Studies/Estudios Mexicanos* 17, no. 2 (Summer 2001): 261–71.

Schell, Patience A. *Church and State Education in Revolutionary Mexico City.* Tucson: University of Arizona Press, 2003.

Schmitter, Philippe C. *Interest Conflict and Political Change in Brazil.* Stanford: Stanford University Press, 1971.

———. "Still the Century of Corporatism?" *Review of Politics* 36, no. 1 (January 1974): 85–131.

Schoenhals, Louise. "Mexico Experiments in Rural and Primary Education, 1921–1930," *Hispanic American Historical Review* 44, no. 1 (February 1964): 22–43.

Scott, James C. "Forward." In *Everyday Forms of State Formation: Revolution and the Negotiation of Rule in Modern Mexico*, edited by Gilbert M. Joseph and Daniel Nugent. Durham, NC: Duke University Press, 1994.

———. *Weapons of the Weak: Everyday Forms of Peasant Resistance.* New Haven, CT: Yale University Press, 1985.

Sheridan, Thomas E. *Where the Dove Calls: The Political Ecology of a Peasant Corporate Community in Northwestern Mexico.* Tucson: University of Arizona Press, 1988.

———. *Landscapes of Fraud: Mission Tumacácori, the Baca Float, and the Betrayal of the O'odham.* Tucson: University of Arizona Press, 2006.

———. "The O'odham (Pimas and Papagos): The World Would Burn Without Rain." In *Paths of Life: American Indians of the Southwest and Northern Mexico*, edited by Thomas E. Sheridan and Nancy J. Parezo, 115–40. Tucson: University of Arizona Press, 1996.

Simpson, Leslie Byrd. *Many Mexicos*, 4th ed. Berkeley: University of California Press, 1969.

Slaney, Frances M. "Double Baptism: Personhood and Ethnicity in the Sierra Tarahumara of Mexico," *American Ethnologist* 24, no. 2 (May, 1997): 279–301.

Smith, Benjamin Thomas. "Anticlericalism and Resistance: The Diocese of Huajuapam de León, 1930–1940," *Journal of Latin American Studies* 37, no. 3 (August 2005): 469–505.

Smith, Robert Freeman. *The United States and Revolutionary Nationalism in Mexico, 1916–1932*. Chicago: University of Chicago Press, 1972.

Solana, Fernando, et. al. *Historia de la educación pública en México*. 2 vols. Mexico: Fondo de Cultura Económica, 1982.

Spicer, Edward H. *Cycles of Conquest: The Impact of Spain, Mexico, and the United States on the Indians of the Southwest, 1533–1960*. Tucson: University of Arizona Press, 1962.

Spring, Joel. *Deculturalization and the Struggle for Equality: A Brief History of the Education of Dominated Cultures in the United States*, 4th ed. Boston: McGraw-Hill Higher Education, 2004.

Steffens, Lincoln. *The Autobiography of Lincoln Steffens*. 2 vols. New York: Harcourt, Brace, and World, 1931.

Stern, Alexandra Minna. "Buildings, Boundaries, and Blood: Medicalization and Nation-Building on the U.S.-Mexican Border, 1910–1930." *Hispanic American Historical Review* 79, no. 1 (February 1999): 41–81.

Story, Dale. *The Mexican Ruling Party: Stability and Authority*. New York: Praeger, 1986.

Sutton, Imre. "Sovereign States and the Changing Definition of the Indian Reservation." *Geographical Review* 66, no. 3 (July 1976): 281–95.

Szasz, Margaret Connell. *Education and the American Indian: The Road to Self-Determination since 1928*. Albuquerque: University of New Mexico Press, 1999.

Tannenbaum, Frank. *Peace by Revolution: Mexico After 1910*. New York: Columbia University Press, 1933.

Taylor, Lawrence D. "The Battle of Ciudad Juárez: Death Knell of the Porfirian Regime in Mexico." *New Mexico Historical Review* 74, no. 2 (April 1999): 179–207.

Tinker Salas, Miguel. *In the Shadow of the Eagles: Sonora and the Transformation of the Border during the Porfiriato*. Berkeley: University of California Press, 1997.

Torres, Carlos Alberto, and Adriana Puiggros. "The State and Public Education in Latin America," *Comparative Education Review* 39, no. 1 (February 1995): 1–27.

Torres, Elena. "Económia domestica: descanso del ama de casa y acción civica del hogar." *El Maestro Rural* 3, no. 3 (1 July 1933): n.p.

Torres Septién, Valentina. *La educación privada en México, 1903–1976*. México: El Colegio de México and Universidad Iberoamericana, 2004.

Trennert, Robert. "Educating Indian Girls at Nonreservation Boarding Schools, 1878–1920." *Western Historical Quarterly* 13, no. 3 (July 1982): 271–90.

Turner, John Kenneth. *Barbarous Mexico*. Austin: University of Texas Press, 1984.

Tyack, David B. "Constructing Difference: Historical Reflections on Schooling and Social Diversity." *Teachers College Record* 95, no. 1 (Fall 1993): 8–34.

Vasconcelos, José. *A Mexican Ulysses: An Autobiography*, translated by W.R. Crawford. Bloomington: Indiana University Press, 1963.

————. *El Ulises criollo.* 3rd ed. Mexico: Jus, 1968.

————. *Obras Completas.* 2 vols. Mexico: Libreros Mexicanos Unidos, 1958.

Vaughan, Mary Kay. *The State, Education, and Social Class in Mexico, 1880–1928.* DeKalb: Northern Illinois University Press, 1982.

————. "Cambio Ideológico en la Política Educativa de la SEP: Programas y Libros de Texto, 1921–1940." In *Escuela y sociedad en el periodo cardenista,* edited by Susana Quintanilla y Mary Kay Vaughan, 76–108. (México: Fondo de Cultura Económica, 1997).

————. *Cultural Politics in Revolution: Teachers, Peasants, and Schools in Mexico, 1930–1940.* Tucson: University of Arizona Press, 1997.

————. "The Educational Project of the Mexican Revolution: The Response of Local Societies (1934–1949)." In *Molding the Hearts and Minds: Education, Communications, and Social Change in Latin America,* edited by John A. Britton, 105-27. Wilmington: Scholarly Resources, 1994.

————. "Primary Education and Literacy in Nineteenth-Century Mexico: Research Trends, 1968–1988." *Latin American Research Review* 25, no. 1 (1990): 31–66.

————. "The Construction of Patriotic Festivals in Tecamachalco, Puebla, 1900–1946." In *Rituals of Rule, Rituals of Resistance: Public Celebration and Popular Culture in Mexico,* edited by William H. Beezley and Judith Ewell, 213–46. Wilmington: Scholarly Resources, 1994.

————. "Education and Class in the Mexican Revolution." *Latin American Perspectives* 2, no. 2 (Summer 1975): 17–33.

————. "Primary Schooling in the City of Puebla, 1821–60." *Hispanic American Historical Review* 67, no. 1 (February 1987): 39–62.

————. "Modernizing Patriarchy: State Policies, Rural Households, and Women in Mexico, 1930-1940," in *Hidden Histories of Gender and the State in Latin America,* edited by Elizabeth Dore and Maxine Molyneux, 199–202. Durham, NC: Duke University Press, 2000.

Vaughan, Mary Kay, and Stephen E. Lewis, eds. *The Eagle and the Virgin: Nation and Cultural Revolution in Mexico, 1920–1940.* Durham, NC: Duke University Press, 2006.

Voss, Stuart F. *On the Periphery of Nineteenth-Century Mexico: Sonora and Sinaloa, 1810–1877.* Tucson: University of Arizona Press, 1982.

————. "Nationalizing the Revolution: Culmination and Circumstance." In *Provinces of the Revolution: Essays on Regional Mexican History, 1910–1929,* edited by Thomas Benjamin and Mark Wasserman, 298–306. Albuquerque: University of New Mexico Press, 1990.

Warren, Louis S. *Buffalo Bill's America: William Cody and the Wild West Show.* New York: Vintage Books, 2005.

Wasserman, Mark. *Persistent Oligarchs: Elites and Politics in Chihuahua, Mexico, 1910–1940.* Durham, NC: Duke University Press, 1993.

————. *Capitalists, Caciques, and Revolution: The Native Elite and Foreign Enterprise in Chihuahua, Mexico, 1854–1911.* Durham, NC: University of North Carolina Press, 1984.

———. "Chihuahua: Politics in an Era of Transition." In *Provinces of the Revolution: Essays on Regional Mexican History 1910–1929*, edited by Thomas Benjamin and Mark Wasserman, 218–35. Albuquerque: University of New Mexico Press, 1990.

Weston, Charles H, Jr. "The Political Legacy of Lazaro Cardenas," *The Americas* 39, no. 3 (January 1983): 383–405.

White, Richard. *The Roots of Dependency: Subsistence, Environment, and Social Change among the Choctaws, Pawnees, and Navajos*. Lincoln: University of Nebraska Press, 1983.

Wilkie, James W. *The Mexican Revolution: Federal Expenditures and Social Change Since 1910*. Berkeley: University of California Press, 1967.

Wilkie, James W., and Edna Monzon de Wilkie. *México visto en siglo XX*. Mexico: Instituto Mexicano de Investigaciones Economicas, 1969.

Womack, John, Jr. *Zapata and the Mexican Revolution*. New York: Vintage Books, 1968.

Yetman, David. *Scattered Round Stones: A Mayo Village in Sonora, Mexico*. Albuquerque: University of New Mexico Press, 1998.

Zingg, Robert M. *Behind the Mexican Mountains*, edited by Howard Campbell, John Peterson, and David Carmichael. Austin: University of Texas Press, 2001.

———. "The Genuine and Spurious Values in Tarahumara Culture." *American Anthropologist*, New Series, 44, no. 1 (January–March 1942): 78–92.

Zolov, Eric. *Refried Elvis: The Rise of the Mexican Counterculture*. Berkeley: University of California Press, 1999.

Zoraida Vázquez, Josefina. *Nacionalismo y educación en México*. México: El Colegio de México, 2005.

Index

A

acculturation. *See* assimilation
Acosta V., Alfonso, 155
action pedagogy, xxv, xxvii, 13, 18, 20, 25
Akimel O'odham, 109
Alanis, Alfonso G., 153
alcohol, 6, 20, 52, 62, 66–70, 94, 96, 131, 142–43, 145, 148–49, 164
Alfonso Andrade, Angel, 155–56
Almada, Francisco R., 69
Almeida, Jesús Antonio, 32, 34–35, 69
anti-clericalism, 38, 106, 116, 127, 130–31, 145, 147, 151, 153–54, 156, 159, 161–62
Apaches, 114, 150
Arellano, Abraham, 143
Article 3 (of Mexican Constitution), 22, 27
Article 123 (of Mexican Constitution), 37–38, 45, 160
assimilation, xv, 135, 147, 152
    indigenous, xxvii, 7, 10, 24, 50–51, 162–63
    peasants, 21, 144–45
    Seri, 79, 83, 88, 92, 94
    Spanish, use of, 16–17
    Tarahumara, 57–59, 71–72, 75
    Tohono O'odham, 105–6, 108, 117, 123, 128–30
Avila, Manuel, 88
Ávila Camacho, Miguel, 45

B

Bahia Kino, xii
Baldíos Law of 1883, 113
Barrera, Gabino, xxii
Basauri, Carlos, 59
Bassols, Narciso, 20, 22–26, 36–39, 43–45, 70, 145
Bautizados, 52
Bay, Alejo, 84–88, 114
Bazán, Delfino, 59, 62, 75
beatas (religious women), 38
Blanco, Pascual, 86
boarding schools, 24, 26
    Tarahumara, 20, 40, 43, 56, 59, 62, 68–72, 74–75, 164
    United States, 109, 132
Bonfil, Ramón G., 101–2, 126
Buffalo Bill Wild West Show, 99
Bureau of Indian Affairs, 83–84, 94, 96, 98, 105–6, 108–9, 112, 115, 117, 123, 126–27, 129–31, 162
Bustamante, Antonio L., 112–14, 116, 123, 126–27, 130–31, 161

C

Cabrera, Luis, 137
Calles, Plutarco Elías, x, xx, xxiii, 90, 165–66
    alliance with Quevedo, 40–41, 148
    anti-clericalism, 6–7, 17, 20, 22, 26–27, 130

221

P

Pablo, José X., 105, 108, 115–17, 122–23, 161–63
Padilla, Ezequiel, 20–21, 36, 45
Paniagua, J. Humberto, 72, 74
Papago. *See* Tohono O'odham
Papago Good Government League, 105–6, 115–16, 123, 131, 163
Papago Tribal Council, 108
Partido Nacional Revolucionario (PNR), 36, 43–44, 142, 145, 165
Partido Revolucionario Chihuahuense (PRCH), 37
Partido Revolucionario Institucional (PRI), ix, xvii
Pequeñas Colonias Agrícolas, 74
Pérez, Nicolás, 58
physical education, 21, 26, 68, 142–43, 145, 149
Piedras Negras, xiv
Plan Sexenal, 43
Pledge of Allegiance, xx
Porfiriato, xviii, xxi–xxiiv, xxv, xxvii, 2, 29, 31, 50, 80
Portes Gil, Emilio, xvi, 36, 68, 149
positivism, xxi, 3, 6
Presbyterianism, 105–6, 123
Pro-education Committee, 14, 34
prohibition, 148–49
Protestants, xviii, xx, 7, 117
public choirs, 141, 146, 156, 161
Puig, José Manuel, 12–13, 16–20, 34, 45, 49–50, 56, 84, 91, 165

Q

Quevedo, Jesús, 151
Quevedo, José, 151
Quevedo, Rodrigo, 36, 38, 40–43, 148, 151, 159, 164

R

radio, 14, 142, 145
Ramírez, Efrén, 65
Ramírez, Jesús A., 91–92
Ramírez, Rafael, 19, 26, 40, 71, 127–28
Rarámuri. *See* Tarahumara
Rébsamen, Enrique, xxii
Reforma, xxi
Reform Laws of 1867, xxi
Refugio Chávez, María, 66
Reyes, Ramón R., 126–29
Reyes Pimentel, J., 149, 164
Rodríguez, Abelardo L., xvi
Romero, Francisco (Chico), 86, 88, 92–95, 97–98, 101–2
Romero, Ignacio L., 85
Ruiz Vadillo, Eliseo, 144

S

Sáenz, Aaron, 21, 36
Sáenz, Moisés, xviii, 12, 17–19, 21, 31, 45, 165
Saint Francis Xavier, 106–8, 117, 130
Salazar, Juan B., 62
San Carlos Cattle Company, 113–14
Sandoval, Indalecio, 58
Seri, xii, xv–xvi, xx, 50, 79–102, 122, 126–27, 161–63
Serrano, Gustavo A., 123, 126
sex education, 22, 151–52, 162
Sheffield, James, 148
Sierra, Justo, xxii, 7
Sindicato de Trabajadores de Educación de la República Mexicana (STERM), 44–45
Sindicato Nacional de Trabajadores de Educación (SNTE), 45